## THE MAN BEHIND THE FAÇADE

David Bowie is an inspiration to millions of fans and budding musicians around the world. Throughout his career he's been consistently, outrageously ahead of the game. Without doubt, he's an absolute original, to many a musical genius, but what was he like behind the scenes? And what were the forces that drove his vision?

## THE WOMAN BEHIND THE MAN

One person knows him better than anyone else, perhaps at times even better than himself – ex-wife Angela Bowie. Now for the first time she describes their life together with shocking candour – David's ruthless ambition to get to the top no matter how many people he had to sleep with or use in the process, his wild bisexual orgies with the stars of the day, and his near fatal degeneration at the hands of Satanist cults and low-life drug dealers. Included here are many sensational home truths never before revealed, stories that will stun the reader and amaze Bowie's fans.

Angela Bowie played a formative role in creating the Bowie legend. For ten tempestuous years she travelled and lived with the star, overseeing his career, promoting his music and engineering headline-grabbing news stories. Since divorcing David she has concentrated on promoting her own talents, including recording her own album. She now lives in Atlanta, though you are more likely to find her on movie location throughout the States. *Backstage Passes* is her first book.

Patrick Carr is a veteran of journalism and rock & roll. He lived in London from 1964–69, then moved to New York to launch his career as a rock critic. There he made a name for himself contributing to *Rolling Stone*, *The New York Times*, *Village Voice*, *Melody Maker* and *Playboy*. During the glitter years of the Bowies' ascendancy, he was in New York writing his *Cheap Thrills* rock & roll column for *Village Voice*, and was privy to many of the characters and scenes portrayed in *Backstage Passes*. He moved to Florida recently and is the author of two previous books, *Gun People* and *Sunshine State*.

# BACKSTAGE PASSES

## LIFE ON THE WILD SIDE
## WITH DAVID BOWIE

### *Angela Bowie*

**With Patrick Carr**

ORION

An Orion paperback
First published in Great Britain by Orion in 1993
This paperback edition published in 1994 by Orion Books Ltd,
Orion House, 5 Upper St Martin's Lane, London WC2H 9EA

Copyright © 1993 by Angela Bowie
Published by arrangement with G P Putnam's Sons,
a division of the Putnam Berkley Group, Inc, New York

The right of Angela Bowie and Patrick Carr to be identified as the
authors of this work has been asserted by them in accordance
with the Copyright, Designs and Patents Act 1988.

A CIP catalogue record for this book is
available from the British Library.

ISBN: 1 85797 108 6

Printed in England by Clays Ltd, St Ives plc

# $\mathcal{A}$CKNOWLEDGMENTS

I would like to thank the following people for their encouragement and moral support during the time it has taken to complete this book: Maggie Abbott, Rae and Dan Adams, Mark Bego, Rodney Bingenheimer, Biker Bob, Kevin Cann, Patrick Carr (for translating my flow into lucid reading), Clarence Cheatham, Leee Black Childers, George Coleman, Ronnie Cook, Jayne County, Barbara Delano, Connie Filipello, Laura Fletcher, Kim Fowley, Dorothy Frey, Dana Gillespie, David Goldman, Hal Gresham, David Groff, Joe Jones, Dennis Katz, Natasha Korniloff, Andrew Lipka, Stasha Lipka, Kevin McShane, Roy Martin, Ray Mayhew, Robert Musselman, Orencio, Fifi Oscard, Gail Parenteau, Dick Richards, Roy Rogers, Tina St Clair, Steven Solberg, Barbara Spitz, Steven Tanton, Cherry Vanilla, Harold Waterman, George Webley, and Tony Zanetta ... and of course my dear ex-husband, David Bowie, without whom none of the adventures chronicled herein could ever have happened.

*Angela Bowie*

To Angie's list I add a few names of my own: Russ Barnard and Rochelle Friedman, A. J. and Pat Bastille, Ivy and Carl Conte, Gayla Jean and Bonnie Fitzpatrick, Martha Price, Kenny Veenstra, John Whitinger, and Lynn Wray and Meredith Keller. I owe special debts of gratitude to my agent, Kevin McShane, and my editor, George Coleman; to my wife and son, Christopher Anne Wright and Walker Carr; and of course to Angie.

*Patrick Carr*

# CONTENTS

PREFACE                                                      I

CHAPTER I
*Swinging London*                                            3

CHAPTER 2
*Evolution of an Ice Man*                                   16

CHAPTER 3
*The Sunshine of Our Love*                                 32

Jimi, George and the Godfather of Soul                     49

CHAPTER 4
*Diary of a Space Oddity Den Mother*                       55

CHAPTER 5
*Rejoice, for the Queen Is Dead*                           66

Questions of Identity                                      77

CHAPTER 6
*The Starship Bowie Boldly Goes ...*                       86

CHAPTER 7
*Pearls in the Oyster, Poison in the Wine*                105

CHAPTER 8
*The Bisexual Boogie*                                      121

# Contents

CHAPTER 9
*Sayonara, Spiders from Mars* 140

CHAPTER 10
*Wonder Woman and the Cocaine Kid* 152

CHAPTER 11
*Brown Sugar and Bullshit* 166

Sticks and Stones 183

CHAPTER 12
*Sex, Drugs, and Diamond Dogs* 193

Skin Pounders and Head Bangers 209

CHAPTER 13
*The Devil Comes to Hollywood* 224

CHAPTER 14
*Queen Bitch and the Man Who Fell* 240

Postscript 254

Discography, 1969–1978 257

# PREFACE

*I* remember exactly where and when David Bowie and I first slept together. It was in London in the early summer of 1968, after an evening at the Speakeasy – the night King Crimson celebrated their new recording contract and Donovan got up and sang Buddy Holly songs with them; just a wild, wonderful rock-and-roll night – and David came back with me to my little room above the Nomad Travel Club in Paddington. The 'colorful' part of Paddington, that is, and really, what a scene: a South African owner, a wrestler from Lebanon who worked security, a waitress from Newcastle who was a really great singer, a band from Mexico who were huge pop stars at home but nobodies in London, a dozen other assorted stars and reprobates, and my Australian roommate and I, selling three-day package holidays in Ibiza to drunken Irishmen as they rolled out of the disco. It was too wild: Swinging London, seamy side up.

That night it was just David and I, though, unless of course you include the much-fabled Lance of Love. Lance was such an active, popular fellow – he never met a stranger, probably never will – that you could make a good case for his being a whole separate character in his own right.

He certainly seemed quite independent in Paddington. David was pretty drunk and we were both pretty exhausted when we fell into my little bed together, but instead of sleep, here came Lance: strong, silent, and suddenly running the show.

It was, I must admit, impressive. Hardly heavenly – although Lance was long on stamina as well as just plain long, he was short on sensitivity – but a convincing performance in David's terms. His pride in the size and staying power of his sexual equipment was quite obviously justified. That night, then, I was introduced in no uncertain fashion to one intrinsic and essential aspect of David Bowie's character: The man is a stud, and proud of it.

The morning brought another insight. David left me early, and he was very abrupt about it. That was startling, an unpleasant contrast to how he'd been at the Speakeasy; it was as if he were saying, *That was then, this is now. I have to get back to what I have to do.* All he actually told me was: 'I'll call you.'

This infuriated me, but I understood what was going on. For David, there was no sentiment involved. What he'd done with me was a piece of work, just a part of the overall plan he was putting together. When he came up to London in those days – he was living in the suburbs, in Beckenham – he had to make the rounds. I'm sure that after he left me that morning, he went on to Ken Pitt, Calvin Mark Lee, and probably a couple of pieces of trade on the side.

But that was okay. It was like having a really mischievous cat. You may hate it, but you don't love it any less. And that was David: just a bad, bad cat. That's how he acted. He used sex the way a cat sprays, to mark his territory. It gets the job done.

Does it ever.

# I

# SWINGING LONDON

London in 1966 was wonderful, the world's greatest city at one of its highest times.

It was a place emerging from the dark into the light; it felt open, free, optimistic, ready for anything. When I picture it today, I see flowers blooming, people laughing, color everywhere. This wasn't the old London, the ravaged underdog of the Blitz or the cold, gray smoggy sprawl of the austere postwar years, but an exciting, playful place alive with art, adventure, and the sublimely civilized eccentricity at which the British, bless them, are uniquely adept.

Britain as a whole was looking up, not back at old glories or down into disaster. Internationally, the sun had set on the Empire and its endless bloody wars and holding actions, while at home unemployment was low, the welfare state in its heyday, and a Labour government sponsoring reform and liberalization on every front.

The entire culture, it seemed, was changing. The Beatles and the Stones and the Who had kicked holes in the old British barriers of class and decorum and inhibition, and other young upstarts were flooding through; for the first time, the stars of the media weren't lords and ladies or the chosen favorites of the elite, but unpedigreed pop singers, artists, models, photographers, designers, whoever had the look or the sound or the attitude. At long last you didn't need a plum in your mouth and a rod up your ass to get anywhere in British society.

Even on the meaner streets, good things seemed to be happening. The pitched battles between mods and rockers – the Mods hip little pill-popping toughs in Italian-cut suits; the Rockers beer-swilling greasers in black leather and Brylcreem; both groups unpredictable, antisocial, and violent – had abated, and it looked as if there was room for everyone in the fun spots of Swinging London.

The high times would end soon enough, of course, and Britain would fall into a nightmare of economic recession, unemployment, gang violence, epidemic drug abuse, revolt and repression in Northern Ireland, and full-scale race and class warfare on the streets of its own cities. But for a few years in the sixties, London was just a gas: beautiful, safe, prosperous, creative, wide open, and wild. You could get whatever turned you on: peace and love, power and money, pomp and prestige, art and culture, hash and speed, call girls and rent boys.

Sex was at the heart of it, just as it was in Paris and Amsterdam and New York and San Francisco, the other power stations on our generation's cultural energy circuit. I really don't think the rest of it – the 'revolutions' in pop culture and politics – would have been possible without the sexual revolution of the early and middle sixties. And that wouldn't have been possible without the Pill, for it was the availability of the Pill that created the most significant fact of the matter: In 1966 my contemporaries and I were the world's first generation able to have sex without pregnancy whenever it pleased.

Talk about a driving force. When people discuss the sixties today, they tend to ignore the sex – more respectable topics such as drugs and politics and war and music get all the airtime – but let's be honest: Sex is what really drove us, the same way it drives kids today. And in our case the sex wasn't just new, but newly safe. We had more sexual freedom than anyone in living memory, and even better, we had more than we ourselves had ever imagined we could have. The Pill seemed to have dropped suddenly into our lives from a clear blue heaven.

So it may come as a small surprise when I admit that in London in the late summer of 1966, at fully sixteen years of age, I was still a virgin.

The fact that I was an American, as opposed to your basic bunny-humping socialist Brit, didn't explain it, and neither did any great claim to innocence on my part. What did was a deal I'd made with my father. He was terrified that I would disgrace him by getting pregnant before achieving my independence, so I'd made him a promise: I wouldn't sleep with man or boy until I was eighteen. And I was keeping that promise. Dad's honor as an American and a business figure in Cyprus, where he worked as an executive for a mining company, and where I'd spent my formative years when I wasn't away at boarding school in Switzerland or on vacation in London, was safe.

The deal didn't mean I couldn't have boyfriends, though, and I did. I just didn't 'go all the way' until a short while after dinner on my eighteenth birthday, when after three glasses of champagne and the gift of a lovely pair of diamanté earrings, my virginity and I parted company in an Austin-Healey 3000 parked outside a pub overlooking the River Thames. Car and penis both belonged to a terrifically nice graduate student from Yorkshire.

After that it was really fun. Having stuck to my end of the deal with Dad, I felt completely free. I didn't have to struggle with the burden of guilt a Catholic education – whether at posh Swiss St George's, where I went, or some local parochial school – usually imposes on girls and boys alike.

That was good, but in many ways the term 'virginity' is relative, and in many ways I had lost mine at sixteen, not eighteen. It was at sixteen that I had fallen in love for the first time, and had my first orgasm with another person. Her name was Lorraine.

I am bisexual, in some circles famously so. My open marriage with David Bowie, the stances he and I took, the philosophies we embraced and championed – these are matters of record in the history of the modern struggle for sexual liberation. David and I may in fact have been the best-known bisexual couple ever. We were certainly the most famous couple ever to admit and celebrate our bisexuality so publicly. So if you didn't know before, now you do.

Until the age of sixteen, I myself hadn't known – but then I'd known with my whole heart and soul: I'd been very much in love with sweet Lorraine, whose name is not really Lorraine but who *was* one of my fellow students during my brief stay at Connecticut College for Women, and what passed between us had been free, natural, honest, true, and beautiful. The school authorities hadn't seen it that way, however, and with what seemed suspiciously like pleasure, they'd separated us, disciplined us, and expelled us. Then Lorraine's parents had shut her up in the first of a series of mental institutions from which she wouldn't go free for four years. I was more fortunate; the experience of being torn from my first and probably greatest love was horrible enough, but *my* parents sent me to college in England.

So as 1966 edged into 1967, the Summer of Love in Swinging London, I knew better than most people my age how things stood on the sexual front. I grasped very clearly and personally that conventional morality, the body of law and custom penalizing anything but monogamy and heterosexuality, was against nature and against the spirit of human love. It was a fearful, vindictive sham, and I wanted no part of it. I wanted freedom.

David Bowie helped me obtain it, and I helped him, and together we helped the world.

My first image of David was enticing: a Polaroid of him posed naked, shot from the groin up. He was very pretty.

That was an intriguing photograph, and so were the other Polaroids on the wall all around it, and so was the man who had taken them and put them there, Dr Calvin Mark Lee.

Oh, Calvin. There was a character: San Francisco Chinese, very beautiful, very sensitive, very clever – the 'Dr' stood for a PhD in philosophy – and as hip as they come. Professionally, he was an A& R (artists and repertoire) man for Mercury Records, and I'd met him through a chance encounter; I'd bumped into his boss, Lou Reizener, in the elevator at Leonard's, a chic Knightsbridge hairdresser's, and accepted Lou's attentions. But Calvin's real vocation was as a collector. He collected people, and not just any people. He wanted the chic, the exotic, the unconventional, the dedicated leaders of fashion, the androgynous.

London in 1966 and 1967 was full of those people, and Calvin would find them in all the likely places, which were also the places his job took him. He would easily walk up and take a likely candidate into that soft, sweet snare of his.

'Oh, what a wonderful jacket! Where did you get it?... Really?
You know, there's an exhibit opening next week I'm sure you'd
really love...'

The Polaroids on the wall in his studio off Sloane Street (a
*very* good address) attested to his success. There were somewhere
between fifty and a hundred of them, all jammed together, males
and females. Calvin told me later that he'd slept with at least half of
those people.

I remember when he first started drawing me into the picture. I
was lying bubbled and perfumed in his bathtub one evening when
he walked gently into the bathroom, took his clothes off, and eased
himself into the water on top of me. As slender as he was, I could
support him easily holding his ankles and buttocks, so I sat up and
turned him around, and he lay there floating in the perfumed water
with his hair haloed out around him, his eyes closed peacefully.

He looked very pretty in that moment, and I hesitated. I didn't
want to make a move he might misinterpret, or do something that
might not suit him, for the waters we shared were, so to speak,
uncharted. At that point, Calvin's sexuality was ambiguous to me.

He sensed my quandary and helped me, catching my hands and
massaging his stomach and chest with them so I knew that my
desire to touch him further was okay. I stroked him, and as soon as
I did, we had action. He reached to swing me on top of him, but
the warm bathroom had suddenly become very hot, and so I got
out of the tub, took a towel, and went and lay on the bed. He came
and sat next to me.

'What do you like?' I asked.

'I like everything,' he said. He waved at the Polaroid collage above
us. 'All these people are my friends. You're my friend. And I want
all of you to know each other, and then we'll all be connected.'

Then he gave me a love jewel and asked me to wear it. That was
one of his things; special people all over London were wearing
Calvin's stones. I promised to, and then I laid him down and took
him.

I gave Calvin a wonderful time that night, and I really meant to.
I wanted no doubt in his mind that I was a very capable young
woman, as serious on other fronts as I was about the sex he was

experiencing: serious about my theatrical ambitions, serious about the music business, serious about working with him, and serious about the loyalty I was offering him. Once he knew that, I calculated, he might possibly formalize our professional relationship. He might give me a job.

A job with an American entertainment company was exactly what I needed – not exactly what I *wanted*, but a very acceptable means to an end. It could move me along the path toward my two immediate ambitions, which were to stay in London and to gain entrée to the theater world.

The theater was the more important goal, and the more difficult one. I had been absolutely passionate about the theater since entering high school, and I'd worked long and hard to develop my skills as an actress, writer, and director on the amateur level. But one large obstacle had been placed in my path already; although I could easily have gained a place in a very good drama school, my father had refused to fund such an education, insisting that I study something 'practical' instead. And now an even more daunting hindrance loomed: now I was both *not* a drama school graduate and *not* a British citizen, which meant that as far as British Equity, the actors' union, was concerned, I could *not* be a part of the professional theater in Britain. As the holder of a mere student visa, I couldn't work legally at any job, let alone the only job I'd ever really wanted, in Britain.

The straight path thus being closed to me, the devious route beckoned. If, I mused, an American company could both sponsor me for a work permit and help me get my foot in the show business door, that would be just too wonderful, wouldn't it?

I don't know if calculation was a significant component of Calvin's consciousness that night. Somehow I doubt it, given what I was doing to him. But I'm certain that it wasn't too long before he realized how, in his 'we'll all be connected' scheme of things, he could best use me to serve his own interests.

Calvin had already had David Bowie in a sexual sense, but he wanted more: he wanted him in a business sense too. He wanted to sign him to Mercury Records. First, though, he had to convince his cabaret music-loving boss, Lou Reizener, that a very odd avant-pop commodity like David could sell big tickets. And then he had to outfox David's manager, the ghastly Ken Pitt.

Connected with sufficient intimacy to David, I could be useful in both enterprises.

I remember my first night at the Round House, which involved two other novelties, my first sight of David Bowie in the flesh and my first rock concert. Strange but true: Somehow or other although pop music was as important to me as it was to almost everyone else my age in the Western world, I'd never actually bought a ticket and joined the crowd. I didn't buy a ticket this time either; Calvin and Lou took me as a backstage guest.

The Round House was a revelation, as was the crowd. So *this* was where all the people from Notting Hill and King's Road, all the most advanced trendies on the circuit, came at night! It was like London's Fillmore, a forum for the more fascinating artists and a place for the tuned-in to congregate, and you'd see them all there: long-haired blondes and afroed brunettes in wispy see-through skirts with delicate Indian-print sashes binding their breasts; better-heeled types in bright velvet capes and wide-brimmed straw hats decorated with ribbons and wildflowers, or top hats studded with badges and icons; and even then, in the pre-metal years, very pale figures dressed in black, carrying a charge of mystery, danger, and eroticism. You knew those people knew how to fuck. They were like crows among birds of paradise. I noticed them; I always do.

David's act fit in perfectly at the Round House. He was intense, intelligent, and 'out there' in the right folky-trippy way. And although he was performing as part of a trio that night – Feathers, with John Hutchinson and Hermione Farthingale – it was clearly his show. Charisma, you call it? Power, I call it.

And, it bears repeating, he was very pretty. Beautiful, actually: his hair cut and permed in tight little curls around that fallen angel's face, his body lithe and strong, his muscular dancer's legs in tight, reveal-all trousers, his sexy ass, his natural grace. Just appraising him as a performer, not a potential mate – my job, after all, was to reinforce Calvin's case for signing the man to Mercury – I could see that he definitely had what it took. A lovely man, I thought. Fans' hearts would flutter.

Hermione, his girlfriend, was lovely too, one of those classic English beauties with delicate tea-rose features and lush, gorgeous copper-burgundy hair. As tall as David, five-ten, she also was lithe, graceful, and physically charismatic. She was a classically trained ballet dancer, and that accounted for the group's emphasis on dance in its performance; David had designed the act around her talents. I think he really loved her, or at least really needed her.

After the show everything went more or less according to plan. David seemed excited and pleased with his performance – I shook hands with him and congratulated him, told him he was great – and I was as effusive as I was supposed to be with Lou. To hear me, you'd have thought the universe would end immediately if Lou didn't sign David Bowie to Mercury as quickly as possible. I might have made a difference too. Lou still didn't seem to understand, but the fact that Angie was so enthusiastic – Angie his close to virginal, ego-flattering young bedmate; Angie the cultured, au courant college girl he loved having on his arm and showing off to his bosses from Chicago – probably hastened his decision.

Calvin was disappointed that when we went out to supper after the show, David, Hermione, and Tony Hutch didn't come with us. He asked me later, 'Why didn't you bring them?'

'Why didn't *you* bring them?' I replied. 'It wasn't my place to ask them. I was there as Lou's date, you know that, so I did well enough talking David up the way I did! I couldn't finesse asking him to supper.' Calvin saw my point; it was okay. In the days that followed he continued his efforts to get David signed, and eventually he succeeded. I heard all about the ups and downs of the deal, including the aggravations caused by Ken Pitt (his managerial style was as bizarre as his sex life) and my role as Calvin's friend and confidante deepened. He came to trust me, and I him. So it was natural that when Hermione broke up with David, Calvin would start thinking about putting David and me together, tightening the circle he was making. He started working my nerves, constantly talking about David and reminding me how handsome and fascinating he was.

By the night of King Crimson's party at the Speakeasy, then, I felt as if I knew David already. I certainly knew a lot *about* him.

We started off with a Chinese dinner in Soho (Calvin knew all the good Chinese restaurants in London), and things went along well. We must have made an odd-looking trio, with Calvin and me dressed fancifully in three-piece velvet suits (mine pink, his purple) and David looking fey and tatty in washed-out Stirling Cooper sailor trousers with buttons up the front, and a light-blue-and-mustard-striped lamb's-wool sweater, your typical cheap-chic art student outfit. On the other hand, this was London in 1968, home of the queers and land of the rent boys; I'm sure the waiters had seen plenty of stranger combinations than us three.

I liked David at dinner, and at the Speakeasy, which was nothing much in itself, just another little basement rock club with a big sound system and a fabulous clientele, I started liking him even better. He was gentle and charming, but at the same time intense, commanding. He moved well, and was treated respectfully by the powerful music business people. On top of all that he seemed vulnerable; I could tell Hermione's rejection was still hurting. So he was hard to resist, and the night started turning special.

We talked about all the things you talk about, and we danced and listened to King Crimson, and as the night went on we knew we'd be going home together.

I worried that if I took David to bed, Calvin might freak. I was pretty sure they had slept together (they had), but I didn't know how it stood between them, what the rules were. So I paid close attention to the signals Calvin was giving out.

Yes, he approved. No doubt about that, none at all. If he had wanted to make himself any clearer, he would have had to push us out the door together. He didn't have to, of course. David and I seemed to like each other. We seemed to be making a bond.

So we went back to Paddington together, and what was going to happen happened. I got fucked.

David was a rotten boyfriend at first, or at least not the boyfriend I wanted him to be. I was still at the age when a girl assumes her lover is going to be nice to her even if he isn't faithful (or in David's case, even if he has the instincts of a bisexual alley cat). But David was cold. One night, I remember, when I was all worked up about some slight of his, in my very best theatrical manner I tumbled tragically down the flight of stairs outside my room at the Nomad Travel Club. He simply stepped over me on his way out and said, 'Well, when you feel like it and if you're not dead, call me.' And naturally I did. I was falling in love; love is blind.

A turning point came in our relationship, though, and it was David who initiated it. He called me one day from Beckenham, the southern suburb where he was living and running the Beckenham Arts Lab with the capable and attractive journalist Mary Finnegan. He was dreadfully sick, he said, and wanted to be with me, so could I please come down and take çare of him?

I agreed and set out from trashy Paddington, traveling the many miles of commuter rail that led to the tranquility of Beckenham. I'd never been there before, or met Mary, but I found my way to the place, a rambling bungalow set among fine old trees, and knocked on the door just after dark.

David answered. He was alone – Mary was off somewhere for the weekend – and he didn't seem nearly as sick as he'd made himself out to be. He did sound a little hoarse, though, so I hunted around for medicine and made him something to eat and generally fussed over him.

By about ten o'clock we were settled in his room. I remember noting that it *was* his room. I'd made the safe assumption that he'd slept with Mary, and realized that he might still be sleeping with her, so it was a relief to find that at least they didn't spend their nights in the same bed; Mary's room was down the hall, across from her two kids' rooms. I was also impressed by how tidy David's room was – until that moment he'd never struck me as the orderly type – and how pretty. He'd done it in colorful Indian and Tibetan fabrics, art, and *objets* of all sorts, creating a warm, hippie-sensuous atmosphere.

We sat down on the bed, and he started playing me tapes of his music – all of it, all the different versions of the tracks he'd been working on for *David Bowie*, his first album for Mercury (*Man of Words, Man of Music* in its American version). A sense of amazement came over me. I'd heard some of the songs before, but only in bits and pieces, never with such intensity; now I listened with wonder to one gem after another. These weren't the usual boy-meets-girl, girl-loses-boy pop songs, but loaded little views into the real drama of life, amazingly original and precise and poetic. And their author, sitting next to me on the bed, wasn't just another pretty pop face (although, God knows, he *was* pretty), or for that matter just another rotten boyfriend: this was a special man, different and great, one in a million or more, a man with a rare and beautiful gift, a star in this world. A new sense of who David was came flooding into me.

He was also behaving in a new way, acting kind and sympathetic toward me, and when we made love he was delicate and sensitive, a *much* better lover than the stud I'd known up to then. Now there were some sweet, heart-melting moments, and as they added up I began to forget all the evidence, initially provided by Calvin and subsequently confirmed by my own experience, that suggested that David was a first-rate user and manipulator. I began seeing a new character and opening up to him. It felt warm and wonderful.

We became intimate that night, revealing the parts of ourselves we'd been keeping hidden and safe. David talked about his childhood in the Brixton area of London; about his father, a gentle Yorkshireman who had worked for the last fifteen years of his life as public relations man for Dr Barnardo's, a children's home; about his firebrand mother, one of the first women in her town to wear trousers, who had had an illegitimate child; and about that child, Terry Burns, nine years David's senior and his great hero. David told me how he worshipped Terry, and how Terry had been such a big influence on him, introducing him to music, politics, and poetry – and also to a haunting fear. Something had happened to Terry while he was serving in the Royal Air Force in Aden during one of Britain's last colonial wars, and whatever it was, it had disturbed him profoundly. Diagnosed as a paranoid schizophrenic, he was in and out of mental institutions until 1984, when he threw himself under a train. He was buried without his little brother in attendance.

Terry was in a mental ward as David revealed himself to me that night in Beckenham, confessing to an awful dread that he might follow his half brother's path. It was an especially frightening prospect, he told me, because Terry was in fact one of several people in his mother's family who had come unhinged. David said that sometimes when he got drunk or stoned, he could almost feel the family madness in him.

He had reason to worry, I think, as events were to demonstrate, but that night in Beckenham we were safe as houses together. We could be trusting and free. He could tell me about his art school days and the rock-and-roll roads he'd traveled and where he'd had to stick the Lance of Love along the way to advance his career, and he could admit how much he'd been hurt when he and Hermione broke up.

For my part, I could bare some truths about myself. I told him about my affair with Lorraine and its bitter conclusion, and I related another formative experience. It had happened on Cyprus when I was about fourteen, during one of the recurrent rounds of fighting between the island's Greek and Turkish populations. The Turks had butchered the wife and six young children of one of their own officers, then thrown the mutilated bodies into a bathtub, photographed the scene, and distributed the picture on leaflets trumpeting the murders as Greek terrorism and crying for revenge. They dropped those leaflets from airplanes; I picked one up and got a sudden, sickening lesson in the ways of the world. I remembered that picture, and the all too typical official morality behind it, when the wrath of the establishment came crashing down on Lorraine and me: We are encouraged and rewarded for murder, it seems, while we are reviled and punished for love.

I made it plain to David that whatever I'd thought before those radicalizing events, I was now beyond the pale: no longer mainstream, no longer respectable, no longer interested in maintaining the status quo. Quite the reverse, in fact. I told him I was ready, willing, and eager to stand up and be counted.

He appeared to accept that, even if the idea of sexual freedom as a cause was new to him; In his own scheme of things at the time, bisexuality meant simply directing the Lance of Love toward whatever male or female orifice would do him the most good; boys who were girls and girls who were boys – and we sat on his bed and talked for quite some time about sexual identity and sexual politics. Among the other things that began that night, then, David's sexual consciousness started to rise.

And indeed, so much did begin: the wild, sexy, sorry saga of David and Angie and their pals in Glitter. I don't know how much love David felt – I suspect very little, and that my main (and powerful) appeal to him was my potential as a nurse, cook, housekeeper, creative ally, and business advisor – but I know I was falling hopelessly in love. I had that weird, almost spooky sense of communion and communication you get, if you're lucky, with very few people in your life. I felt that I could read David's mind; that I knew what he wanted and needed as well as or better than he did; that I was almost inside him. I'd felt that way only once before, with Lorraine, and to be finding it again, so soon and in a man, was wild. It was exciting, and it felt very good and right.

It also felt lucky. I realized that in addition to finding love, I had found myself a job and everything that went with it. If I played my hand well with David, I could stay in England, get into the musical side of show business, and work my way into the theater from there. I should add that I realized these things rather quickly, as if perhaps I'd known them all along.

Don't be surprised. If there's anything I've learned from my time in the music business, it's that the truly sublime and the utterly selfish can exist simultaneously in a person, and very often do. That is certainly true of David Bowie, and it's true of me too. I aim for the stars, and I do what I have to do down here.

That's my character in a nutshell, and this is my book. If you read on, you'll find that as well as being a chronicle of sex and sin and sleaze in glamorous places, of the cavortings of the rock-and-roll rich and the contortions of the celebrity sick and decadent, it's also a study on several contrasting airs – high motives and bright hopes, low doings and lost illusions – and one very solid, basic theme: survival. *My* survival. Against all the odds, I'm still alive. And that's amazing.

# 2
# Evolution of an Ice Man

*L*et's have a portrait of the man I had fallen for. Who exactly was David Bowie, and where had he come from?

He was, exactly, David Robert Jones – 'Bowie' came later, an exotically American, slightly dangerous new name to glamorize just another suburban English singing boy – and David Robert Jones entered this world at nine o'clock on the morning of January 8 1947, in the working-class district of Brixton.

Since that date there has been some tabloid press-fed controversy about David's class origins. While I personally find the English obsession with that subject unattractive – I'm from the land of the free – I should make the facts as clear as possible before going any further. In English terms, David was born into a reasonable facsimile of the middle class, his publicist father, John Jones, being the son of a successful Yorkshire shoe manufacturer, and his mother, Peggy Burns, having grown up one of an Irish Catholic professional soldier's six children in the genteel southeastern English town of Tunbridge Wells. In the exquisite way such things are calculated, the social mobility of David's father was lateral – from childhood in a well-funded sector of the upper trading class to adulthood in a significantly less prosperous division of the lower professional class - while his mother's class track tended unambiguously upward; a publicist is far above an noncommissioned soldier in social prestige, no matter where he happens to live. And while money alone neither admits one to the English middle class nor ejects one from it (within a generation, anyway), the Jones family was funded well enough to maintain respectable lower-middle-class appearances. In 1957 the

Joneses moved out of their two-up, two-down little house and moved into a very similar structure in the solidly respectable south London suburb of Bromley.

That move, in terms of social status if not actual living comfort, was a very distinct step up, and so young David Robert Jones, enrolled at Bromley Technical High School, could be said fairly to have matured almost exactly in the center of English society, somewhere in the populous segment between the top end of the working class and the middle of the middle class.

I should add that the term 'middle class' in England doesn't mean what it does in the U.S. of A. In England in the fifties, a thoroughly respectable middle-class family might or might not have owned a used car (and would never have conceived of owning two new ones). They would have lived in a house that would qualify as a hovel in the United States, set on a minuscule piece of property in a neighborhood most Americans would describe as a slum. They would have relied exclusively on public health care and public (in the American sense, that is) schools, would have approached a purchase as minor as a schoolchild's shoes with prudence and planning, and in the unlikely event they ever set eyes on an American steak dinner, would probably have fainted dead away in disbelief and wonder.

So much for the class issue, then – but before you conclude that David's upbringing must have been typical English petit bourgeois, think again. David's family really was odd.

He was, for a start, born illegitimate. On January 8 1947, John Jones's divorce from his first wife had not become final; he and Peggy Burns, whom he'd met in her capacity as a cinema usherette and wooed into an affair that was to end his thirteen-year marriage, were living in sin.

Such circumstances were, apparently, par for the course in John's and Peggy's lives. Peggy's history included that other illegitimate child – Terry, born in 1937 from an affair with James Rosenberg, a Jew with whom she fell in love despite her active membership in Oswald Mosley's fascist, pro-Nazi Blackshirts – and John too had another child, Annette, whom he'd adopted in 1942 after an extra-marital affair with a nurse. Put all that together and add a little more spice, such as the fact that John had begun his career as the owner of a small Soho nightclub catering (according to David) to wrestlers and gangsters, and you have a picture very much at odds with the social mores of the day. Despite the hunger for gentility that was a significant feature of Peggy's adult life, the Joneses were hardly backbone-of-the-middle-class material.

John's club, incidentally, consumed his entire inheritance of Yorkshire shoe money before it went bust and forced him to find steady work. He landed on his feet, though; his job with Dr Barnardo's, which involved dealing with show business celebrities as well as wining, dining, and otherwise spreading expense-account good cheer around the scenery, suited him perfectly.

It's said that John was a drinker and a philanderer, and I have no trouble believing that. I liked him – I found him intelligent, funny, down-to-earth, charming, and very supportive and loving toward David – and I was saddened by his death in 1969. Flaws and all, John was okay.

Peggy, on the other hand – well, I had my problems with Peggy. I could empathize with her after John's death, and make some allowances for her inability to handle herself, but even so, I thought her diatribes against me – calling me a tart and a slut and every other word in the book – went beyond the acceptable into the contemptible, especially when you consider the lady's own youth. She was a kettle exceptionally well acquainted with the various shades of black. I mean, perhaps I *was* sleeping with her son outside the bonds of matrimony, but I wasn't getting pregnant with illegitimate children, and I wasn't running around in jackboots with a bunch of fascists. Peggy mellowed out eventually, but in my early days with David she could be very trying indeed.

Yet she never really lost it, never got to the point at which she had to be taken away and locked up, as others of her family had been and would be. For a while Peggy and John's household sheltered three children: David, the darling of the home; his cousin Christine, who arrived when her mother, Peggy's sister, succumbed to schizophrenia; and Terry, reluctantly accepted *chez* Jones after his grandmother's descent into schizophrenia removed her from the arrangement that had been in place ever since his scandalous birth.

Terry's place in the Jones family was always a problem. Although I wasn't aware of any difficulty John might have had in accepting Peggy's illegitimate son, others have written about it, and I can see how it might have been true. I can see also how Peggy, who had never taken daily responsibility for her firstborn, might have felt he didn't belong in her marriage and her new family. But whatever the mixed emotions and precarious rationales of the situation, it's clear that Terry was never treated as David's equal. He seems to have been tolerated rather than welcomed, and then only when he didn't have anywhere else to go.

The problem was that Terry was David's great hero, and his periodic banishment from the household hurt and bewildered David, driving a wedge between him and his mother and also, I think, teaching him a cold and destructive lesson: If your best-loved ones disappear on you, maybe you'd better not love in the first place. And watching his revered big brother mutate into a raving psychotic right there in front of him – a metamorphosis especially extreme when Terry came back spooked from Aden, a war zone, and began drinking heavily – couldn't have been reassuring at all; this was definitely not the medium in which trust, intimacy, and warm, fuzzy feelings are likely to flourish.

Biographers, music critics, and other amateur psychologists have made much of those family circumstances in particular and the Burns family madness in general, and to a certain extent I believe they've been on the money. I think David was indeed terrified of losing his wits the way Terry had lost his (he told me so, quite often and quite clearly). Furthermore, I agree that David's 'Ice Man' persona, and his great need for control, were functions of his fear of emotionalism: extreme emotion sent you out of control into madness, and so if you wanted to survive, you simply didn't get extremely emotional.

That's why David's songwriting, and his whole stance as an artist, have been such an analytical, distanced affair. As a writer he's chosen to avoid working from his feelings, instead approaching his material as an elegant anthropological exercise among you fascinating humans, and as a performer he's chosen the even more impersonalizing tactic of creating fictional characters to present the finished work to the public: Ziggy Stardust, Aladdin Sane, the Thin White Duke, whoever.

Which has worked, of course, and brilliantly. David's art has been fascinating and, God knows, his commerce healthy enough. But personally his flight from emotionalism has cost him dearly.

His problem has been obvious enough: You simply can't have a life without strong emotion. The best you can do in that direction is put on a convincing show, and that gets you only to dangerous places: straight into emotional isolation and escalating paranoia until more often than not, sooner or later, you arrive at the bright idea that medication – booze, dope, coke, smack, prescription drugs, whatever – will make it all feel better.

What am I doing here? Describing a classic addict personality?

Exactly. Moreover, if you want my opinion – and want it or not, you're getting it – David was never 'insane' the way most of us understand the term, despite the impression he's tried to create at various points in his career and despite his period of very bizarre behavior in the mid-seventies. David was in fact one of the most coldly calculating, tightly controlled human beings I've met. His only real psychological problem in the years I knew him was his emotional frigidity, the cure in his case being worse than the family disease. The really crazy stuff, the mania, delusions, and paranoia he exhibited during the second half of the decade I spent with him, coincided precisely with his ingestion of enormous amounts of cocaine, alcohol, and whatever other drugs he had on hand; his 'madness' simply didn't happen unless he was stoned out of his mind.

I should add that I don't regard my ex-hubby's extreme self-absorption (or, if you like, plain old egomania) as a flaw in itself. In the pop star business, as in politics and business and the military, you need all the egomania you can summon in your race to the top. But you know what recovering alcoholics say about themselves – that they're egomaniacs with inferiority complexes (think about that) – and very deep down, where nobody was allowed to see it, I think that's what David was hiding.

On that level, the David Bowie I met in 1968 was a poor sick puppy, headed more or less inevitably for a very hard time a few years down the road.

But none of us knew then what we know now – we never do – and what I saw in David was anything *but* trouble. Or rather, it was all the right kind of trouble and none of the wrong: an invitation to adventure, to the exotic, the fast lane, the wild side, and to something uniquely his: a wonderful combination of great delicacy and great strength. David was a very startling, sexy, unusual, and powerful young man.

As vivid as it was, that impression was hardly original. Many a citizen of greater London before me had marked, and fallen for, the Jones/Bowie charisma. David had always been adept in the art of charismatic self-presentation.

At Bromley Tech, for instance, one unscheduled entertainment was David's varying hairstyle; he would suddenly show up one day with some radical image change – a Teddy-boy quiff, an orange-dyed mod cut, whatever would attract the most attention – and likely as not he'd have a new name to go with the new 'do ('Luther,' a handle perhaps as hiply American as 'Bowie,' being the first of his alternative identities).

He loved the grand, shocking gesture. When his classmates were fixated on electric guitars, he talked John Jones into buying him a white plastic saxophone he'd seen in a shop window, took four months of secret lessons, and then came to school one day and floored 'em. When graduation rolled around and each member of the class stood up in front of the headmaster to state his or her intended line of work – technical draftsman, typographer, adver-tising layout artist (this being the specialized art form at Bromley Tech) – David went for the gold: 'I want to be a pop idol.'

History doesn't record whether anyone who witnessed that moment put any credence in it, but certainly some of them might have. David was such an item – beautiful, charming, talented, intelligent, sexually precocious, patently ambitious – that a clear-eyed observer would have recognized: Wherever this boy was headed in life, it was Somewhere.

Where he actually went was The Design Group, Ltd, an advertising agency in which he started at the bottom, as a messenger and tea boy, in the summer of 1963, and worked his way up to the position of 'junior visualizer,' producing sketches for ad campaigns. Which of course was not his destiny, which of course he knew. He really *was* going to be a pop idol. He quit his job at the first sign of pop progress, a successful audition at Decca Records by him and his Stones-clone band, the King Bees, in the spring of 1964. So much for commercial art.

Pop idolatry did not ensue automatically, however. Davie Jones and the King Bees were just one of scores of bands signed more or less willy-nilly by British record labels on the theory that if you cast your net wide enough, you might just snare the next Beatles or Stones. The record company executives of the day, mystified by the Beatles/Stones phenomenon but desperate to duplicate it somehow, would simply market a single or two on each of the groups of likely-looking lads they'd dredged up, retain the ones that surfaced within range of the Hit Parade, and cut loose the ones that sank (nothing changes, does it?). The King Bees went down without so much as a ripple, and that was that.

Ditto, with minor variations, David's next attempts: the Mannish Boys (more Stones-style rhythm and blues); the Lower Third (R& B verging into Who-style bombast and then, after David discovered the whimsical Cockney *chanteur* Anthony Newley, a very odd cutesy pop-rock cabaret), and finally the Buzz. It was with the Buzz behind him, on a Sunday afternoon in 1966 at the Marquee Club, that our hero first stormed the sensibilities of Ken Pitt, singing a version of Rodgers and Hammerstein's 'You'll Never Walk Alone' that must have given the older gentleman some truly tantalizing ideas.

Among them, we know for sure, was the notion that amid the uncouth, feedback-fixated young yobbos and ersatz Mississippi blues belters of Britain's new pop culture, here at last might be something worthy of a cultured show business professional's loyalty and toil: a personality, an artiste, a Star, a – corny but true – Judy Garland for the rock generation. And so the ball began.

Now, to fit that Sunday afternoon into its cultural context, you have to know something about sex, style, and music in the Swinging London of the early and middle sixties, and that means you have to know something about the mods.

I knew very little – the mods were history by the time I arrived on the scene, replaced in the cycle of mini-generational turnover by a potpourri of hippies and skinheads and protopunks – but David was an authority, and he used to tell me about everything. I don't remember his words well enough to quote them, but as luck would have it, here he is in print, talking to music journalist Timothy White in *Rock Lives*:

'There were two batches of mods in England, the first lot being in 1962–3. The initial crop called themselves modernists, which reduced itself down to ["mods"] . . . These weren't the anorak mods [who] turned up later on motor scooters. . . . The first mods wore very expensive suits; very, very dapper. And makeup was an important part of it; lipstick, blush, eyeshadow, and out-and-out pancake powder . . . It was very dandified, and these were James Brown lovers. Elitist. Pills always played an important part; everything was fast . . . You earned your money somehow, wheeling and dealing . . . You'd get dressed up, go 'round the Marquee Club, and just get loony and listen to rhythm and blues.'

He goes on to talk about some of the little tricks of the mod trade, like sorting through the trash bins behind the first generation of Carnaby Street boutiques for barely flawed garments that would be thrown out in those days, and getting your suits tailored inexpensively in Shepherd's Bush from quality material that had 'fallen off a truck' somewhere else in London. He doesn't go into some other aspects of mod culture, though, such as the fact that those pills and clothes (except the bin discards) were often paid for in sex sold to the older queens, many of them theater and music business insiders, who trolled the mod clubs.

Don't get me wrong here. David never told me he'd sold either end of himself for money, and I have no reason to suppose he did; all he told me in those early days was that he was bisexual and had had 'boyfriends.' But the club-trolling of queens was certainly an important factor in his rise from obscurity, and so was the mod ethos of intense narcissism, fashion competition, and all-around gender-bending. In David's teenage scene, the boys often knew more than the girls about eyeliner, lipstick, and the creation of a good bouffant. So ten years later, when David made his legendary first public appearance in a dress and shocked the hell out of establishment England (and most of pop America, for that matter), I'm sure it was no big deal in more than a few London households. I can just see some typical ex-mod sitting at the kitchen table in his undershirt, the wife frying up the Walls pork sausages, him trying to ignore the kids and gazing at David swishing proudly in *News of the World*, his mind drifting happily back...

David's walking of the bisexual edge had been going on for years before I met him, as had his sexual success. At Bromley Tech, according to his own and his classmates' memories, he scored both boys and girls at a high rate, and the girls he scored were usually older, prettier, and more glamorous than those his contemporaries could dream of seducing.

What happened to my dear friend Dana Gillespie is a good example of his style. When David slipped up behind her as she was fixing her hair in a mirror one night at the London Club, then gently lifted the hairbrush from her hand and began brushing her gorgeous long tresses, she was probably the catch of the night: fourteen years old, astoundingly beautiful, physically developed and intellectually talented far beyond her years, and a real-live Austrian baroness to boot. She bought into David right then and there too; took one look at the lovely boy with the waist-length bleached blond hair, soulful, weirdly mismatched eyes, and decadent, delicate fuck-me mouth, and made up her mind. She took him to bed that very first night, sneaking him into her family's townhouse and past her sleeping parents' bedroom to do it.

In the homosexual arena (I really don't have any juicy firsthand, ah, blow-by-blow accounts), David has boasted publicly of his teenage success with boys, though, and in the early days I certainly observed his homosexual *effect*. I saw those queens, rent boys, transvestites, and good old-fashioned everyday gays going gaga for him, and him enticing them on. I saw the way he flirted with Ken Pitt. I saw the intensity of Pitt's interest in him, and Calvin Mark Lee's, and I have no doubt that sex – given, promised, implied, even strategically withheld if that's what got the job done – was a very significant factor in his rise through the gay mafia of the London music business. That soft intensity of his, the way he was able to suggest profound intimacy simply by looking you straight in the eye, was a potent weapon, and he used it often and well: there were lots of goose bumps, hot flashes, and warm shivers down the spine when David targeted a chap.


When I first laid eyes on him at the Round House, three years after Ken Pitt caught him at the Marquee, I was aware immediately of David's power, and his poise, and his very special appeal. Here was a great beauty (and I use that term carefully) who knew how to hold and present himself in a very specific, androgynous way.

You don't find that kind of sexually ambivalent, physical self-awareness very often, but in the world of dance it's virtually a benchmark. And that's where David was coming from. Before I entered his circle he had spent a full two years performing, traveling, and living with the infamous Lindsay Kemp's Underground Mime Troupe, a rad/lib/mystical/multisexual communal organization he described later to rock journalist Timothy White as 'wonderful, incredible. [It was] a great experience living with this sort of rancid Cocteau-ish theater group in these bizarre rooms... decorated and handpainted with elaborate things. The whole thing was so excessively French, with Left Bank existentialism, reading Genet and listening to R&B. The perfect Bohemian life.'

Hints of sarcasm aside, he loved that scene, which opened his eyes and broadened his horizons. It put plenty of sex – heterosexual, homosexual, bisexual, multiparty – his way, of course, but it also gave him something more important: his edge over his competition in the music business. For when push finally came to shove in David's career (at *Ziggy Stardust* time), what hurtled him ahead of the field wasn't his rock-and-roll chops but his out-front androgyny and his absolute theatricality – his thorough grasp of dance, mime, makeup, staging, lighting, and the exploitation of sexual outrageousness in a theatrical context. And he learned all that in Lindsay Kemp's traveling circus. I think it was in the Underground

Mime Troupe that David fully grasped the fact that quite apart from his talent, he could command and receive real, useful respect as a beauty. So by the time I got to him, when he was through with the troupe and had moved on into Feathers, he knew exactly how to present himself. Even in those fey, raggedy hippie-student-dancer clothes of his, he projected power directly and electrically. He could be playing the naif or going in the opposite direction, commanding the scene, but in either role his charisma was obvious and immediate. He was so poised. What a combination he was: beauty, vampire, victim, angel, innocent, user, stud, commander. He was gorgeous, and it was wild.

Philosophically he was interesting, but very depressive. That wasn't unusual in bright English boys of his generation – Britain in the fifties, ravaged by world wars and torn by class struggles, was nothing like the good-life Shangri-la across the Atlantic – but David had added layers of bleakness and perversity beyond the norm. Under Terry's influence he'd established an early, thorough grounding in the stars of down-and-decadent modern literature – Kafka, Genet, Burroughs, Kerouac, Isherwood, Duchamp – before going on with the teenage-rebel crowd into an obsession with American pop culture up to and including Bob Dylan, his role model for 1966. So when I met David, the paranoid vision and the language of life's darkness were second nature to him. 'Space Oddity,' 'Wild-Eyed Boy from Freecloud' – that's how he really thought about the world.

He wasn't *all* gloom and rebellion, of course, and in fact, again like many of the brighter members of his generation, he had a wonderfully ironic sense of humor. David in a living room was a hoot, full of natural charm and his father's down-to-earth Yorkshire insight, the Ice Man nowhere in sight.

He was a lot of fun, in short, and I've often wondered what his art might have been and how his career might have gone – whether he would have been as popular as he is, for instance – if he had allowed that funny, natural side of himself into his music. The frigidity of his work seems especially striking when you look at who his entertainer heroes were: natural, broadly humorous, ultra-earthy British vaudevillians such as Gracie Fields, George Formby, Albert

Modley, and Nat Jackley, as well as such contemporary warm bodies as John Lennon, Tiny Tim, and Anthony Newley.

Also significant in David's worldview was the component he'd acquired most recently when I met him. Basically, he'd gone hippie. He'd studied Buddhism after the Beatles did (although he didn't, as some biographers have written, live at Chimi Youngdong Rimpoche's monastery in Scotland and 'come close to taking his vows'; that impression, I suspect, resulted from his habit of gilding the lily somewhat when he thought it might impress), and while he'd been with Hermione he'd lived in hippie-central Notting Hill, learning to eat muesli and macrobiotics, intoning chants and positive affirmations, and otherwise embracing the peace-and-love life-style. He'd had a great time and had, I believe, been infatuated with both the wonderful Hermione and the package the relationship came in, the creative, liberated, living-in-sin, working-in-love, happy-hippie hash-smoking scene. Of his relationship with Hermione, he once said in an interview: 'We had a perfect love – so perfect that it burned out in two years. We were too close, thought alike and spent all the time in a room sitting on the corner of a bed.'

I don't really know for sure why Hermione went her own way, but I think it had more to do with her goals and career than with a surfeit of perfection in her relationship with David. She was a professional ballerina capable of making real money and advancing her career in first-class productions, as opposed to subsisting on the few coins and flutters of outer-fringe interest Feathers could generate from time to time. But whatever the cause, hippie heaven fell apart. David moved out of Notting Hill and back under the wing of Ken Pitt in his house on Manchester Street until he found his digs *chez* Mary Finnegan.

Which was, approximately, where I came in, advancing my own agenda while soothing David's ravaged ego and providing our star with a new, improved, formidable ally.

So what did I see when I first really looked at my new man? What was the physical entity that so seduced and compelled me?

He was, as I've said, a beauty, a young man blessed with a

lovely face and body. His face was perfectly structured to classical proportions – forehead-to-nose and nose-to-chin measurements being equal – with high, wide cheekbones pulled tightly down into a mischievously chiseled chin. His skin was creamy smooth, his beard very light (for me, just right). His hair, bleached ash blond like mine, bordered his face in a halo of soft little curls, and his eyebrows, as finely blond as his hair, arched gracefully to frame that one divine asymmetry – one green eye and one blue, erotic and compelling.

David stands between five-foot-ten and five-foot-eleven. His shoulders are broad, like mine, and although he's always been slender, the sinew and muscle I saw first in his arms and legs foretold the powerhouse I would find in his chest and pelvis. His fingers were long and artistic, with strong squared-off fingernails, and usually they held a cigarette.

David speaks softly, and the timbre of his voice is rich and intelligent; it's an almost hypnotically effective instrument. He has full, sensual lips which demand kissing, perhaps gently, perhaps not.

Now you know David; you need to know some details about me.

First, though, I want to clarify an issue about my years with David. I'm fully aware that lurking somewhere in most readers' minds (probably somewhere quite prominent) there may be some doubt about me. Might I not be someone who shared David's life for a while but was never really important in its creative and professional aspects? Just another semi-relevant ex-spouse cashing in?

Many of the crucial business moves, musical and professional connections, and marketing and imaging strategies were my work, as were, much of the time, the daily minutiae. For a number of years David's career was my *job*.

Let's make that a little clearer. Let's look at my qualifications. What was I bringing to the workplace? Who was I?

Well, I *wasn't* the girlfriend you might expect, the standard sub-urban British wannabe rock star's wannabe first wife. I *wasn't* some dim, peroxided little golddigger with a headful of hash, a drawerful of last year's body stockings, and an outlook stretching all the way to Portobello Road and back on a clear day. I was transcontinental and bilingual. I had Swiss schooling and theatrical experience – years of it, everything from the principles of direction to the nuts and bolts of lighting – and I knew how to *really* cook and *really* sew and *really* run a house (they turn out good old-fashioned ladies at expensive Swiss finishing schools, you know, not half-baked girls). And of course, unlike David and his friends and associates, including the people in charge of managing and promoting him, I had nine-tenths of a degree in marketing and more than enough savvy to make up for the missing piece of paper. So all the little shits who have denigrated my role in the launch of La Bowie, and all the chauvinists of every sex and stripe who at one time or another have dismissed me as 'the wife,' can kiss my highly credentialed, much more than adequately competent ass and feel damned lucky I let 'em. Okay? Do we have that straight?

Let's hope so, and proceed with some biographical details.

I was born Mary Angela Barnett, an American citizen, the daughter of George and Helene Marie Barnett, in Xeros on the Mediterranean island of Cyprus, in 1950. My father's parents were English, my mother's Polish. I have one brother, sixteen years my senior, who works as a mining engineer in New Guinea; in that respect he follows in the footsteps of our father, who spent most of his professional life as an engineer with the American-owned Cyprus Mining Company. He had served in the U.S. Army in World War II as a leader of guerrilla fighters on Luzon in the Philippines. His book *Three Fields to Cross* details that heroic campaign, from which he emerged a much-decorated full colonel. Both my parents passed away in 1984. We were practicing Catholics.

I was educated at the Cyprus Mining Company school (lessons in English) until I was sent to St George's School near Montreux, Switzerland, at the age of nine. I graduated from St George's at sixteen, spent a mercifully brief few months at Connecticut College for Women, and then studied marketing at Kingston Polytechnic College in suburban London. I was denied eligibility my final degree because – well, to put it bluntly, I did the work and knew my stuff well enough, but I didn't show up for class the way they'd have liked me to. I was having too much fun.

So far in my life I have lived in Cyprus, Switzerland, Connecticut, London, New York, Los Angeles, northern California, and Arizona, and I've also spent significant amounts of time in Frankfurt, Berlin, and Vienna, and on the islands of Hydra, Mykonos, and Spetsai. At this particular moment I live in Atlanta, Georgia.

I have two children. Stasha, born in 1980, lives with me. Her father is Andrew Bogdnan Lipka, aka Drew Blood, located near London these days. My son, Joe, born to David and me in 1971, and then named Zowie, is in England. His father has had sole custody of him since our divorce became final, on February 8 1980. As I write, it's been two years since I talked to Joe, and more than ten since I talked to his father. Which is just awful, terrible.

When I think about how David and I were together and how we came apart, I keep returning to the matter of emotionalism: how he hid his feelings and denied his vulnerability all the way down through the depths of alcoholism and drug addiction to the destruction of our relationship and the threshold of his own death.

In particular I remember sitting with him in a café in Switzerland immediately after we signed our final divorce papers. I was pretty far gone into the dark myself then – betrayed by my own flaws, certainly, but also worn away by years of David's coldness and broken by his final, ruthless campaign to erase me completely from his life – and I expected nothing from him but more of the same. I'd come to think of him as a person so utterly uninterested in loving or caring for me that he might as well have been my executioner.

That's not how he acted, though. He was quite gentle and solicitous, even sweet, and he talked with openness and genuine regret about what had happened between us, and how he'd behaved. It was almost as if he were trying to build a bridge back to me.

That was so strange for me, and so hard. I just didn't understand. Why was this conversation taking place now, with signed divorce papers in hand, instead of two or three years before, when it might have meant something?

I don't know. Maybe the therapy he was involved in was helping him reach his feelings at long last, or maybe – Oh hell, I really don't know. He closed me down completely after that day, saying not a word to me since, so I'm just stabbing in the dark.

Back to the further and better past, then.

# 3
# THE SUNSHINE OF OUR LOVE

Nineteen sixty-nine was a very fine year. David and I became close in the spring, after our weekend together at Mary Finnegan's, and our love grew and flourished in the sunshine of that summer.

I can't remember our being apart at all. I'd moved from Paddington after some poor Irishman turned up dead on the street outside the Nomad Travel Club (his final verdict on the neighborhood?), and technically speaking I now lived in Blackheath, a suburb not too many miles from Beckenham but three days by native bearer and London Transport across a maze of middle-class greenery. In reality I spent my time on David's turf, at Mary Finnegan's or one of his other occasional homes; or at Dana Gillespie's place in Knightsbridge; or at the Earl's Court flat where Tony Visconti, the producer of *David Bowie*, lived with his girlfriend, Liz.

I smile when I remember those days: waking up wherever I'd gone to sleep, stuffing my used underwear in my shoulder bag, and going without until I could get back to my flat and do laundry (it was a while before I started taking things for granted and traveling with a toothbrush and a change of panties). I smile even more when I remember how David and I were together. We held hands and locked eyes a lot, and we were sweet. When we were in public or with our friends, we used to say to each other 'In your ear' when we meant 'I love you.' Shy about it.

I was a young lady of leisure that summer, having abandoned my job at the Nomad and my studies at Kingston Polytechnic; I was free and life was easy. David could become my focus, then, and he did – and since *his* focus was recording his album at the Trident studio on Wardour Street in Soho, in the heart of London proper, that's where I spent a good many of my days.

For David it was a time of great clarity and creativity. The recording process of *David Bowie* was almost entirely pleasant, productive, and cooperative.

For one thing, his collaborators were great. David has always been adept at incorporating other artists' ideas and talents into his work (and knowing just whom to use when; he's kept his serial-stylist career rocking along on the energy of collaborators as diverse as Brian Eno, Luther Vandross, John Lennon, and Stevie Ray Vaughan). The people he assembled for that album, his second with Tony Visconti but his first for Mercury, were typically wonderful.

Tony was, and is, just brilliant. I love him both personally and professionally. An American abroad, in his early twenties, he'd come a long way from Brooklyn; as he sat behind that console in the little Trident control room he was already a very accomplished musician, songwriter, arranger, engineer, and producer. He was only a year or two older than David, but he was so much further into his profession that he and David had a big brother–little brother relationship.

Tony was terrifically hip, as transatlantic musical transplants tended to be, and sexily chic. Tony was a keeper; when David and I started living together, he and his girlfriend came and lived with us.

Tony is intelligent, funny, and just plain nice, a genuinely pleasant person, with an endearing macho streak. I like the story behind that too: It came, he told me, from his teenage years in an Italian-American neighborhood, where carrying a violin case on the street, as he did, didn't exactly conform to peer group standards of male behavior. Tony was in the unusual position of being able to say that he'd fought for his music – bled for his art, man! – and mean it literally.

His machismo didn't show at Trident, however. Far from it. As the producer, he was the boss in the studio (the artist was a relative novice, not a star), but you'd never have known it. His input came in the form of an associate's suggestions to the other players, musician to musician: none of that executive director, taste-führer attitude.

There was actually a triad in charge of the *David Bowie* sessions: Tony, David, and a wonderful engineer, Ken Scott. Ken was like many a studio engineer, overqualified and upwardly mobile. He didn't just set levels, place mikes, control effects, and otherwise manipulate mechanics and electronics at the producer's behest; he was a full creative partner with an extraordinary musical vocabulary and a refined sense of nuance and atmosphere, on which David and Tony drew frequently and liberally. As a pure engineer he achieved levels of sound manipulation his peers couldn't approach until they'd listened to his final product and figured out how he'd done it. He was one of *those* guys.

In personal style he was straight, sane, normal middle-class, as engineers often are, and honest and unaffected. I thought the world of him. David liked him a lot too, as did Tony. Those guys really got along.

They worked wonderfully together too. During the six weeks of recording and mixing there was a magical communication in the studio: fast, intuitive vibes at a high level of creativity and technical expertise. Everyone was turned on – David by Tony's and Ken's depth and expertise, Tony and Ken by the quality of David's songs and his perfect-pitch vocal performances.

The musicians also were great. The marvelous songwriter/ guitarist and Beckenham Arts Lab regular Keith Christmas, a singularly intelligent, dashing young man with a slow, potent fire in him... Tim Renwick, the hippie lead-guitar genius in long Pre-Raphaelite curls, headed for his job in Pink Floyd... Herbie Flowers on bass – wow!... Rick Wakeman, pre-Yes at that point, keyboarding beautifully... and of course the divine Paul Buckmaster on cello. Even now, just seeing Paul's name makes my heart beat a little faster. He was my kind of lunatic: turquoise eyes, long eyelashes, auburn curls, dimpled chin, handsome as they come, and an inspiringly eccentric musician and string arranger. He actually got some record company, I forget which, to give him a contract and fork over money for an album of 'intergalactic' music played exclusively on instruments he invented.

Paul, I must confess, impressed me very personally: turned me on like a Ferris wheel in a blackout, in fact, and presented me with quite a dilemma. I'd met him only two or three weeks after I'd met David, so in the beginning I had a period of delicious indecision: Which one did I want the most?

I never resolved that question. I chose David not because he turned me on more, but because he didn't happen to have a girl-friend at the time. Paul did, but he griped about her; that fact both offered me an opening and warned me off; I certainly wouldn't want him acting that way toward *me*. So I went for the blond.

There we were, then, working well and happily on Wardour Street. The musicians showed up at the studio every morning, ready and willing, worked all day until early evening, and quit in time for dinner. They broke for lunch, and actually ate it. They didn't, in short, behave the way David and many another rock legend behaved in later years. They weren't drunk, doped, wired, cranked, tranked, tripped-out, or significantly trashed in any other way. They weren't manic or paranoid. They didn't have to wait until darkness before emerging from their hideouts and venturing to the studio, and when they worked they didn't have to do so within a cocoon of bodyguards, drug dealers, sex providers, and assorted other syco-phants and leeches. They were working musicians in every sense of the term.

During those six weeks, some of my hours were spent in the studio, where Tony and Ken used me as an extra set of hands during the mixing (thus beginning my education in the art of record production); but while I must admit that I spent a fair amount of time just sitting rapt in the control room, watching David and making eyes whenever we connected, I hate the girlfriend-getting-in-the-way role, so I also spent a lot of my hours elsewhere. I went out to fetch lunch and run errands here and there, and I roamed around. Wardour Street is in the center of Soho, an utterly fas-cinating area of clubs, restaurants, delis, boutiques, record stores, street markets, and all other manner of holes in the wall, and Soho in turn is in the middle of central London's many other diverse attractions, so I had a great variety of routes to take from the Trident door.

You can look into myriad worlds as you walk around Soho, but much of the time I kept my attention on the world awaiting David and me. My path took me to the hip-pop cornucopia of Carnaby Street boutiques or, nearby on Regent Street, the array of gorgeous fabrics at Liberty's. Many of David's image changes and fashion statements began as I pondered my way around that magnificent establishment.

Most days after I ended up back at Trident, I would wait until the boys had finished recording or mixing for the day, and then David and I would roam. We'd visit Calvin in Chelsea or Ken Pitt on Manchester Street.

One day David took me to Dana Gillespie's house. We banged on the door, and there she was, my new best friend. Dana was a great singer, songwriter, actress, athlete, and beauty, and her accomplishments ranged from winning a place on the British water ski team to playing Mary Magdalen in the original West End production of *Jesus Christ Superstar* to amassing a body of sexual expertise uncanny in one so young. She was something else; one look and you were an instant fan.

David had said, 'You two are really going to get along,' and he was right (and I realized how well he knew me already). There was no physical resemblance between us, since I was built like a boy and she was very voluptuous, but we both knew we were in this world to celebrate it: to eat, to play, to make art, music, love, whatever was creative and productive. She and I and David and Ken, her boyfriend, all made love together that night. London was our oyster; all we had to do was reach out and touch it, and it would respond. Something would start, something would happen.

Sometimes that summer, on the street or in stores or studios, I would catch glimpses of the people who had already made it on the scene, the royals of Swinging London going about their business – Twiggy, maybe, or Ray Davies or Pete Townshend or Rod Stewart or Terence Stamp or Marianne Faithfull – and I'd feel my dreams getting closer. Those feelings had a growing sense of reality too. The music at Trident was very strong. My love the blond was leaving no doubts at all about his potential.

*

And now I have to tell you something important, crucial really. Although I'm uncertain about it these days, I must confess that as I watched David committing his art to tape in that studio, a feeling inside me became a conviction: David was one of the Light People.

This belief was an integral component of my attraction to him, and a powerful factor in the loyalty and trust I (mis)placed in him. So I'll tell you about the Light People, and you can scoff all you want – or maybe, if you were there in the sixties (and I mean *there*, not just catching the whole strange trip on TV), you will understand.

The Light People, in my scheme of things, were aliens: extra-terrestrials, inhabitants of some other planet or space or dimension. They were infinitely more advanced, intelligent, and powerful than earth people, and indeed, we may have been their creation; it was possible, I theorized, that Earth was a science project of sorts for the Light People, and human society the equivalent of an elaborate ant colony they could observe and manipulate at will. They did this chiefly by monitoring crucial junctures in human development, and sending in entities to influence events toward the course they desired. Such entities were spirits, basically, which would dwell and operate within otherwise entirely human beings.

My theory posited that many of the great individuals in human history, those who advanced our progress far beyond contemporary reason or pulled our fat from the fire when all seemed lost – Leonardo, Galileo, Newton, Gandhi, Churchill – were hosts to Light People spirits. And as I lived and breathed and went about my business in the cosmic atmosphere of sixties alternative London, it made perfect sense to me that David, along with a handful of other unique voices – Bob Dylan, John Lennon, Jimi Hendrix – was Lit from within.

Thus there were in my rationale the very best of reasons for my long devotion to David. I was serving the Light.

Ultimately, the Light People philosophy served my purposes very well. It was like a good pair of shades and a particularly effective set of earplugs all in one: it kept the sunlight out of my eyes as I focused dead ahead on my goals, and it diminished the din of reality as I moved resolutely forward. Reality is fine, you know, but it can really get in your way when you're chasing a dream.

*

By the early summer of '69, David and I had begun to act as a team. I was the person to whom he played the tapes of his day's work in the studio, inviting reaction and comment. I was the one with whom he discussed philosophy, religion, history, society, and the doings of humanity around us, the raw material of his work. I got on the telephone for him and went with him to business meetings, both advising him and acting the heavy in the bad good-cop, bad-cop routine we were developing. More and more, I became the person who put his ideas into action, found and secured the resources he needed, and kicked down the doors he wanted to walk through.

It was fun. I'd been educated, brought up, and perhaps even born for this role, and I relished it. Apart from loving, there's nothing I love more than being effective.

One example was the Beckenham Free Festival, an outdoor hippie shindig that epitomized David's folk-populist values and his Arts Lab approach to the music scene. He arranged for the musicians and other performers from the Beckenham Arts Lab to put on a free show – and he was very successful. About five thousand spectators and participants showed up, people of all sorts, and things went off peacefully, pleasurably, and properly. The local mayor and chief constable went so far as to congratulate David publicly on a job well done.

David played for a good hour and a half that day, performing among other numbers a reggae version of 'Space Oddity' (yes, really!), but I wasn't aware of what went on entertainmentwise. Having worked my tail off helping Mary Finnegan line up the acts and deal with the authorities, I spent most of the festival day itself obscured by grill smoke, serving endless platters to streams of stoned, munchies-crazed young suburbanites. Which, I must say, pleased me greatly. The feeding of the five thousand was a very successful feat indeed: they ate well and heartily – not your macro-biotic mush, mate, but good old charred flesh hunks, and plenty of 'em – and we made out like bandits. My catering operation cleared a good £2,000, which then equaled about $5,000 and in those days that kind of money went a long way. The more than slightly shaky finances of the Arts Lab, not to mention of David himself, had improved considerably when the day was done. From a profit perspective, a free festival could be pretty cool.

Another coup began with an international phone call from David to Mary Finnegan's, where I was staying while he went about his business of the moment, a round of international song contests. He was calling from Malta, and he wasn't happy. He hated the middle-of-the-road musical scene around him, hated the elegant dark blue suit he had to wear, and hated the fact that the man 'making' him wear the suit, Ken Pitt, was at his side night and day. David couldn't stand the idea that the circumstances were going to continue as he, Ken, and the whole cast – six-foot-tall Nordic ice goddesses, little Italian twin boys singing to their teddy bears, yodelers, crooners, handsome Eastern bloc superstars, your typical bush-league Euro-vision song contest talent – shifted location to Monsummano Terme, a mountaintop spa resort near Pisa.

I listened to all that, did some quick mental calculations, then said, 'Okay, David, I'll meet you in Monsummano Terme.'

There was a sudden silence until he said, 'What?'

'I'll meet you in Monsummano Terme, is what I said. If you're having such a rough time, I'll just come and deal with it. Okay?'

Those were the magic words. His tone lost its edge of misery, we discussed a couple of quick details and said a sweet thing or two, and he hung up. I was going to Italy.

In those days, not yet the time of our great success, neither David nor I simply 'went to Italy'; we didn't have the money. But as it happened, I was holding a plane ticket home to Cyprus, so I arranged for a stopover in Italy, booked a flight, and went. I took a cab up the mountain, found the very beautiful spa, established myself in the gorgeous room booked for David and Ken Pitt, and awaited the arrival of my man. Hey, *presto*, boys.

David was thrilled. Ken wasn't. He had to find another room, and I don't think it was the inconvenience that really bothered him. Talk about a snit. There's nothing, thank God, like the ire of a queen whose affections have been spurned.

It didn't get any better for Ken either. Before I left England, I'd gone to the Kensington antique market and bought appropriate outfits: for the young hippie lady a lovely, ultraromantic Victorian white lace dress to be worn with flowers in the hair, and for the handsome, delicate young gentleman a cream-colored balloon-sleeved Victorian silk shirt and very, very tight black satin trousers.

It was in these clothes, not the cabaret suit that defined Ken's vision of him, and with his damned *girlfriend* on his arm, that David made his grand entrance to the song contest – and it was wild, let me tell you. I remember our sweeping down the stairs at the hotel into public view, and the great collective gasp that went up. I don't think those people had *ever* seen high-class hippies before, but whether they had or hadn't, they loved us; we absolutely made their day. And wouldn't you know it, David went right ahead and won the song contest.

It was a grand show we put on, and David was very pleased. It was nice that he'd won the contest, but nicer still that he'd done it *his* way, in *his* style; he'd made *his* statement. He appreciated what I'd done for him, and I think he learned the lesson very clearly: Angie had made the right things happen for David.

Ken Pitt watched David learning that lesson, and I don't believe he enjoyed the experience. I felt for him, but it was his problem, not mine. It would be mine soon enough, all right – but that's another story.


A new level of affairs between David and me began with another international call from him. This time he was at his parents' home in London and I was at my parents' in Cyprus; I'd gone there after the song contest adventure, while David had flown back to England with Ken.

The news was tragic: John Jones had died of pneumonia shortly after the plane carrying David and Ken had landed at Heathrow.

David wanted me with him as soon as I could get there. My father very generously made that possible, and I arrived at the Jones house in Plaistow Grove in time for the funeral, about which I recall almost nothing.

I remember the following weeks quite clearly, though, because they were among the most difficult of my life. David and I stayed at Plaistow Grove to help Peggy through these days (me in one bedroom sleeping with Peggy, David in another: a seemly if entirely odious arrangement), and basically it was awful. Peggy was extremely depressed and incapable – both bereaved and incompetent, since John had handled virtually everything for her -and David wasn't much better. He was grieving for a father he'd really loved and depended on, but he was also angry and having a hard time with that. For one thing, he hated the idea of having to take care of his mother now that his father was gone. For another, he couldn't reconcile the manner of his father's passing: Peggy had waited too long before summoning a doctor, and in the end John Jones had asphyxiated alone in an upstairs room, trying to get to an oxygen tank just outside his reach.

David's relationship with his mother had been difficult for a long time, so the dire unspoken accusation took root in fertile soil. It was horrible: Peggy dragging around, saying that her life had been meaningless (she didn't yet know she'd given birth to the great David Bowie); David moping and resentful; the two pecking at each other like psychotic vultures in that closed little house while I bounced around in the middle, handing out helpful hints – 'David, why don't you take driving lessons now that you can use your dad's Fiat?' or 'Mrs Jones, shall we take the dog for a walk?' – and trying to make the good old Angie Barnett life-of-the-party happy face. Ugh.

Peggy's attitude toward me was awful. She turned on me the way she must have turned on Terry, and I began to understand what drove David to distraction about her; until those days I'd thought she was relatively pleasant, certainly not the difficult and demanding woman David described whenever she pushed his buttons. But there she was, in all her mournful glory, as mean as she was miserable.

Her abuse came in multiple forms, from out-and-out diatribes to low-level harassment. David, for example, didn't like tea; he drank only coffee. So whenever Peggy made a pot of tea, she would make David his coffee at the same time, serve it to him, and then serve herself a cup of tea. I'd be sitting right there all the way through this charade, but she wouldn't acknowledge me until she and David had settled down with their beverages. Then she would look at me, all innocent surprise, and say, 'Oh, I didn't know you wanted anything. Did you want a cup of something?'

Thinking about my nature, I'd like to say that I almost told Peggy what to do with her misery. I like uneasy peace more than open warfare, though, so I bent over backward to placate the poor woman. I was determined not to trigger a fight or give her a legitimate reason for hating me, and I *really* didn't want for David to stand up and take sides with me against his mother. That was a confrontation I knew he didn't need and would regret deeply. So every night I climbed into bed and lay next to the poor awful woman and prayed for sleep to take me away. As often as not, it would be a long time coming. Horrible.

Great things can come from hard times, however, and from the emotional muck of that swamp at Plaistow Grove, David and I made a new bond.

He came to depend on me in new ways. Aside from his advisor and effectuator, I became his road manager, going out with him on the weird assortment of gigs Ken Pitt had booked him into – workingmen's clubs, cabaret lounges, anywhere but the scene in which he belonged. And as he watched me wire amps and hump speakers and deal effectively with the attractive, honest, warm, and wonderful individuals who typically ran the places we played in (and me without so much as a set of brass knuckles!), he came to realize just how much more than 'a girl' I was. His prejudices were challenged (and despite his liberated talk, David was as chauvinistic as any man of his generation), and he began to see the possibility of real friendship and camaraderie in a manly girl like me. So we gained more common ground, and our relationship expanded into it.

There were other factors drawing us together. We couldn't sleep together, so we filled our need for intimacy with talk. I revealed myself to David more than I had before, and David reciprocated. Being back at home on Plaistow Grove called up a lot of memories for him, some of them painful (particularly his feelings for Terry), and he shared all that with me. I was drawn closer, happy to be hearing direct emotion from my cool and distanced man.

Looking back on the melting of the Ice Man, I think David was beginning to turn to me in place of his father. John Jones had always been the supportive, accepting person in his life (and a strong force standing between his son and Peggy's disapproval), and now he was gone. David needed someone else in that role. I qualified well enough – I loved him and supported him unconditionally and, moreover, could *do* things for him, just as John had – so I was it.

There came a formalization of sorts: nothing legally or religiously sanctioned, but a commitment fully binding in my heart, soul, and conscience. We were sitting together in the upstairs back room, the room where David had slept during his youth, with and without his half brother, in good times and bad. I forget what hour of the day it was, and what led up to our discussion, but I remember the crux of the matter. I offered David a deal. He and I would stay together, I said, and embark on a joint course: First we would work together to accomplish his goal – to make his dream of pop idolatory come true, to make him a star – and then we'd do the same for me; we would power me into a career on the stage and screen.

David listened to me, then said, 'Can you deal with the fact that I'm not in love with you?'

I didn't even have to think about that. As far as I was concerned, David's version of being 'in love' was what he'd had with Hermione – sitting on a bed holding hands for a year or two, suffocating each other emotionally while the clock ticked and their careers went nowhere – and I wanted no part of *that* kind of love. I wanted movement, growth, freedom, mutual inspiration to creative action, mutual respect for separate identity, mutual support for individual ambition. I wanted us to make each other's world bigger, not smaller. I knew too that David loved me in ways that really mattered: he really needed me, respected me, and cared for me. And ultimately, as we both knew and had told each other more than once, we were kindred spirits. We were *alike*. We belonged together.

So I told him 'Yes, David, I can deal with that. I can deal with anything.'

'All right, then,' he said, and agreed to my agenda. Freely, willingly, he accepted both my commitment to him and the trust I was placing in him.

And so I'd taken my leap of faith. Right there in that little Bromley bedroom, looking out over the coal shed and up into the brilliance of a fine, free, star-bound future, I'd given David the best years of my life.

It was time to get moving. Certain matters needed attention, some seriously; changes were needed in certain areas of David's career. With an album about to be released on a new label and the successful 'Space Oddity' single just behind him (after languishing for two long months, the haunting story of Major Tom's dilemma had risen to number five on the pop charts), David had a case of momentum crying – screaming – for direction.

No aspect of our situation needed attention more urgently than the most basic: David and I had to have a place to live and work together. He was still at Plaistow Grove with Peggy, but for the sake of everyone's sanity I had retreated to my room at the end of nowhere in Blackheath; consequently, the swift, spontaneous joint operations required by our mission weren't exactly our specialty.

I went house-hunting, then, and oh my, did I ever do well. Haddon Hall was its name, and it was spectacular.

Picture this: You're on the slow uphill gradient of the main road south from Beckenham, which, as I've said before, is one of the leafier, gentler south London suburbs – plenty of greenery and muted graciousness, a quiet and substantial civilization – and you're facing a structure, at 42 Southend Road, that is as distinct from the usual run of rental property as you can imagine.

It was a candle manufacturer's mansion originally, a bastion of the great lost British industrial empire, built in concert with one of the dominion's last great spectaculars, the Crystal Palace Exhibition of 1851. As you might expect, Haddon Hall is a thoroughly Victorian edifice: solid red brick, ornately embellished with solemn white fasciae, and of course righteously, haughtily churchlike in basic aspect, so much so that the dominant feature of the rear face (which looks out over a long, lush garden toward a lovely green expanse of a full-sized golf course) is a huge stained-glass window.

The front is almost as imposing. The door opens, and the first thing you see is that magnificent stained-glass window rising above a short staircase at the far end of a central hallway fully forty feet wide by sixty feet long.

You enter the hallway, a wonderfully high, imposing space, and move toward the window. On the right you pass a bathroom, then a dining room twenty-five feet square, then a music room twenty-five by thirty; on the left are a tiny kitchen, then a massive living room, forty-seven by twenty-five feet.

Hoy, who began his career as the gardener to the family of the candle king, got lucky when the last patriarch willed him the property to spite a generation of errant offspring. I found Mr Hoy a nice gentleman, but he was a difficult project. It took me several months, ever since I first saw Haddon Hall during my stay at Mary Finnegan's, to convince him that David and I could afford the fourteen pounds (about thirty-four dollars) per week in rent, meet the expense of curtaining the towering windows, cope with the minimal kitchen facilities, and so on. John Jones's death, however, delayed our own cohabitation schedule, so that it and Mr Hoy's decision-making odyssey coincided rather nicely. He was ready when we were, and we moved in.


David and I had a little work to do. I had some big plans for Haddon Hall's decor, as did David. Everything had to be white. We all pitched in – David, Tony Visconti and Liz, and I – and it started coming together. It was thrilling to watch a wonderful environment emerge from the gloom; as the clean white background spread, I began to see the shapes and colors of an inspiring stage set for the social performances of my rising star. Haddon Hall could be David's showplace, and a superb creative cocoon.

It was a home David and I were making together. We felt proud of ourselves; we'd struggled through some difficult days, and now we told each other that we'd found the place in which our dreams could come true. Great things could happen now.

We felt daring too, and in that sense I was particularly pleased with myself. David had already lived in sin during his Hermione period, but this was my first such experience. I loved the freedom, and the excitement of going against convention, propriety, and Peggy.

Not for long, though. Dear Peggy saw to that, and so did

David's other dead-weight albatross, Her Majesty Mr Pitt.

Peggy struck first, by telephone. I can't quote her verbatim, and really wouldn't want to, but the gist of her message was somewhat more strident now that I was actually living with her beloved/hated golden boy: Angie the slut, the tart, et cetera, et cetera. For a woman of such fervently claimed gentility, Peggy knew her way around the language of the gutter rather well.

Sarcasm aside, her behavior was just horrible. It hurt me deeply. I'd been brought up in an accepting environment, in a family whose members respected each other and acted accordingly, so I had a very hard time dealing with the poisonous fruit that dropped freely from the maternal branches of David's family tree on whoever – sons, sisters, strangers – sought shelter there. I was aghast, appalled.

Ken Pitt had much better manners, but he too tested my tolerance beyond its natural limits, bit by bit. The climax came when, after inside moves I'd rather not think about, he succeeded in getting his colleagues in the music business gay mafia to name David the Most Promising Newcomer for the Ivor Novello Awards of 1969.

The sheer incongruity of the award itself didn't disturb me much - it was akin, say, to giving Jimi Hendrix a Lawrence Welk Memorial Citation – but the fact that Ken chose to exclude me from his boy's achievement bothered me greatly. I wasn't, I was told, welcome at the awards ceremony. The award was Ken's doing and the ceremony was going to be Ken's moment, a shining bauble in his queenly crown, and *he* was going to be at David's side that night.

I must admit that I went over the top about that, verging into hysterics and causing more than dust to fly at Haddon Hall (such things happen; I'm not exactly the mellow type), but all my raging won me nothing. It was going to be boys' night out, and that was that.

So that *was* that. I'd had it. The price was too high. David himself was an exciting proposition, but the baggage he'd come with belonged in the trash. I decided to abort my mission at Haddon Hall and head to Cyprus to rethink my plans. David could face his queens and demons alone.

I converted my ticket to go home for Christmas, and took my

flight in November. Good-bye, Bowie nearest and dearest; hello, mine.

According to the most readable of the many published accounts of David's career, Tony Zanetta's and Henry Edwards's *Stardust*, what I have just written is not the whole truth. As they tell it, before I went to Cyprus I 'gave David a vital piece of information: she believed she was pregnant. Nothing was said directly but it was clear to David that the right and noble thing to do was to marry her.'

Boys will be boys, I guess, and I suppose I shouldn't be too disturbed by that rather important untruth. Tony and Henry, after all, were relying on secondhand information at best (Tony didn't set foot inside Haddon Hall until long after the Christmas season of 1969, and Henry never did), so let's be charitable and assume no evil intent. I love Tony, by the way. I might like Henry too, if I'd ever been close to him, but I never really wanted to be.

Let me be clear about this; I wasn't pregnant, didn't think I was pregnant, and didn't tell David I was pregnant before leaving for Cyprus. Nor did I remind him, as the authors of *Stardust* allege ('in case that wasn't enough'), that I 'did not have English citizenship' and therefore 'could do nothing official on his behalf.' What I did was go off to Cyprus in a huff, leaving him to fend for himself, in November (not 'shortly before Christmas').

Let me be even clearer: I did not, as *Stardust* nastily implies, trick David into offering to marry me. In fact, when I read the words on the card I got from him in Cyprus after a silence of several weeks - *This year we will marry* – I had mixed emotions.

It's true that marrying an Englishman was the most obvious way of solving my visa problems and making myself eligible to work legally in Britain, and thus bringing my goal of a career in the theater closer.

Should I marry a Briton, then? Well, perhaps – but not a Briton with whom I was in love. I had in fact researched the matter, going so far as to consult immigration lawyers, and I'd decided that if I chose that path, any marriage I entered would be a business proposition. I wouldn't want it subject to the turbulence of romance – liable to end at any time and requiring enormous amounts of time and energy for its basic maintenance – and I certainly wouldn't want my partner to come in the form of an incorrigibly promiscuous, self-obsessed young starlet. And I'd already had other offers, which I'd refused. I'd concluded that if I were going to marry anyone British, it would be a waiter, taxi driver, bank clerk, or whoever might be amenable to some sort of mutually beneficial arrangement.

So, do you understand, honey? Have I made my position on marriage in December 1969, clear enough for you, Henry? Can you see how, when I first read the words *This year we will marry*, my reaction was: *Wonderful. That's just what I don't f*****g need!*

David called me the very day I received his card. It had come in a bundle of his letters, delayed by a postal strike. The letters were charming and affectionate, and I'd been reading them one by one and softening as I did so, and by the time I heard his voice I was very well disposed toward him; romance had reentered my feelings.

He was very sweet too. He played me a tape of his new song, 'The Prettiest Star,' and told me it was written for me. And then he asked me to marry him, and I accepted.

What can I tell you? I knew it wouldn't be easy, but I loved the man. I told myself that marrying him would solve some of my existing problems, and I'd just deal with the ones it created. I was Angela Barnett, child of heroes and survivors of wars, learner of lessons and leader of finishing-school girls, closer of deals and kicker of doors, and banisher of demons. I could do anything. I could move *mountains*.

# JIMI, GEORGE, AND THE GODFATHER OF SOUL

*N*ow that the story is rolling along at a reasonable clip, let me digress.

If you look at my life as a river, then my rock-and-roll decade with David was the main current, and thus it will form the main narrative flow of my book. There have, however, been lots of tributaries along the way, some of them just as lively as the waters David and I shared, and I'd be selling you short if now and again I didn't take you wandering from the main channel with me. Some interesting characters lurk up those streams. Jimi Hendrix, for instance.

I must say how lucky I feel to have seen and heard Jimi play. He was outrageous. Hearing him play in person was like hearing the electric guitar played for the first time ever; it was as if he were creating a whole new instrument, made of his own flesh and blood and soul somehow, and he was just soaring inside that left-handed spirit Strat. Talk about a Light Person.

I wasn't prepared for him at all; I had no idea. I was just my stylish, well-bred young self, accompanying my music biz gentleman friend Lou Reizener on an evening of pleasurable business at Blaise's, a hip little Kensington club (this was late in 1966, before David). I was sitting with Lou and some other Mercury Records people, and I looked up, and *wham!* – there he was. Just *wild*: the tightest pants I'd ever seen, bright screaming yellow, topped by a knee-length crushed-velvet frock coat (silk velvet from the antique market, not the cheap modern stuff), with a gorgeous purple-and-yellow Indian silk scarf looped loosely around his magnificent exploding-Afro head. Jimi was the very first great psychedelic dandy, the maker of the mold, and man, did he do it well.

Lou saw him just after I did, and went over to him, then beckoned for me to join them. So I did, and said hi and shook the lovely man's hand, but it was a non-encounter. Lou was saying the usual things about looking forward to the show and so on, but Jimi was unresponsive and unsmiling, blank. His eyes didn't register seeing me at all.

I thought that was interesting, so after he'd moved away I said to Lou, 'He's so self-possessed, isn't he? He must be really concentrating on his music.'

Lou laughed, the man of the world enlightening the sheltered teenager. 'No, Angie, that's not it,' he said. 'He's stoned.'

I thought that was even more interesting, but quit thinking entirely a few minutes later when Jimi and a drummer (Mitch Mitchell, I guess) took the stage and started playing. It was like being hit with a tidal wave and a lightning bolt at the same time. I was flabbergasted. I couldn't believe that that much music – wonderful music – was coming from one man with one guitar.

Jimi came back to sit with Lou and me after the set, and this time he was much more communicative, apologizing for how he'd been before and explaining that he'd been worried because his bass player (Noel Redding, I guess) hadn't shown up. He introduced himself to me very charmingly, and we chatted a while about something or other, I don't remember what; I do remember his making a very good impression. And I don't think he was stoned. He was very clearheaded and sharp when he talked to me, that first night and the three or four nights Lou and I went back to Blaise's in the following weeks.

I think, in fact, that sometimes Jimi may have *pretended* to be stoned. For one thing, my generation's great romance with hash and grass and acid was in its first, most powerful flush, and so a person obviously stoned was a person beautiful in the eyes of peers (remember that, hippies?). A seriously spaced-out demeanor was virtually de rigueur in all the right places. For another, musicians who appeared stoned were in a good position to observe the straight people circling their action. A&R men such as Lou Reizener, who were mostly older and alien to the drug culture, tended to let their guards down when they thought the target of their interest was off in a psychedelic fog. They were a little too candid, a little too free with their business secrets, a little too like themselves as opposed to how they might prefer their prospect to see them. Jimi, I think, was playing *that* game.

I was more straightforward. Lou was very hesitant about committing Mercury to Jimi, and I couldn't believe it. 'Why don't you sign him, Lou? I mean, sign him *now*. Take a standard contract from the office, have them cut a check, and get his name on the paper! He's incredible! He's *gorgeous!* He's going to be huge!'

Wrong approach. My enthusiasm seemed to discourage Lou rather than inspire him, perhaps because he felt threatened by Jimi's very obvious sex appeal (not an unusual reaction in older white men), and he didn't enjoy the spectacle of his own much-prized teenage girlfriend's joining the stampede. I know he was pleased when I told him I'd turned Jimi down – relieved that I hadn't gone home with him, and doubly thankful that I'd been tactful in my refusal. I pretended I hadn't heard when Jimi suggested we leave together, and I went on talking; while that certainly wasn't how I *wanted* to act, prudence prevailed. I was under eighteen and therefore still committed to my deal with my father, and then too, I was sharp enough to predict Lou's likely reaction if I went skipping off with a burning-hot young black guitar god. So, sorry, kids, no Jimi Hendrix sex stories here.

I'm sure my avoiding his invitation made no big difference to Jimi, who wasn't exactly short of willing admirers then or ever, and it helped the tone of our future encounters, when we met more as peers, as colleagues. He asked me if I was sleeping with Lou; I told him I wasn't and explained my reason (Daddy again), but other than that we talked music, clothes, and business. Jimi was curious about Lou and the other Mercury guys; he wanted as much inside dope as he could get, and he was looking with an intelligently critical eye at the various suitors for his hand in business. He was leaning away from Mercury, he told me, because the company hadn't had any rock hits in its recent past, and it might not be able to do a good job of promoting him. He was right too. Mercury had plenty of financial resources, but the bosses in Chicago were jukebox guys. They just didn't think in terms of artist development and big promotion budgets.

Another odd factor in any prospective deal with Mercury was Buddy Miles, the great and grossly girthed jazz/rock drummer who would, oddly enough, join Jimi's Band of Gypsys a few years later. Basically, I think, Buddy saw Jimi as his rival. *He* was the heavy black act on Mercury (pun intended), and he wasn't about to encourage the label to sign an artist capable of diverting attention away from him.

That's my assumption, anyway. What I know for sure is that Buddy passed along to Lou the buzz among black musicians that Jimi was unreliable. I don't know how true that was. The American black music community had, after all, rejected Jimi's radical approach to blues and R&B, and would continue to make him a pariah in the few remaining years of his life; reports of his unreliability thus might well have been covers for deeper, darker misgivings. The whole sad, stupid question of where Jimi's loyalties lay, with the unaccepting brothers of his root community or the welcoming hippies of the white middle class, was a potent and ugly undercurrent even then.

But I don't know whether Buddy himself bought into all that stuff. I doubt it. I do know for a fact, however, that it was he who drove the nail into the coffin of any deal Lou might have been contemplating with Jimi, because I heard him do it. Lou asked Buddy about his experience playing with Jimi in James Brown's band, and Buddy said that Jimi was always being fined for being late, and that he eventually was fired for doing acid.

Buddy was a trip all to himself, though. While he was making one of his albums, he and I got to be – well, I suppose 'messmates' is the proper term. Buddy ate quite a lot, and that's putting it mildly (these days he'd have an 'eating disorder'; back then he was just a glutton), and he loved me because I was the only person on the scene who could even begin to keep up with him. When I showed up at the studio, it was 'Oh, good, you brought Angie! My girl! There's a girl that can *eat*! Okay, sister, what you want?'

I'd state my preference, and we'd order vast quantities of it – fried chicken, Cantonese food, whatever – and then hunker down in the studio and have at it. I couldn't approach Buddy's enormous intake volume, but I'd sit there with him, serve him whatever he wanted, and clean up after him. He loved it. So did Lou, who could keep the recording sessions on schedule as long as Buddy stayed in the studio rather than lumber off in search of the food of his moment.

I liked Buddy. Later he got into some pretty bad stuff and ended up in prison in the States (with three separate convictions, no laugh), but that's okay. Drummers as a breed are like that. One of my favorites, a man who was my lover for a while, actually killed a guy by putting him through a plate-glass window in a fight, and plenty of others have come close – although usually it's themselves they end up sending prematurely to the Great Beyond. There's something about the boys who wield the sticks, and something about me too: I've certainly loved my share of them. More later on that, though.

Apropos of Buddy and Jimi, I remember sitting in Madison Square Garden in New York City years later, watching Tower of Power and those divine Parliament/Funkadelic folk, George Clinton and Bootsy Collins and the whole brilliantly tripped-out dandy-poet-intergalactic gang, as they (finally!) picked up where Jimi left off. I had just about the best time I've ever had in public at that show – I can't think of anything I've seen that would match it musically or theatrically – and I recall watching the guitar player fly over my head (yes, he actually flew, in a harness, across Madison Square Garden), and thinking: *This should be Jimi! This should be him! This is his doing!* Jimi went away when he had to, I suppose, but I wish he'd stayed longer among us.

I'll continue my rambling – now, however, at the New Music Seminar in New York in 1985 or thereabouts. The event is boring except for one magic moment in which George Clinton and James Brown find themselves in the same room. Naturally, something has to happen.

The Godfather kicks it off. 'Hey, George! I understand you're in good shape. You going to do some splits for us?'

George looks down his nose. 'Old man, old man, why you talking like that? Do the splits – *huh!* You think I'm gonna get up there and embarrass you?'

'Now, now, come on,' says the Godfather. 'Do three splits!'

George comes back. 'I'll do *three* if you'll do *five*, old man.'

James gives a little laugh and looks at him. 'Why don't I save you the trouble? Why don't I just do *ten*, and then you see if you can do that many?'

So they start doing their splits, and the scene is wild to watch. By the time they're finished, James Brown has done twenty-seven - twenty-seven full splits! – and the considerably younger George Clinton has fallen over, gasping and defeated (*really* defeated?) after twenty-three. So the founding spirit of funkadelica lies there on the stage, looking up at the Godfather of Soul, who stands bright-eyed and beautiful, sweating like a stallion; and George says the perfect ceremonial words: 'You're still the boss, James.'

Those guys are just too cool for words.

# 4

# DIARY OF A SPACE
# ODDITY DEN MOTHER

*O*h, what a lovely wedding! It was *exactly* in tune with the times. I wore someone else's dress (a lustrous silk number from the twenties, bought the day before at the Kensington antique market); we held our ceremony in a register office and didn't invite any family members (although Peggy showed up anyway, alerted by Ken Pitt); we forgot about the legal requirement for witnesses and had to drag along our house-mates at the last minute; neither David nor I had any intention of obeying the laws or observing the moral or social conventions of marriage; and rather than send the groom off on his last night as a bachelor to get drunk and make out with some stranger, we went off together and made love with a friend.

The only non-seventies aspect of the affair was that neither of us was stoned when we said our words (I hate to call them vows). But we made up for that by proceeding straight from the register office to the Three Tuns, our local pub and the venue of Beckenham Arts Lab performances, and getting as drunk as possible with our buddies.

So voilà! One perfectly Alternative wedding for one perfectly Alternative couple. And lest there linger any doubt about just how Alternative that was, why don't I make it perfectly clear?

We didn't, for a start, marry from any romantic impulse. As I've said already, I myself took the plunge with David to end-run the United Kingdom's all too efficient immigration authorities and thereby bring my professional goals within reach (and to shut Peggy up). For his part, David was taking care of similar needs: getting a shot at *his* professional goals by keeping his door-kicker by his side (he'd had a stiff dose of his own resources during my retreat to Cyprus, and had found them wanting), and shutting Peggy up.

We were simply soothing a major irritant and removing a massive obstacle from our path to the big time. It didn't hurt that my parents had undertaken to add a wedding present of three whole thousand British pounds. That kind of money bought a lot of curtains, even great big long ones for great high Haddon Hall windows.

I must also say, however, that when David and I tied the knot, I got a real old-fashioned girlish glow. The moment was sweet, significant, all those things: romantic, in fact, and I *really* liked it. Yet I did my best to play those feelings down. It wouldn't be cool to start acting like a real girl all of a sudden: better to stay strong, steady, competent, capable, motivated, aggressive – good and butch, in other words, the way David liked me.

So much for romance. Now for convention.

Oh, spare me. David, son of Lance, subscribed to the vision of monogamy shared by most males on the planet – absolute fidelity until the first better offer – and moreover, he was an up-and-coming star in a world where better offers were abundant, if not actually overwhelming, on a more or less daily basis. So even if he had committed to a marriage to one woman on pain of something genuinely threatening, say eternal banishment from the pop charts, I would have been a fool to accept.

Besides, monogamy wouldn't have appealed to me in the first place. I was anything but a one-man-or-woman woman. As long as we held true to each other and respected the love between us, David and I were perfectly free to romp and dally with whoever else might tickle our fancy.

We'd already made a good start in that direction. Our prenuptial night together, with a gorgeous dark-haired actress friend of David's and Calvin's, had been great fun. We went to her flat for dinner, got tipsy, fell into bed together, romped *à trois* until we all passed out, then woke late and rushed in a panic to the registry office. I remember once stumbling back to Haddon Hall from the Three Tuns for a frolic with David and a folksinger named Tina, and a lovely evening with Dana Gillespie and her boyfriend Ken (my first foursome), and I recollect David and me being tempted to try to take Mary Finnegan into our bed but not doing it. I'm pretty sure she wouldn't have gone for it.

We were young and free and this was London, ground zero for the bold, beautiful, brave new world; free love was natural, and simply what one did.

It wasn't only the times, though, or at least for me it wasn't. I'm hot on the subject partly, of course, because I'm bisexual, and I was traumatized and radicalized early in the game by the dire conclusion of my affair with Lorraine at Connecticut College. I'd felt the lash of the sexual bigot's whip, understood its power, and decided it needed fighting.

Another root of my philosophy goes a little deeper and further, into my childhood. Its fruit is a powerful disdain for the human vices of jealousy and possessiveness – low emotions, based in fear and imprisoning the spirit, the most profoundly destructive forces in relations between individuals, and the threads that bind the fabric of monogamous society. Not only do I disapprove of them; I abhor them.

I remember where and when my path to this ideology began. I was eight years old, and had just returned home to Cyprus after receiving my First Communion in the States. I had very long hair then, and one day at school a gang of boys in my class caught me and put lizards in my lovely hair. The frightened lizards tried to get away, and they shed their tails as they fought to escape; panicked lizards and their detached, still-twitching tails were squirming and scrabbling in my hair, for God's sake!

When my father came home from work I wasn't hysterical anymore, but I was upset enough for him to know something bad had happened. He asked, and I told him.

First he offered a piece of advice I've held on to all my life, even if I haven't always followed it: 'Baby, don't ever do anything that lets people know what you're afraid of. If they know what you fear, they can hurt you.'

Then he took me outside and caught half a dozen lizards for me, and although I was afraid of them, he stayed there with me and we played with the lizards until I started to enjoy it. Then we let them go.

'Are you ever going to be upset by lizards again?' he asked. I told him I wasn't, and I meant it (and I never have been).

I feel I got lucky through that experience. Most people, I think, don't learn the lesson I learned as early in life as I did, if indeed they ever do. So thank you, Dad. The colonel came through.

I don't recall that his advice was ringing in the back of my head as I married David, but I know I was following it. With David I was entering uncharted, potentially frightening territory. I had no idea whether the open-marriage commitment between us would work, or could work; whether either of us had the emotional resources to handle it. But there I was and there he was and there we were together in a decidedly unconventional, intriguing situation. Why not go ahead and find out if a person could really handle it?

I found out, all right. A person could. Or at least *this* person could. Having a love partnership with David, plus very satisfying love relationships with other people, plus whatever fleeting encounters floated appealingly down the stream, meant a wonderful way of life.

It's an awful shame that while I could handle it just fine, David couldn't.

But now I'm way ahead of myself. The reality in 1970 was that David and I subscribed to the theory of open marriage but behaved more or less monogamously. I say 'more or less' because now and again we romped and dallied together with other people, and David probably accepted the occasional offer when he was off without me on the rock-and-roll circuit. I myself didn't have other lovers, male or female.

For one thing, sex with David was nice, and encouraged intimacy, but was not the kind of overwhelming experience it can be. He was a stud, not a sensualist, and I found myself in a situation all too common among young women: the sex frequent and vigorous, but the ultimate pleasure elusive or, as in my case, unattainable.

For me, in fact, it was still true in those early days at Haddon Hall that Lorraine remained the only person to have taken me to orgasm. You can probably imagine how large she still loomed in my daily consciousness, how loudly *that* voice still rang in my head. I still carried her book of love poems with me (even now I can smell the acrylic paint on the cover she made for me), and I still carried her love in my heart. And that would be the case for a while; it would be a couple of years before I began any serious dalliance with other women, and several before I met a man capable of taking me over the sexual top. Men were a big disappointment.

But sex wasn't the mainspring between David and me. In our partnership the primary imperatives were creative expression, philosophical growth, and the achievement of our separate, mutual, and equally bright-burning ambitions.

And in those domains we were very intimate, very trusting and cohesive, very intensely together. We sat together in Haddon Hall's blooming beauty, talking about Buddha and Confucius, Newton and Einstein, Kafka and Dalí, Egyptian hieroglyphics and the Arab alphabet, all the great mysteries of history and creativity, struggling to align them and ourselves in our brave new world. We went antiquing, hunting the Deco treasures David loved and whatever other pieces told us they needed to take their place in our home. We wandered London, visiting friends and absorbing art of all sorts. We entertained – oh yes, did we ever entertain; even in those first days Haddon Hall was a stellar salon. We listened to pirate radio stations and watched the few pop moments the telly offered in those days, an hour or two a week at most, and picked apart the performers we saw; precious few were worth watching, we concluded, and almost none worth copying. We plotted and planned and dreamed and schemed, and of course we acted and we accomplished. We spent whole days and nights together; we touched a lot; we held hands.

It was special, it was intense. We'd each found the person we needed to make our dreams come true, and that was a *very* powerful bond for people like us. We were almost embarrassingly grateful, almost maudlin about it . . . the two of us alone together against the world; kids claiming the future; dawn breaking on the house where a Light Person and his guide awoke and readied themselves for the journey of their lives . . .

\*

To business, then. Our first priorities were taken care of – David's door-kicker was by his side, his home base secured and operational – so now we needed the rest of our Stairway to Stardom shopping list. Next item: one band.

Which wasn't exactly a new requirement. It had in fact been obvious for a while to everyone sensible, most notably Calvin and me, that the versions of David Bowie available to the public in 1969–70 – David's fey young folksinger and Ken Pitt's cabaret up-and-comer – weren't at all in tune with the times. It simply didn't work, for instance, for David to walk bravely out onstage, alone except for his acoustic guitar and his fine sensibilities, and face a hall full of drunken East End yobbos primed and loaded for Humble Pie, a band distinguished above all by its pioneering mastery of planet-crushing volume. And as to his cabaret career . . . well, people who wanted to watch Judy Garland should just stay home and rent *The Wizard of Oz*. This was 1970, for God's sake. Anyone illuminated by even the dimmest of bulbs knew that whatever flavor you came in, you just *had* to rock.

So David needed a band. He had the foundation already – Tony Visconti on bass, John Cambridge on drums, himself on elementary rhythm guitar – but he didn't have the vital ingredient, the power and the glory of any real rock band: a lead guitarist. No problem, though; John Cambridge knew a very likely lad who might be open to offers. Mick Ronson was his name, and he was to be found far from the lights of Swinging London, in the south Yorkshire industrial port of Hull.

To Hull we went, then. I don't remember much about the city, although a fair amount of rain and an almost eerie lack of hills or even inclines come to mind, as does my first taste of northern-waters skate in a place I had no trouble accepting as the world's largest fish-and-chip shop. I have, however, a very vivid memory of meeting Ronno.

What a lad. Hull's finest. Leader of the Rats, the closest the city ever came to its own Beatles or even Gerry and the Pacemakers (which might tell you how it compared, scenewise, with its mirror city, the industrial port of Liverpool directly across the country on the other coast); a born and bred Mormon; an incorrigible ladies' man who was fast and loose, blond-god handsome (oh Lord, how handsome!); and one of the nicest, best-hearted men I have ever met. Dear Mick, how lucky we were to have coincided.

He needed some persuading, however. We had to go to his parents' little council house and meet his family – lovely welcoming folk, living proof that the farther north you go in England, the nicer the people are – and pass muster with them, particularly with his mother. Mick wasn't going anywhere with anybody, apparently, until Mum had assessed the situation and approved of it. Which Mum did. She got along nicely with David, and she took to me too. As I did to her.

'Now, you will look after 'im, won't you, Angie?' The dear woman was all motherly concern, sitting there surrounded by her gorgeous towheaded children, every one of them a little English Mormon with beautiful manners, an unwavering sense of morality, and a wild streak a mile wide. 'He'll be all right down there in London, won't he?'

'Oh yes, Mrs Ronson, we'll take very good care of him. He'll be all right with us.'

... Oh, yes, Mrs Ronson; he'll have a nice warm balcony to sleep on with his mates, a nice cozy van to ride around to gigs in, three squares a day, free guitar strings, a few quid in his pocket now and then, as many girls as he wants, and the best doctors the National Health can buy. He'll be just *fine* in London ...

Ronno's own doubts were expressed over great golden gobs of batter-encrusted skate ('Yiv never 'ad *skeeat*, lass? Ooh, it's *luvly*!') served in reeking vinegar and hard-boiling lard in the afore-mentioned fish-and-chip shop, the Gainsborough – that's what they called it, all five floors of it – and he was concerned mostly about practical matters. Where would he live? What was the pay? We answered to his satisfaction (he'd live with us, the pay would get better), and by the time all that delicious ultra-saturated animal fat was on its way to our arterial walls we had ourselves one very wonderful lead guitar player, great new friend, and happy hippie housemate.

A hot body filled the lead guitar slot, then, and so the band was ready to begin competing seriously in the pop marketplace. By now the major personnel requirements, including that of the roadie, had been met.

Our roadie, Roger Fry, some kind of Australian Yorkshireman or Yorkshire Australian, was a beauty. I have no idea where or when the original connection with Roger was made – it feels as if he was always there, as if he had jumped full-blown out of my womb one day – but he must have been somebody else's roadie before, because he had all the essential roadie style points covered cold.

Wherever you've got a roadie, of course, you've also got a van (until, that is, you've got a truck, or a bus, or a bus and a truck, or several trucks and buses, or an airplane, or an airplane and several trucks and buses, or several airplanes, trucks, and buses). Roger had a van, and a good one too: a brand new Bedford (what else in 1970?), baby blue, which David had bought with 'Space Oddity' money and given him in lieu of wages. The way it worked, Roger got his three meals daily, just like everyone else in the Bowie operation, but he had to earn his cash by being a roadie for other bands on a free-lance basis. This was a very intelligent arrangement: David secured long-term access to a vital tool, the van, while he had the means to do so, took advantage of the tax break for the capital outlay, avoided the ongoing financial burden of both the van's upkeep and Roger's salary, and kept Roger busy and loyal. It was a characteristic move; although I was the one who pointed out the need for a van in the first place and conceived the outlines of the deal, David appreciated and endorsed it – John Jones's son, with all that Yorkshire blood running through him, was usually sharp with his money – and he did it in style. He had a little boy's enthusiasm for motor vehicles, and buying that van was great fun for him. He and Roger went off together and visited about six different pubs before deciding what color it should be.

Roger, like Ronno, was one of the balcony dwellers at Haddon Hall, others at various points being our first drummer, John Cambridge, and our second rhythm section, Mick Woodmansey and Trevor Bolder (Ronno's fellow former Rats from Hull). The balcony also served as more temporary bedding space for whomever we and the boys dragged home with us for purposes high or low, plus random guests too tired, stoned, drunk, or simply far from their own beds to make it home at night.

That balcony was a great and significant asset, then. Basically, it made it possible for David to have a band, which in turn made it possible for him to have a career in rock. I'm glad I didn't have to sleep up there, though. The people who did were usually startled out of sleep at some ghastly hour before the crack of rock-and-roll dawn – sometimes as early as nine o'clock (and that's *a.m.*) – by me, barking orders or cajoling favors on the telephone in the hallway near the front door.

That was my routine. While David slumbered happily in our bedroom, I'd get up and start doing business as soon as people arrived in their offices, or crank up the sewing machine and start turning out rock-and-roll finery, or begin whatever other task called most loudly for my attention. More or less anything I did involved noise, though, so I my poor babies on the balcony didn't get their sleep the way the boss did. Or perhaps I helped teach them how to stay comatose through whatever din I could generate, a useful talent in a rock-and-roller.

David's usual stirring hour was noon or so, at which time I'd squeeze him his orange juice and make a fresh pot of coffee and point him in the day's direction, which could be anywhere, really: writing songs or rehearsing with the band; visiting his agent or his song publisher or La Pitt; shopping for knickknacks; going to the Three Tuns for lunch with the Arts Lab family; getting in the Rover (yes, 'Space Oddity' had bought us semi-posh personal transportation) and tooling over to Richmond Park to stroll and frolic, or up into town to smoke hash, listen to music, plan creative-world conquest, and generally entertain ourselves *chez* Dana. Good times.

Some processes were taking their course during those months just before and after our marriage. One was the increasingly efficient, intuitive teamwork between David and me. Haddon Hall was in many ways our stage as well as our home, the place to which we brought people we wanted to dazzle, impress, shock, or seduce into our creative sphere, so quite often David and I were working consciously together on our guests.

It wasn't as simple as the basic good-cop, bad-cop routine we used in business negotiations, but it broke down along essentially the same lines. I was forthright where he was reticent, usually; frank where he was subtle; forceful where he seemed (but wasn't) compliant. I got it going, whatever it was, and I changed its direction when it needed changing and stopped it when it wasn't working. I was the spark plug, the accelerator, the brake. David was the fuel, the journey, and the destination; it was he who really swept them up and carried them away with him to Bowieland. We took turns steering, according to the need.

It worked well. The David & Angie show, playing Haddon Hall for several successful seasons, got to be a pretty hot ticket in the hipper parts of town.

Another process was the increasing self-confidence David's lord-and-mastership of Haddon Hall gave him. Being free to decide how to decorate the place, to play his music whenever he wanted, as loudly as he wanted, to have his meals on his own schedule, to pay for it all and be the person responsible – these were liberating changes for a young man previously dependent on, and confined by, the hospitality of people (his parents, Ken Pitt, Lindsay Kemp, Mary Finnegan) older and more established than him.

Haddon Hall, in short, introduced David to a brand-new state of personal affairs. For the first time, he was in charge of his own life. And for that I take full credit. And yes, it was good to watch him begin acting more the man than the boy. I liked David strong and responsible, the way he liked me.

Nineteen seventy really was a good year. Our days were certainly goal-oriented, and pointed in many ways, not at all aimless, but I wouldn't call them stressful. *Fun* is what I'd call them: productive, optimistic, gregarious, challenging, pleasurable.

I was in my element. I dealt firmly with Peggy, and I cared for Terry when he came to live with us after being released from the mental hospital. I grew to feel deeply for the poor lovely (funny, brilliant) man, and I fed all the other boys from my new kitchen with the fabulous gas range David had provided (what a husband!). I wined and dined David's old friends and our new ones, everyone from the great puppeteer Brian Moore to Lionel Bart, that ultra-bright leading light of the British theater. I finessed a sweet little deal to buy an adequate PA system for David and the Hype (his band) by talking Philips Polygram, Mercury's European distributor, into signing the Hype as a separate act (and getting the advance check made out to the sound company, in the exact amount required, on the spot). I rattled cages. David and I would go to the various music offices in our loop, doing business and getting people crazy too, just for fun: saying David's new songs were all about lesbian love, or that we were teaming up with Paul Buckmaster for an album inspired entirely by whale song, or whatever came to mind. It was such a hoot, watching those poor guys trying to play it cool and figure out whether or not we were kidding.

I was feeling my oats that year – powering up, approaching thresholds. For one thing, I was spending time with Dana Gillespie, and going places. She was the first person I'd known who had a fully formed philosophy of self-liberation through sex and drugs, and she encouraged me. Dana introduced me to the pleasures of smoking hash and helped me begin to see my own attractiveness; she brought out my femininity and challenged my conviction that my butch side was my only high card in life. I found a lot of new confidence in Dana.

With David I was also expanding. Our potential was becoming clearer, our horizons broadening, my hopes rising high. I remember one day in particular: We were sitting in the Giaconda, a hip Soho coffee bar, and he was waxing lyrical about what fun it was when he was sixteen, playing Eel Pie Island with the Buzz or the Lower Third, doing Black Beauties and staying up for days on end, hanging out with his mod mates right there in the Giaconda. Ah yes, he was saying, *that* was rock and roll. *That's* what it was all about.

I looked at him and thought, Oh no, my man. There's got to be more to rock and roll than that; it's got to go further. I don't want just the roar of the Benzedrine, the smell of the crowd, and some clammy little coffee bar to call home. I want the fucking *World!*

# 5

# REJOICE, FOR THE QUEEN IS DEAD

We had our home, we had our band. Next item? Oh dear, a sticky one, full of ambiguity and conflict for me, and perhaps not such a happy, breezy read for you. Still, it has to be done.

La Pitt. How did he offend me? Let me count the ways....

No, no, not yet. First a less vague impression of the man than I've created so far.

Middling tall, of medium build, in his mid-thirties in 1970, with ginger hair going to gray and his hairline receding prematurely, Ken was above all else very well groomed: tailored in Savile Row, barbered exquisitely, scented discreetly. Perhaps he made up in style what he lacked in natural physical attributes, but I think not; I found his face, thin-lipped and Teutonically broad below the eyes, unpleasant.

He spoke with all the languid arrogance of the ruling class, but I detected none of that aggregate's real badge of rank, the truly steely grace educated into successive generations of British Brahmins by the better public (that is, private) schools. So while he wasn't Eton (or Harrow, or Wellington), I've no doubt he'd been to some public school or other, where the boys got a thorough grounding in cold showers, frequent canings, lots of sadomasochistic peer-approval rituals, and plenty of plain old buggery. He was deeply, unredeemably misogynistic, and of course he worshipped his mother.

I don't mean to disparage Ken's education, for he was a very cultured person with a broad appreciation of history, literature, and the arts, and David certainly learned a lot from him. I don't think my Bromley boy's cultural horizons would have been nearly as wide as they were if Ken hadn't taken it upon himself to expand them.

Ken wasn't by any means an incapable manager either. He was very sharp and exceptionally well connected in the you-kiss-mine, I'll-fondle-yours world of British singer handlers (Angie, you bitch!). If David had wanted to take the cabaret-cutie route to fame and fortune, he and Ken might well have danced their exquisite, little pas de deux a good while longer and done reasonably well for each other.

But it was not to be. The words writ large on David's wall were ROCK and RADICAL, not CABARET and CONFORMITY, and there you had it: one essential, irreconcilable difference.

The problem was clear enough, yet there was a lot to it. One element, the most important, was the big daddy of all generation gaps. This being 1970, the cultural/attitudinal distance between David at twenty-three and Ken at circa thirty-five was daunting. Ken simply couldn't fathom David's passion for Zen, macrobiotics, universal love, and other manifestations of the hippies' new world order. For him, I'm sure, going to a show at the Round House was a deeply alienating experience, probably very much like a dream I had the other night: I suddenly found myself at a rap concert with no idea of how I'd gotten there, surrounded by people twenty years my junior wearing $150 sneakers, and baseball caps, backward. The rappers bellowed bombast at a bazillion decibels – threats to their fellows, insults to women, obscenities about this, that, or the other – and everybody just loved it. So I know it's difficult, having your sensibilities offended and your values violated, and I'm sure that Ken's brushes with peace, love, and liberation back in 1970 were as uncomfortable as my encounters with today's embrace of egomania, misogyny, and dog-eat-dogism.

One arena in which David's and Ken's values diverged very widely was, unsurprisingly, sex. David was bisexual (or *sort* of bisexual, anyway; more like hetero with a homo sideline), while Ken was pure queen. You can probably imagine, then, the dust that flew *chez* Pitt because of David's heterosexual conquests, especially his big-time love for Hermione. I wasn't there, but David told me that Ken's jealousy of Hermione, although largely unexpressed for fear of alienating David completely, was considerable. Perhaps it colored his more freely vented disdain for all things – fashion, art, dance, music, politics – emanating from hippie headquarters Notting Hill. Perhaps not; perhaps his queenly loyalty to the established cultural and social order threatened by the hippies was enough of a force all by itself.

His loyalty to the status quo was ardent, and in that respect he was very much a man of his generation. He and his contemporaries were queens who knew their place: safe in the closet. They wouldn't dream of challenging the system that dictated that the closet was their only choice, and therefore somebody like David, or me, was dangerous to them. To make no bones about one's deviance from the one true sexual path – to flaunt one's bisexuality or homosexuality in public – was an invitation to disaster. The establishment wouldn't stand for it, the logic went, and the lash would come down, and life for all the quiet, respectable queens of the land would get that much harder.

Ken's position had some logic in a certain cringing vision of real-life sociopolitics, and in his defense I must point out that two decades ago the gay liberation movement, and therefore gay power, didn't exist. David and I weren't following a trend or reinforcing a message already circulating; we were pioneers, originals, and our voices were the *first*. So I can't really blame Ken for finding our openness threatening, or for regarding me and my radicalizing influence as dangerous to David's career.

Or maybe I can. It wouldn't have taken much imagination for him to grasp the truth: that the social walls built so intricately around individual homosexuals and such cliques as the music business gay mafia were about to be smashed asunder; that all the convoluted rules, all the limits on how far what kind of queer could go where and when with whom before the straights stamped down, were about to get chucked out the window; that David and I weren't lone voyagers but harbingers of massive change – the first swallows, if you will, of our generation's sexual spring.

It was a shame, really. Ken could have done wonders with David. He didn't have to be a genius to figure it out either. It wasn't as if David didn't have obvious potential and even real, concrete successes in the career direction he wanted to take. His 'Space Oddity' single had done very well, going all the way to number five on the British pop charts once American radio refused to play it (disaster in space being judged an un-American, perhaps subversive theme in the summer of the first moon landing) and the BBC, typically, reacted by plugging it especially hard. Critical response to David's music, never hostile, was especially enthusiastic in 1970; he was gathering 'most promising' and 'best new' accolades in all the right places. So everything was on the up-and-up. David's career as a hip act was well under way.

But no. According to Ken, 'Space Oddity' was a fluke, a novelty, which meant nothing to David's future. There was no career to be had in rock. The Mercury guys were doing everything wrong; they were pushing him in all the wrong directions. He needed to be an Entertainer. He needed to be in movies. Wasn't *that* his kind of niche? Hadn't he done well in that part in *The Virgin Soldiers?*

David would repeat all this to me, venting his anger and confusion and looking for sympathy whenever some new contention arose or some old resentment surfaced for further embellishment, and slowly it became evident to me that the distance between him and Ken wasn't going to decrease, even when Ken was making a good point. On the issue of a film career, for instance, Ken was absolutely right as far as I was concerned; the small role in the independent, low-budget *Virgin Soldiers*, which he had secured for David, was a very promising beginning.

You couldn't tell David that, though. The mere fact that it had been *Ken's* initiative, and that a film career was *Ken's* idea, sent him running in the opposite direction; he'd be a rock star no matter what Ken wanted, and he'd be damned if he'd go anywhere near a movie set (the prejudice endured; I had a devil of a time motivating him toward *The Man Who Fell to Earth,* and almost didn't manage it). My husband, I must say, possessed the unfortunate character defect of needing everything he did to be his own idea, even when most of his ideas really came from other people.

In practical terms the career direction fight came down to what kinds of gigs David was booked to play. Ken kept pointing him toward work that followed naturally in the track of his song contest success – ballrooms, workingmen's clubs, the places where you're expected to work the crowd and give them all the popular numbers, *then* (maybe) throw in one of your own tunes – while David kept resisting and trying to head off to the hip rock-festival scene.

The band was a big factor in all this, and a sticking point with Ken. David Bowie as the singer in a rock band was not at all what Ken had in mind; and as his most convincing argument against such an arrangement, that David simply couldn't afford a band, dissolved in the face of ingenious solutions – the Haddon Hall balcony, the Bedford for Roger, the PA money from Philips Polygram, my feeding and clothing of all the boys – the issue of bookings became more and more divisive.

It got rather gruesome. Booked by Ken, we'd have to strap the PA system onto the roof of our Fiat 500, a vehicle which strongly resembled an adolescent turtle and made a VW Bug look like an ocean liner, and head up the M1 motorway to Birmingham or wherever, hoping the wheels didn't collapse or a modest gust of wind didn't simply pick us up off the asphalt and tumble us into some cow pasture and a dog's death. Then, usually after arriving with only nerve damage, we'd have to face the hard part: crowds of generally very warm, down-to-earth industrial workers who would become drunker and drunker and warmer and warmer as long as David delivered the songs they knew and liked and expected of a Saturday night, or, alternatively, drunker and drunker and meaner and meaner if he didn't. And all this for the princely sum of fifty pounds per gig or even (heavens! such blessings, such managerial foresight!) a few quid more.

I remember one night when we were doing a double-header down south in outer London rather than the usual two hundred or more miles away up north. I was having a hard time that night. I'd been hauled off by the cops for trying to throttle some yobbo who'd been flipping lit cigarettes at David's face while he was singing for his supper, and I'd slipped out of that mess only to find myself shivering and shaking in the rain and the dark, trying to load that bloody PA onto that ludicrous little car so we could go get our fair share of abuse from the *next* crowd of yelling, puking, beer-sodden idiots, and it hit me: I'd had enough.

'David?' I said. 'I'm over this, man. This has *got* to stop.'

'I know what you mean.' He sighed, and the angry-dof look in his eyes told me he was speaking real truth. 'I've been over it for two bloody years.'

For quite a while, several months, we tried to work around Ken, to go out by ourselves and secure the gigs we wanted without having him lecture us about David's compromising himself. We went to NEMS, a hip booking agency – I made the whole pitch, as we'd agreed beforehand – and told the people there exactly who David Bowie was, what we wanted, and how we wanted it. It was a hard sell, but effective. Through NEMS we started working the few tuned-in places available at the time, and David saw once again that by pointing me in the desired direction and letting me do my thing, he could actually get where he wanted to be. And of course, here again was evidence that he didn't need Ken Pitt.

Now there's a question lurking: Why was all this conflict still unresolved? Why hadn't David simply sat down with Ken, made a determined effort to talk him into moving his career toward rock, and acted on whatever came out of that confrontation? I don't think the Brits, circumlocutory as they are, have a term for such an exercise in direct action, but here in the USA we call it 'fish or cut bait.'

The answer lies in David's psychology, an interesting if somewhat unimpressive area. His habit was to whine a lot and resist, passive-aggressively, never really speaking up for himself or taking charge of a situation. When I first met Ken, in fact, I was quite puzzled: Could this charming, cultured, beautifully mannered gentleman really be the ogre I'd already grown weary of hearing David bemoan? And was Ken not a very desirable resource, a powerful, experienced businessman who was obviously, deeply, professionally, *and* personally devoted to his client? What more, I wondered, could David wish for in a manager?

What he actually did wish for, I think, was his father. The roles in the relationship between David and Ken were all messed up along *those* lines. David wanted a father figure as uncritically supportive as his real-life daddy: a caregiver/benefactor whose basic function was to make his boy's dreams and schemes come true, and *never* tell him what to do. Ken's profile of the ideal son/client/sex object, on the other hand, was a young man eager for direction, convinced that Daddy knows best. And so the relationship staggered along under all that baggage, Ken trying harder and harder to mold his boy, and David, resolutely unmalleable but absolutely non-confrontational, wishing it weren't so, subverting Ken's plans in subtle ways, and whining a lot to me – expecting, of course, that eventually I'd reach my tolerance level and take the action he wouldn't (or couldn't). I don't doubt for an instant that when David proposed to me, a major item in his mission profile for me was the hit on Mr Pitt. Protector, effectuator, door-kicker, *dragonslayer*.

Sex, of course, was a significant component of the deal between Ken and David, but on that front I don't have much hard information. I often wondered whether at some time early in their relationship David might have let Ken do a number on him. But after that it was all desire, no action.

Such a setup would certainly fit a pretty standard queenly profile. Queens don't really want to be gay, so they seek the affection of straight or bisexual men more eagerly than that of pure homosexuals, and often they're most comfortable with a scene in which the object of their desire either doesn't reciprocate physically or doesn't engage fully in the sexual relationship. So an attractive, flirtatious, bisexual young stud with a legitimate reason to visit often but not be underfoot all the time – David – would be just about perfect.

And that's my take on David and Ken. Ken really wished the best for David, really worked hard for him, and really loved him. And of course he really hated me.

It's easy to see why. I was the latest in a string of serious competitors for David's creative ear and personal affection, from Lindsay Kemp to Hermione and Calvin Mark Lee, and I was turning out to be more formidable than any of them; David had *married* me, for God's sake. So unless I'd made a point of burying myself in the kitchen and/or mindlessly supporting every move in Ken's spectacularly misguided campaign to mold David into the British Liza Minnelli, I was bound to taste his venom. As it happened, he didn't really come down on me (and I didn't turn on him) until he made such a point of excluding me from David's moment at the Ivor Novello Awards, several months after we'd become inseparable, but the timing was probably arbitrary. Every queen in history has feared and hated the wife of her *innamorato*, so the basic arrangement of conflicts and loyalties between Ken and me was a done deal from the start.

It's sad. Ken once said about me, 'She was a storm trooper who yakked at him [David] twenty-four hours a day.' Interesting, that. *Storm trooper. Twenty-four hours a day.* Sounds more like Ken's fondest wish than my reality.

All of which lands us squarely, if not very comfortably, in the lap of a subject often mentioned but not really addressed so far in this narrative: the British music business gay mafia.

Let's cut to the chase on this. Was the British pop music business in the sixties and seventies run by gays, and if it was, am I going to tell you who it is your heroes had to blow in order to become your heroes?

Yes and no to both questions. The British music business in the sixties and seventies wasn't exactly *run* by gays, but many of the key middlemen in the game, especially managers, were self-proclaimedly, obviously, or covertly homosexual. Among them were the late Brian Epstein, who so intelligently saw our future in the Beatles; Robert Stigwood, who came from Australia with the Bee Gees, made Cream a supergroup, launched his own record label, and perpetrated a string of middle-of-the-road extravaganzas including *Jesus Christ Superstar,* the movie and musical versions of *Sgt. Pepper's Lonely Hearts Club Band,* and other properties too numerous and/or awful to mention; the outrageous Seymour Stein, founder of Sire Records and launcher of Madonna, the Talking Heads, the Ramones, and many another wonderful act, who was American but such a frequent troller of the London scene that he might as well have been a native; Ken Pitt, of course; and oodles of others.

They made up, I guess, roughly a quarter of the middlemen in the British rock/pop business during my years. And it takes no great feat of genius to figure out why. The bees go where the honey is. Just as British television was heavily infested with *Killing of Sister George*-type lesbians feeding off the medium's endless supply of comely, ambitious young actresses, the lusty young lads of rock drew the queens.

I don't think, however, that your idols actually had to suck their way to the portals of the big time. At the very worst, the young knights errant of rock and roll just had to relax a little now and then and not worry too much about the gender of the lips lubricating their lances – not, in rock-and-roll terms, much of a stretch at all. Or maybe they didn't even have to try that hard. In a lot of industry situations, escorting one's queen in a purely social sense would suffice, the queenly ego drawing perhaps as much sustenance from the semi-public appearance of intimacy as from the private satisfaction of lust. And of course a powerful music business queen is hardly doomed to a dry spell even if her headliner *does* display reluctance. The rock scene isn't exactly short of less stellar but still attractive, sexually adventurous, willing and eager young trade.

Drugs are of crucial importance to this subject. The story of your sixties and seventies rock idols was, in most cases, the saga of young men readied for the big time in scenes featuring plenty of recreational, reasonably low-risk, thorough peer-approved substances – mostly grass and hash, with some psychedelics now and then, maybe a little speed on the side, plenty of good cheap beer – and then very suddenly confronted with the big time: big money, big fame, big drugs. So among other things, our lads went straight from beer and joints to cognac and cocaine, quite often making great strides forward in their journey from drug fun to drug dependence as they did so.

This is unremarkable in most ways, just the story of our generation, except for the issue of supply. Rock and roll being such a high-profile profession and its practitioners such desirable targets for law enforcement or whomever, secure lines of supply for highly illegal substances are a very high industry priority indeed, one that can't be left to amateurs, or to chance. Therefore, the typical seventies rock-and-roll management operation featured a reliable, high-quality, high-volume narcotics connection with as much graft as possible going for it, and a designated individual within the organization (typically the tour manager) whose job it was to distribute the goods as needed.

Quite often, then, a musician would be hooked on heavy drugs, coke or smack or big-time downs, and dependent on his management for his supply. Think about it: What would *you* do if, say, you were out there on the road in some nowhere you couldn't even find on a map, really stoned – *really* stoned – and the man who made it all possible for you and loved you so much was just really, *really* horny, and nobody would ever know? Or if, like one famous New York New Waver we all know and love to marvel at, you were such an out-and-out smack junkie, and so broke all the time, that the only way you could make it was to blow the man at your record company every time you needed a bag?

It's very unseemly, all this, and I'd rather not be thinking about it. A large part of me is very attached to the world as it should be. But I also have an affection for the real world as opposed to the one erected for our benefit by hypocrites, and I'm seeing more and more of the latter these days.

So what do I really want to say about the music business gay mafia? Well, how about this:

I don't think that providing the occasional blow job in exchange for significant career advancement is all that terrible. Very large numbers of women and girls do it, and worse (or better), all the time. They do it for *dinner*, for God's sake, and that seems just fine with everybody concerned! So if you, dear reader, find yourself just horrified by the very idea of your rock-and-roll heroes lubing the ol' executive tube steak, so to speak, perhaps you should bend over, grasp that homophobic double standard of yours firmly in both hands, and ... Or at least look to the logic of your values.

Now think about this: None of the most significant musicians mentioned above – the Beatles, the Who, David Bowie, Madonna – got anywhere worthwhile in the business until the talent and energy of a gay man was added to the act.

So take note, all you young thugs, musical queer-bashers, and run-of-the-mill guitar homophobes. I see a lot of you around these days, some of you sounding very good indeed, and sometimes I cringe when, after I tell you about so-and-so in New York, possibly a wonderful manager for an act like yours, you come back with, 'Yeah, he's interested, but we heard he's a faggot, so . . . '

I'll ask you a question: Would you rather spend your life jerking Slurpees in Bumfuck, Georgia, or take the risk of actually working with a queer?

# QUESTIONS OF IDENTITY

*I*'ve got the riff going, so I might as well carry it on. Who's who and what's what; confusion, controversy, hypocrisy, homophobia . . . It's such a pervasive theme in the music business, and often the reality can be elusive. So many people have so much invested in some image they think they need.

Elton John, of course, is the classic case. Poor Reg (I still can't call him by his stage name, even after all these years): so confused for so long, and getting honest only in the last few years, after what seems to have been a painfully misguided attempt at marriage and what was definitely (no 'seems' about it) one of the nastiest imaginable lawsuit-and-tabloid maulings in public. Reg is too nice to endure such crap, especially after he'd spent so many years making a wonderful show of his dance-along-the-sex-identity razor's edge. You really can't deny that for our generation, Elton John in his full-blown Glitter period was every bit as entertaining as our mothers' boy, Liberace (whom I met as a child, by the way, and of whom thought very highly). More so, in fact: our boy had much better songs and bigger shows.

And like Liberace, Reg has always been a kind and caring soul. He's done more than his fair share for good causes, and from what I've seen he's always treated people with respect. He's certainly been very nice to *me*.

I met him early in the game, during my first magic summer with David. We'd gone up to the Essex Music offices to get a cash advance from David Platz, and that gentleman had as usual handed over the fifty pounds with great good grace. (Now, *there* was a music publisher who knew his business; he always made his writers feel valued, especially if they hadn't yet realized their sales potential.) As we emerged from his office, we ran into more of the Essex crew: Tony Visconti, Gus Dudgeon, and Reg.

'Bloody hell!' David Platz joked. 'It's a songwriters' convention!' And indeed it was; that was quite a hallway full of talent. All it needed were a couple more of the Essex gang – Marc Bolan, maybe, or the guys in Procol Harum – to make it a summit conference, not just a convention.

The subject of 'Space Oddity' came up, and Tony said he thought it was too much of a novelty song (a discreet way of expressing what he said later in an interview, that it was 'a spectacular cheap shot'). Sure, he said, he'd produce David's album for him – that was *serious* material – but maybe Gus Dudgeon should produce 'Space Oddity.' Gus had a better feel for 'that kind of thing.'

'Sure,' said Gus. 'I'll do it. I like that song. I think it could really go places.'

David Platz agreed. 'Yeah, David. It's the most commercial thing you've got. It's got hit written all over it. We'll cut it as a single, and I know Gus'll do a great job with it.'

At this point, Reg joined in helpfully. 'Gus really is a great producer, David. It'll work out, you'll see. He'll do you right.'

That turned out to be a good call, as we all know. The conversation was a turning point, perhaps *the* turning point, in David's career. Who knows what would have happened without Gus's sure hand in the studio? Major Tom might never have left the launch pad, let alone achieved orbit in the pop charts. Ziggy Stardust might never have come down among us. There might be no Tin Machine today.

I glanced at Reg while the others were agreeing with each other about David's hit potential, and felt a flash of sympathy. He looked a little dejected, and I thought I understood why. He'd been struggling for as long as David had, after all, and nobody was talking about potential hits in *his* songbook. So there he stood, just another bright, sensitive, dowdily dressed, penniless-art-student type (though not quite a *starving* one; he was a touch chubby even then), doing his best to be helpful behind a brave little smile.

My heart went out to him that day, and so I was especially

delighted when, a few months later, I saw him on the telly with a hit going up the charts. 'Look, David, it's Reg!'

David professed good feelings, but then again, with him there was always an edge of competitiveness. I saw that pinched look around his mouth when Reg came out with 'Rocket Man,' and felt it necessary to reassure him. 'It's okay, David. Other people can sing about space travel too, and besides, imitation is the sincerest form of flattery.'

That pleased him, I could tell. I didn't, however, raise the same point when he began composing his *Hunky Dory* songs on the piano instead of his acoustic guitar, just like Reg.

I was even happier for Reg when, with several hits behind him, he started flowering as an entertainer and a person. I loved his mouse-to-marvel-man metamorphosis and his 'Top *this*, boys!' approach to stage dressing, and I enjoyed seeing him relax in his success. Good funding and star status improved young Reg's mood immensely; he got funny as well as nice.

He threw fabulous parties in his Glitter years too. I remember one in particular, at his beach house in Malibu in '82 or so, a sumptuous affair with a dance floor on the lawn out by the beach, superb gourmet catering, the works. I walked up to him and introduced myself – I hadn't spoken with him for several years at that point, and of course I looked very differrent in the post-punk eighties from how I looked in the post-hippie seventies – and I was happy to find that he was still the same old amusing, unassuming Reg. When I reminded him of how long I'd known him, and told him how proud I was of what he'd achieved and how he'd handled himself, he actually blushed.

I didn't know, of course, that he wasn't handling himself very well at all. He was great in public – I *never* saw him obviously stoned, or even sloppy – but privately, I guess, it was another story. I don't know.... Maybe people susceptible to substance abuse, such as Reg and David, are doomed to end up with a problem no matter what, but in Reg's case, I can't help wondering whether facing his sexual identity crisis earlier in life might not have preempted some of the pain he went through later.

I'm glad he's past all that now, though, and he's sober, seemingly happy, and settled (for now anyway) with his boyfriend in the city I too call home (for now anyway). If anyone deserves a little love, peace, and happiness, Reg does.

I'm not so sure about Rod Stewart, though.

Rod was another vibrant figure from the old days in London. There's never been any great love lost between him and me.

It's the blondes. I'm (usually) not one, so I don't think Rod has ever had any reason to take any interest in me. He's like that. I can't remember ever seeing him out in public without some stunning young thing crowned by a healthy headful of gold- or wheat- or otherwise light-colored hair (or two or three such creatures), and I'm certain I've never observed him directing his energy toward anything else, except perhaps clothes. He does exhibit a powerful love for his threads – and for his own headful of streaked hair, and his profile, and his tight little bottom, and everything else he sees in the mirror.

He's not one of the lads, Rod isn't. I've never seen *him* hunkered down around a table at Tramp's with his fellow musicians, talking music. Or maybe I have, but in that case the musicians around him would have been the Faces, and I'm afraid that in that case they would have been holding all my attention. Current Rolling Stone and former Face Ronnie Wood, you see, is my idea of the ultimate golden-hearted rock-and-roll gypsy. A fabulous man – and talk about a *face!* And Ronnie Lane, God bless him, is one of those wonderfully smart, deep, funny, down-to-earth, natural gentlemen British society can sometimes produce just perfectly. In my book Rod doesn't hold a candle to either of those two, on any level. Neither does he measure up to Steve Marriott, the original Small Faces singer who formed Humble Pie with Peter Frampton when his band went off to work behind Rod. I spent some time with Steve in his studio, and came away with enormous respect for him as a writer, composer, producer, and thinker – and Rod just isn't in that league. I'm sure he's very sharp and his head's well screwed on businesswise, but I simply can't imagine advanced creative concepts thriving in the space between those shapely ears.

He *is* gorgeous, though. Photos of him by my friend Leee Black Childer's *are* pretty much the ultimate in pure rock-and-roll sex appeal, wherever you happen to be on the gay/straight/bi/multi axes. And I love the way he's kept that ultramacho ethos alive down the decades.

There are situations where 'everybody in the business,' and sometimes even the whole 'community' has heard all about so-and-so's supposed sexual orientation, but there are other worlds of people who have no idea, who haven't heard so much as a whisper. Are country record buyers, for instance, aware of the rumors about a country and western singer? Or have the girls who swoon for one of today's most famous pop stars heard the rumors that I've heard about him – that he might be that sorry soul, a homophobic homosexual?

As you've already surmised, I'm for total honesty. It just works better and helps out all around. Wouldn't it be terrific, for instance, to hear women sing about love between women if they are really bent that way? Wouldn't it be refreshing to be honest, as Elton has been, as Freddie Mercury of Queen was? And hell, while we're on the subject, let's hear from Pete Townshend, and more current figures. And shall we ask about one of the hottest singers of all, whose band's name is a series of letters?

God knows, Madonna has been up front about swinging both ways. But what about the 'rumors' regarding a member of that famous seventies rock band? What about that legendary dark-haired, lithesome pop singer/actress? God knows, a lot of men have been through her life, but why doesn't anyone ask her about that certain woman in her life?

As we all know, appearances can be *so* deceiving. And not just on the sexual front.

The ultraspectacular, pyrotechnic, supershowmanly and very straight Gary Glitter, for example: I remember him when he was still Paul Raven, known for his solid cabaret career and his low-key, all-around nice-guy manner. And as it happens, my sharpest memory of him is from the days just before he detected a change in the show biz wind and transformed himself, calmly and thoroughly, with great good humor, into the rock-and-roll Glitter critter.

It was the week in 1972 when David's admission of his bisexuality hit the headlines, and I was sitting in the Gem Music reception area, reading *Billboard*, with Paul sitting opposite me, absorbed in the *Melody Maker* featuring (or rather, trumpeting) the infamous interview with David. We read on in silence for a while, and then Paul, having assimilated the news and its implications, lowered his paper and favored me with a deadpan look.

'Well,' he said coolly, 'there's not really much else to say, is there?'

'No, not really,' I replied, and that was that. No further comment. I *loved* that. It was so typical of him, today as well as way back then; he has a dry, gentle wit about him. Sometimes when I've seen him onstage in his Glitter persona, all crazed and sweaty and supercharged, ringed with roaring motorcycles and bathed in laser light, I've had a difficult time believing it was really good old Paul up there.

We are talking about *show* business, though, so such dichotomies aren't all that rare. To this day I can't imagine that nice Ozzy Osbourne summoning Satan or biting the head off a chicken, even for big metal money; he's such a pleasant, mild-mannered, down-to-earth, *decent* bloke.

Ditto Alice Cooper. If you could talk to him without looking at him, you'd probably think you were chatting with an articulate, even-tempered, well-informed golfer type, perhaps a midlevel executive in a politically moderate think tank or charitable foundation. My clearest memory of *him* remains a dinner party I threw in London circa 1973: a civilized little soirée with David, Alice, me, and a few others, including Arthur C. Clarke. The main topic of conversation was Kirlian photography, at the time a very exciting new field offering opportunity for all manner of scientific and philosophical speculation, and Alice was great. He addressed the subject with as much enthusiasm, and almost as much erudition, as the famous science fictionist and speculative thinker himself did. Alice drank Budweiser all the way through, of course, but then, everyone's entitled to his own little peculiarities.

My friend Boy George is a case of 'what you see is what you get,' except that he's bigger than you expect him to be, a tall, handsome boy. I've known him since he was a kid coming up on the scene, and I've always been charmed by his openness, gentleness, and idealism. When a boy was found dead from an OD in his house and the full scandal broke in the press, I admired the way it was handled. The head of his recording label, Richard Branson, didn't sneak him off to a Betty Ford Center and try to sweep the whole thing under the rug as quickly as possible. Instead he got him into rehab and took a public stance that was very antidrug but very pro-Boy George, and stood by him all the way. That was the responsible thing to do, I think. It sent just the right message to teenage junkies and establishment hypocrites alike.

The last time I saw Boy George, backstage after a gig he did in Atlanta, he was surrounded by mind guards. That might be a good idea, if you consider the stakes; it just felt very strange.

And very nineties. Can you imagine that kind of thing in the sixties or seventies? People in bands used to be scared of getting dosed without knowing it – the classic acid-in-the-punch scenario - but I don't recall *anybody* losing sleep about the possibility of getting high on *purpose*.

Sometimes, I think, we forget how it was back then, and how quickly it got really crazy. By the early-to-middle seventies in my scene, the hardest drugs were *everywhere*. There was more white powder, smack and coke and whatever, in Tramp's and the back room at Max's Kansas City than you find at some ski resorts.

The price got paid, of course. Look at the New York Dolls, the one great band in which, in the early 1970s, everything came together – punk, Glitter, unisex, genius, and total mayhem – and check out the score: three survivors today from a starting lineup of six. Dead, one after the other, over the years (no private-plane crashes here) are my drummer ex-lover, Billy Murcia; his replacement, Jerry Nolan; and that wonderful archetypal rock-and-roll lunatic, Johnny Thunder. Johnny and Jerry are still together, in adjacent graves.

Johnny was wild. I went on tour with him and his post-Dolls band, the Heartbreakers, in the late seventies, and one of the weirdest things about it is that I almost can't recall his speaking voice. That's probably because the only time I ever heard him talk, as opposed to sing or grunt or mumble incoherently or moan with pleasure, was when he would go to his manager, my friend Leee

Black Childers, and say 'Leee, have you got any money?'

Leee would reach into his pocket, pull out a roll, and peel some bills off. 'Okay, Johnny,' he'd say. 'Go eat now. Don't spend it on drugs, all right?'

Johnny would look at him with an expression somehow both sad and mischievous, and say, 'Right, Dad, I'll go eat.' But of course he never did, and soon enough he was dead.

Like most other people, I try to make some sense of such things. In Johnny's case, I do that by telling myself that he really wouldn't have *wanted* to live longer than he did. He was a rock-and-roll kamikaze, and that's the script he followed, with great flair and diligence, to its inevitable end.

And that in turn brings to mind Mr Elvis Aaron Presley.

I saw Elvis perform twice, once at Madison Square Garden in 1972, where he was fabulous – still vital and virile, but also aging with confidence and dignity – and then again in 1976, in Las Vegas.

That second time, I was appalled. The tacky, excessive elements of his act which had been mere hints at the Garden were virtually the whole show in Vegas. He looked like a cross between a baby elephant and a wedding cake, moved like a slug, and sang with a weary, distracted formality I almost couldn't bear. He seemed lost. I was very sad for him. I wished somebody close to him would help him.

I was in Vegas on Elvis business, as it happened – he was interested in recording one of David's songs, and RCA had asked me to deliver the demo tape in person – so after the show, some of his people came to my room to escort me to his hospitality suite for the meeting. Unfortunately, I told them, I had to decline the invitation. I had a case of laryngitis I surely did *not* want to pass along to Elvis, and so if they would kindly convey the demo tape themselves, with my regrets...

I wasn't exactly lying about the laryngitis – I did have a mildly sore throat – but that wasn't my real reason. The fact is that I just didn't want to meet the poor sad travesty of Elvis that Elvis had become. I preferred to remember him as he was before the drugs took him down, with the power and the glory of rock-and-roll in his hands.

I wonder if Johnny Thunder's way of going down might not have been better for everybody concerned  Ultimately both he and Elvis lived fast, then killed themselves with drugs. But there the similarity ends, because Johnny died young and left a beautiful corpse.

# 6

# THE STARSHIP BOWIE
# BOLDLY GOES...

*B*ack to the late summer of 1970, and the final stages of business relations between David and Ken Pitt.

Tiresome processes in those days... Calvin Mark Lee withdrawing from friendship with me as David and I grew closer... Ken taking his best shot at Calvin – telling him he would handle press invitations for a 'Night with David Bowie' showcase at the Royal Festival Hall's Purcell Room, then inviting just one gay-newspaper journalist, then telling David the whole mess was Calvin's fault – and David buying it and freezing Calvin out for good... Ken and Tony Visconti in unlikely alliance over the worth of 'Space Oddity,' and David having to wonder if his first real success was the fluke they told him it was, and credibility being strained all around ... David intensifying the passive-aggressive chill on Ken, avoiding his calls, neglecting to visit Manchester Street when he went up to town... Ken complaining, then stepping off the edge into quicksand – calling Peggy and having her give David messages. Wrong move, Ken darling; you just allied yourself with Private Enemy Number One in David's mind. Into the quicksand, then; through the murk, down to bedrock, no way back. Good-bye, Mr Pitt.

It took a while – months, in fact, as we traipsed around from very respectable lawyer to very respectable lawyer, getting the same terrifically polite but deadly frustrating opinion every time: Nothing to be done, old chap, the fellow has a *contract*. But in the end I had a minor brainwave of the crucial kind and went to talk to Ralph Mace, the dear man who was head of A&R for Philips Polygram at the time (and who went on to head RCA's classical division for many years). Ralph and I got along very well; it was he who had done the PA-money-for-Hype-tapes deal with me, arranging things with great grace and humor. So I had no qualms about popping the million-dollar question to him: Did he know a lawyer who could break a management contract?

As it happened, he did. Or rather his boss, Olav Wyper, did. The man in question wasn't a lawyer, just a very shrewd operator; lawyers came to *him* for advice. Tony Defries was the name.

This was information, I should add, rendered gladly. Both Ralph and Olav took the news of Ken's impending departure with relief. They could see David coming on strong, they believed he could be huge if his career were handled correctly, and they knew his future lay in rock, not folky cabaret. I'm sure too that they hadn't enjoyed the many irritants he'd inserted between artist and record company, and I assume they saw a more harmonious future should he and his baggage depart the scene.

I took their information back to David, and we agreed that it sounded good. I called Mr Defries's office for an appointment, and a few days later David and I were sitting in an office in a square behind Oxford Street, assimilating our first impression of Tony Defries.

He was a big man, quite handsome. He wore his dark hair slicked back at that meeting, and presented two immediately outstanding features. First was a rare, deadly combination of great intelligence and lightning-fast wits; here was a man who knew exactly where you were going, and who got there ahead of you every time. Second was his nose. My God, what a nose! A peninsula of a nose, a protruberance of proportions beyond Cyrano, beyond compare; a lunar probe of a nose, a *Graf Zeppelin* of a nose! Everything else about Tony receded into the background behind that one amazing asset. Not that, as assets go, it did much good; so much air-intaking acreage, and still he was asthmatic.

It didn't require long for him to judge the matter we laid before him and conclude that – Well, no problem. Simple. Sure, Ken's management contract could be null-and-voided. He would take care of it, worry not, end of problem. Our wishes would become reality posthaste.

The look on David's face was as if a forty-ton anvil had just been lifted off his big toe – or perhaps more to the point, as if his father had come miraculously back to life inside this suave, soothing, superbly self-confident (married, heterosexual) thirty-year-old. To describe the expression on my poor dear boy's face as 'relieved' would be a very grave understatement.

And of course I was delighted too. What I liked immediately about Tony was his refreshing lack of Englishness. Here at last was a person born on the Scepter'd Isle who didn't consider it his job to tell you why you couldn't do what you wanted to do. He didn't want to sympathize, commiserate, explain the particular rules and regulations and mores and conventions standing in the way of the particular enterprise you had in mind, or get down and simply whine in harmony with you; it didn't even seem to occur to him. He just looked at the problem, then solved it. I dunno: I still suspect that Tony might actually have been born in New York, then smuggled across the Atlantic to grow in Golders Green, sharpening his wits and moving inexorably toward the destined moment when David Bowie would walk through his office door.

All in all, he was impressive. He did indeed handle things. I have forgotten exactly how his approach to Ken was geared, and neither am I sure about the terms of the settlement with Ken, but that's significant in itself: *Tony* took care of the whole deal; neither David nor I had to, and we had to visit his office only a few more times and sign some documents, and that was it: Bob's yer uncle – bye-bye, Ken.

Which of course meant *Hello, Tony!* in a big way, somewhat bigger than we'd anticipated. We'd had only three or four meetings when he made his move and said *he* should manage David. But more on that (much more) anon.

Having lived through more than my fair share of foolishness and turmoil caused by Ken's wrongheadedness about David's career and his jealousy of my influence, I had to wonder: How was the new guy likely to work out in those terms?

Tony Defries promised very well. He was very friendly toward me and seemed perfectly willing to deal with me as seriously as he dealt with David, and he was much more willing to follow our campaign plan than Ken had been, much more interested in our concerns, and much better tuned in to our generation. So circumstances stood a good chance of working out just fine.

If they didn't, though, and another fight developed, I would be in combat with a whole new class of cat. For one thing, Tony had demonstrated levels of cunning, speed, and ruthlessness the gentlemanly Mr Pitt could never have achieved and wouldn't have wanted to, even in the worst of his snits. For another, Tony knew my mettle already. Unlike Ken, he didn't think he was dealing with some female appendage of David Bowie who could be snubbed, offended, and dismissed without consequence. No. He knew I was the person who, when management displeased me sufficiently, had gone and hired a hit man.

He understood the implications, I'm sure, and made his moves accordingly right from the start.


So David had a home, a door-kicker, a band, and a manager he could handle. Now he needed something else. He needed to stand up and stand out. He needed to quit moving with the crowd.

Consider the crowd. Put yourself in our shoes, among the crowd at a typical 1969–70 rock concert – in London, New York, San Francisco, a Kansas college town, wherever.

For one thing, it smells. You have the basic grunge of the hall, which until recently (perhaps as recently as the afternoon before the show) may have been functioning as a triple-X porn-movie house, attracting odors closer to the dead-fish than the fresh-popcorn end of the spectrum and inviting, most likely, a certain degree of flea infestation – ah yes, little biters up your Mother Earth macroskirt, what *fun*! Then too, the promoter probably hasn't seen fit to have the bathrooms cleaned before the show, so beneath the scent of stale semen you have an olfactory undertow of ancient urine, the odor sharpening as the show proceeds and legions of your stoned-senseless brethren migrate through the bathrooms, doing their business in every conceivable way but straight down or forward. Impaired flushing apparatuses, both mechanical and human, lead to increasingly severe and widespread toilet blockage, adding a richness one recalls with something very close to horror. At times a kind of sickening sympathetic resonance gets going...

There are of course powerful scents competing with the basic grime and fetor. Incense may be burning, although, this being '69–'70 rather than '67–'68, that would be a trifle retrogressive. Dope is very certainly on fire: grass and hash in joints and in pipes of every conceivable size, shape, and material. And of course almost everybody is smoking cigarettes as well as dope, and almost everybody (particularly in Britain) is in serious need of a bath, new sweat over old sweat under long-worn hippie threads being pretty much the personal-hygiene hallmark of the psychedelic era. In some circles in these years, you'll recall, body odor is a *virtue*.

Maybe you've gotten the idea by now. Perhaps you're back there, led by the nose, and you're starting to squirm in your seat, which is exactly what I did in many rock halls in that period. Oh yes, another thing: the sticky floors, those sworls of evil black-brown goo and snaky ridgelets of crusty stuff under your precious all-organic tootsies in the dark, and your having to handle this shit on *drugs*...

I mean, bless us all, it was so much fun, but it really *was* sloppy. And not just the venues either. The shows themselves were – well, I guess 'loose' is a good word. People stumbling around onstage, the roadies bumping into the drummers, bass players tripping over cables, pints of beer and gallons of wine sloshing all over hot amplifiers, nobody ever getting it straight about which mikes did what, lights fizzing out or flaring suddenly bright, PA systems either humming low and mean like alligators contemplating poodles or belching apocalyptically when some tripped-out guitar god stuck his Fender in the wrong hole...

This stuff was routine, and more or less often the whole crowd would have to experience at least a good half-hour of it before the band even started tuning up – and *that* could be a marathon too, especially if the various musicians arrived onstage separately, according to their own highly individual schedules. You know: *first*, brown rice dinner with a hit of acid, then a few 'ludes and tequila chasers; professional blow job *second*; alternative-press interview *third*; privileged-fan greetings and amateur blow jobs *fourth*;

assembly of onstage stash-and-bottle kit *fifth*; and – ready? is the karma right? – *up* the nose with the pre-performance coke jolt (but only if you're American and very hip indeed; coke use hadn't spread widely in the United States, or anywhere in Britain, in 1970) and *yes!* – to the stage *now!* Plug in and tune up while the other lads amble around, then get a bit more stoned, touch up their hair, slip back behind the amps for another last-minute lance lube or maybe a few more bites on that delicious unpasteurized all-organic peanut butter sandwich on seven-grain bread with wheat germ sprinkles and the mescaline-laced homemade blackberry preserves Susie Morning Glory brought in from Marin (or Manchester) as, like, something *really* trippy for the head....

When the first note hit, of course, the interminability of the wait was irrelevant: you were off – and I mean *off* – on whatever journey the band had in mind that night. But why did it have to be that way? Where was it written in the rock-and-roll bible that a band had to be so incredibly untogether in every aspect of performance but the actual playing of their music? Why did they have to stand with their backs to the crowd, dress as if they had a date with a broken sump pump, intro their songs (while tuning, of course) with gems like, 'We... ah... wrote this one in, ah... uh... yeah!... mmmmmmmmmmmmm... New Mexico,' and never even consider the idea that total electronic failure (at least once per show, usually more often) wasn't a preordained natural phenomenon.

I know, I know. Showmanship was for Elvis and efficiency was for straights: business guys, soldiers, cops, uptight mothers anywhere. Shit happened when it needed to, musicians were just people, like you and me (but richer); machines had their own rhythms, time was a circle, everything was cool.

Me, though – Miss Finishing School, Ms Marketer, Angie of the theater – I loved my macrobiotic munchies and my personal enlightenment and most other aspects of the times, but I couldn't stand *that* nonsense. Neither could David. We two would sit watching these guys (brilliant musicians, wonderful!) stumbling around in the dark, tracked by spotlights that never seemed to catch them until they'd finished their solos, then snorting up goobers and wiping coke snot on their blue jeans in beautifully illuminated view of thousands of their fans, and we would almost die of embarrassment and frustration.

These guys didn't seem to care, but we wanted *our* act halfway together. At least, we thought, you could tune in a back room before you went onstage. You could set up your equipment behind a curtain, darken the house, raise the curtain, then hit the spotlights and stagelights, and *boom* – make your *appearance*! That's where the first note belonged, for pity's sake!

Notions modest enough, those, but they were the start of modern rock staging and showmanship, and the seed of David's great difference, and the beginning of Glitter.

In the matter of image, or more accurately presentation, we had to begin with the most basic unit, David's body. My gorgeous lad didn't have a personal-hygiene *problem*, exactly – he wasn't rank in the hard-core hippie manner – but you could never describe him as immaculate, or crisp, or even fresh. He was in the habit of bathing only every three or four days, so he often appeared a little off, wilted; 'moldy' is the word that springs most forcefully to mind.

Well, that just wouldn't do. No way. I didn't nag him about it, or diplomatically suggest more frequent tubbing, or even confront him in a forthright but caring manner; I simply drew a bath for him every morning and took him by the hand and led him to it. Which was fine with him; David loved being taken care of. End of problem, then, one fresh body out there in the world.

New clothes were more a joint operation, and David's evolution here was a more gradual process. In those early days of ours, as I've said, his sartorial style was a combination of penniless art student and hard-core hippie – dull colors, cheap fabrics, potato-sack tailoring. While such a style was fine, I suppose, if all you wanted to do was study Buddhism and steam organic vegetables, it didn't impress me as effective dress for pop success. You could look hip in the hippie way without looking scruffy, for God's sake, and nowhere was it written that the tuned-in young man of 1970 need eschew the bold, bright, and beautiful colors.

It wasn't that David wasn't interested in fashion. He was. It's just that he was stuck in the hippie rut and his experience before that, as a dress-to-kill mod, didn't translate into our new world. It was one thing to achieve fashion parity by tightening yourself up into one of the same dark, sleek, conventionally macho sharkskin suit-and-tie outfits your mates wore, but it was another thing entirely to let yourself go into the wild, free, sexually ambivalent direction that (to me, anyway) was obviously awaiting the fashion leaders of 1970. To boldly go where no man had gone before.

He needed help, and he was ready and willing. I'd bought myself an outfit up in town, a knitted gray two-piece with a V-neck sweater and tight, slightly flared trousers, and one morning when we were getting ready to go out for the day, David asked me if he could wear the trousers. Sure, I said. We were the same height and almost the same shape, both of us built like dancers, so why not?

He looked very good in those trousers, and at day's end he was delighted; they'd been so comfortable, he'd felt so good. I told him he could wear them anytime he liked, and he did. He pretty much monopolized them.

It went on from there. Knowing how my lad's mind worked, remembering how things had to be *his* idea, I never actually suggested anything outright. No point giving him a chance to dig in his heels and balk the way he had with Ken Pitt. Instead I shopped for both of us, buying and trying outfits I judged to be safely within his existing taste – if they fit me, I knew they'd fit him too – but also picking out items for him that were more to my taste, on the wilder and brighter side. These I'd hang in *my* side of the closet in our bedroom, and wait and see. More often than not he'd take the bait, come sniffing over from his side, see the new stuff hanging there, take it down, look it over, try it on, thinking he was being naughty, pulling a fast one ... and I'd lie there on the bed reacting innocently. 'Oh, you like that? It *does* look good, doesn't it? Oh yeah, David, it's you. Take it ... '

Thus was he seduced, very gently, toward my vision of how a unique, lovely man like him should go out and about in the world. He began appreciating the fine fabrics I loved, the bright and lustrous colors my Mediterranean upbringing had introduced me to, the art I'd learned to esteem in a good tailor's workmanship; he began moving into the realm of high style and sensuality. It was manipulative, the way I went about it, but so what? It was the wifely thing to do.

It helped, of course, that my style of dressing was as far from female convention as his was from the male mainstream. I was inclined toward wilder clothing for men rather than toward what girls were supposed to wear (not that I have anything against dresses and such; I like the way *girls* look in them just fine, yum!), and in fact, when I first met David I was dressing almost exclusively in very flamboyant men's suits, the way Calvin Mark Lee dressed. So what David and I were doing, really, was meeting in the middle – outwardly now as well as inwardly. It felt good. It was bold, provocative, sensuous, and very liberating.

A significant step in this process – significant because it was so public, and such a clear marker for the beginning of something different in rock and roll – wasn't directly or even indirectly my doing. I executed it, but the impetus came from David himself. The original force was Lindsay Kemp's.

We had spent a week in Glasgow with Lindsay and his troupe, working on a show for Grampian TV, which in those days was a marvelous experimental organization. We had a wonderful time doing the show (despite the ravening cold of a Scottish winter, which permeated every inch of our boarding-house bedroom and made us curl up close and cuddle every night), and David, who performed 'Space Oddity' and did a reprise of his part in *Turquoise*, one of the shows from his days as a member of the troupe, was at his creative best. He was very happy, and I think the whole experience – just being back in Lindsay's world, watching that genius of staging at work – rekindled his theatrical passions. So I wasn't at all surprised when, a week or so after we got back to Haddon Hall, I walked into the music room and found him and the boys in the band, Mick Ronson, Tony Visconti, and John Cambridge, talking about costumes. They had a show coming up at the Round House, opening for Country Joe McDonald (!), and David had tabled the idea that they do something new, exciting, and theatrical.

Which certainly lit *my* lights. It was one of my little things to tease Ronno and the lads about their blue jean addiction – endless bloody denim, you'd think it had come down the mountain with Moses! – so I was tickled pink. It was *Point me at the sewing machine! Let's go!*

David was the easiest. It was all his idea, of course, so he was ready and willing, and then too, I had the ideal material at hand, a three- or four-yard remnant of some wild silver netting I'd found in town. Back that with turquoise silk or whatever, I thought, and you'd have one hell of a stage cape. If David wore it over an all-white outfit, with his lovely golden curls above it, the light would bounce beautifully. That would get the audience's attention. And of course the silver tied in with the 'Space Oddity' theme – the astronauts' suits, the shiny skin of the alien archetype, the starry strangeness of the impression David was working to create.

He loved the idea, and I went to work.

Tony was also an eager customer. He came up with his own character, the ironic superhero Hypeman, and that was just fine. His trim, well-muscled body would look great in a basic super-hero leotard, and all we really needed on top of that were Hypeman insignia, which I cobbled up in no time. We decided against a cape for him, since David was wearing one, and went for a collar cum shoulderpiece I built from petticoat wire. Voila! Tony was happy.

The others weren't so smitten with the whole idea. They weren't very articulate about it, but that was okay; I understood. It was one thing to be the good, straight macho rock-and-rollers in David's band, I'm sure, but quite another to go dressing in silly outfits and poncing about the stage like pooftahs. People might start to wonder.

It was okay, I told them. They didn't have to wear tights or capes or anything like that. They could be whoever they wanted to be, as long as it wasn't their usual selves.

That brought them around. John Cambridge, who was drawn to things American, decided to be a cowboy (simple enough: big fringed shirt, boots, and so on; he got it all together himself), and Ronno, after much agonizing, agreed that if he *really* couldn't be his usual sex-appealing self and wear his usual tight jeans and crisp white open-chested shirt, he'd get into the spirit of the thing and be Gangsterman. So we went up to town together and found him a brand-new Carnaby Street suit, an extraordinary piece of work in shiny gold velour, double-breasted, and a great bargain too; about sixty quid, if memory serves. A few accessories later he looked stunning. I'd have oiled *his* Tommy gun anytime (if, that is, I didn't have to stand in line behind every other girl in London).

That, then, was the lineup for the Round House show: the Space Star, Hypeman, Gangsterman, and the cowboy. If you think it sounds like the prototype for the Village People, you might be onto something. If you suspect it was a little ahead of its time and therefore a little hard to relate to, you're definitely onto something; the Round House crowd reacted to the new and different Hype with a lot less enthusiasm than they displayed for Country Joe's more familiar all-denim act. I've read, in fact, that David 'bombed' that night, and that most people in the crowd were 'baffled'.

Critical subjectivity aside – who really knows *what* the crowd thought? – baffled is good. Stunned is better, but baffled is at least a step in the right direction. Bafflement begets curiosity, which creates a buzz. So something could have started on the underground grapevine that night. There might have been a little flurry of interest among the trend-hungry, the people one step ahead of the pack. The nucleus of David's natural constituency might have stirred.

We knew it had been good for us, if not for them. Putting that show together had been a blast, and it felt like just the right thing to be doing. I was very happy; I saw David's star emerging from a vast, featureless sea of sixteen-ounce indigo-dyed cotton into something lighter, brighter, crisper, more colorful. *Much* more colorful.

The real coup, of course, was the dress. Or rather the dresses (there were two, one pale green and the other a wild salmon-pink-blue number). Or rather the gowns. They weren't dresses at all; there wasn't a dart in 'em. They were contemporary inspirations on the theme of garments worn in medieval times by kings, and whatever other nobles were allowed such luxury.

Mr Fish, the designer best known for his kipper ties and sharp-boy suits he tailored for such sartorially nonadventurous sixties rockers as the Dave Clark Five, was the man responsible. It was in his shop around the corner from Savile Row (in his downstairs studio, not the upstairs showroom where the regular stock was displayed) that I first noticed what he'd done. I almost fell over. I couldn't believe it. They were *gorgeous*: silk velour of the best, softest quality, exquisite Chinese frogging across the front, V-necks, ankle-length hems; amazing work.

I showed them to David and he flipped too. He knew good costuming from his days with Lindsay (and Natasha Korniloff, the great costume designer with whom he'd had an affair even with Lindsay's concurrent claims on his affections), so he realized immediately that here was a rare and wonderful find. He scooped up the robes and headed for the fitting room despite the price Mr Fish had quoted us, a prohibitive £300 apiece.

When he came out you could have heard a butterfly swoon. Mr Fish and I both stood there openmouthed, silent, awestruck. David's dancer's grace, his fine features, his luscious long blond hair, and that fabulous robe – it was as if we'd died, gone to heaven, and awakened in the boudoir of the best, gentlest, most manly Sir Galahad one could imagine. God, what a sight he was. What an image.

Mr Fish was the first to speak. 'I'll let you have them for fifty pounds apiece,' he said. 'Just swear to me you'll tell people where you got them.'

We did. We were good to Mr Fish, and Mr Fish's dresses were very, very good to us. Wearing them on his first trip to the States, a promotional tour of radio stations instigated by Ron Oberman, then Mercury's head of publicity in New York, David shocked the straights and tweaked the antennae of the trendsetters as he might never have done on the strength of music and message alone.

Really now, just imagine: An (important) English singer/songwriter in a dress, wearing eye shadow and a shoulder bag, talking on the air about having been 'a shaven-headed transvestite,' garnering press characterizations like 'a mutant Lauren Bacall,' and brazenly fucking anyone he fancied coast to coast? Can *you* conceive of a more gossip-worthy item in the back room at Max's Kansas City, or any lesser cutting-edge space, in the winter of 1970–1?

That recognition among the New York ultrahip was a crucial factor, of inestimable value to David's career, but Mr Fish's creations did even more for us. Photographed in the light green robe in our living room for the cover of *The Man Who Sold the World* album, David achieved even greater notoriety.

It wasn't only that strange, seductive image of him in that stylish, sensuous room that buzzed whoever saw it; it was the fact that nobody in America, or at least nobody in an American record store, was allowed to see it. Mercury Records' bosses couldn't see themselves being associated with a product featuring a picture of a guy in a dress, and they made it quite plain: Give us another cover, or this album won't be released in the United States.

These days, of course, getting your original cover banned has become, if not commonplace, rather low-watt in terms of creative outrage and publicity. Back then it was really an event. The only British artists to have suffered/benefited from such treatment before were the Beatles.

David was furious. I remember him at Haddon Hall when he got the news, cursing and fuming. Bloody philistines! Fucking gangsters! Censors! Fascists! How *dare* they dictate how *his* art be presented? And had his cover not been calculatingly and effectively pre-promoted – worked up to, as far as marketing – by his robed and mascaraed radio tour, which Mercury had funded and endorsed? What, then, did those bloody clowns think they were doing? Did they have any fucking *idea*? And so on.

But there was nothing to be done about it. Once set on their course, the guys from Chicago were *not* going back on their decision, and David would have to come up with another cover if he wanted his album available in the United States.

He did that, then, getting his friend Mick Weller to paint a new cover, a cartoon so far removed from the original photograph in theme, mood, and everything else, and so unconnected in any way to the music it represented, that there was no mistaking his intent: Up yours, gentlemen, and may everybody know it. And should anyone miss the point, his Mercury ally and advocate Ron Oberman made sure that reviewers of the album were informed unofficially, in detail, of the nature of the original cover. Which naturally encouraged much empathy (most rock critics in those days still felt that record company bosses belonged with the pigs running Dow

Chemical and the White House) and lent extra vim, vigor, length, and prominence to the reviews in the States, as well as stirring up a healthy dose of piss-on-the-Yanks publicity in the Scepter'd Isle.

So it was as they say, and as most of you girls and some of you boys know well: It's just amazing what the right dress will do for you.

Bit by bit, Haddon Hall came up in the world. David did the living room in a dark green and painted scarlet the woodwork on the gothic chairs I'd had reupholstered in crushed velvet, and I dyed twenty-six lace curtains that same brilliant red (that's the room you see on the cover of *The Man Who Sold the World*). Our antiques and David's growing collection of Art Nouveau and Deco pieces really popped in their new settings, and our guests lounged and frolicked in luxury. Yes: high style, getting higher; a salon of distinction, a setting fit for a star.

A star needs a firmament, though. A great salon needs great characters, flamboyant personalities, sparkling guests. A fashion leader needs followers. A spokesman needs people to speak for. David's case called for all these elements. The wonderful thing is that he found them all in one place.

The Sombrero Club, it was. This red-hot basement dance club on Kensington High Street – a disco, not a live-band place – catered to people who worked in the fashion industry, everybody from sales assistants and boutique managers to hairdressers and designers, in Kensington and across the broader swath of fashionable southwest London.

It was visual, dance-oriented, and gay. David loved it, and so did I. It was the first club we'd ever seen with a dance floor lit from below, so it had a new edge of atmospheric excitement. It was set up for watching and being watched too: a wide, curving staircase for making grand entrances, plenty of perches from which you could see the whole dance floor, and – very important – enough square-footage. You weren't jammed in there like so many cockroaches to writhe around together in the dark; you had room to move and breathe and circulate.

It had a sizzle to it. The music was all hard-moving American R&B (not a note of rock or anything British), and the people were up there with the music; high energy was the theme, sex the undercurrent, speed the drug of choice.

There were some bright and brilliant characters, and among them Freddi Buretti was the brightest, clearly the star.

Dear Freddi, there every night, and never the same outfit twice. Not that he really needed such great clothes. At six feet, with blond hair, big blue eyes, fine high Scandinavian cheekbones (from his mother) and a voluptuous mouth, he'd have been a showstopper in any old threads. He worked for a designer named Andreas somewhere on King's Road, making shirts and jackets, but his own craftsmanship and sense of style far transcended anything he did at his job; his outfits were all his own, and they were all wonderful. A *very* talented lad, Freddi.

Colorful too. He had great stories. One of the best, I recall, was about picking up a policeman in Holland Park and blowing him right there and then, in uniform. What an image: the blue-black serge trousers straining, the truncheon swinging rhythmically back and forth, the sacred helmet hung safely on a railing... Oh, my. How come you can never find a Nikon when you really need one?

Freddi's circle was also really something. There was the gorgeous Mickey King, all turquoise Celtic eyes and auburn hair, of whom I had the very personal pleasure a year or so on from early 1971 and who, a little later than that, had the error of his rent-boy ways demonstrated rather too conclusively. A colonel he'd been black-mailing grew tired of paying and sent a couple of his lads to resolve the situation, and they did: Mickey became one well-bayoneted, thoroughly silenced rent boy, and the very first of my dead lovers.

Then there was Mandi, another incredibly gorgeous person living out there on the edge, making her money as a very high-rent call girl for Arabs and spending a good deal of it on various kinds of speed. Freddi would dress her as Marilyn Monroe or Betty Grable or some other great icon of his peer group, and she'd make entrances to the Sombrero that left you gasping – and then, fabulous actress that she was, she'd stay in character, improvising all sorts of won-derfulness as she moved among us. What a beauty; what a trip.

Another of Freddi's models was his teenage girlfriend, Daniella. She was called 'the negative' by the Sombrero crew because of her bright white-blond hair framing a coffee-colored face and huge, deeply beautiful dark eyes. Born of Indian parents and reared very respectably in suburban north London, she'd hit the ground running when she'd first come to Kensington, falling in with Freddi and his friend Antoriello, a hairdresser, and embracing the scene, the gay life, the drugs, the works. Freddi and Antonello made her their own dress-up doll, designing clothes for her and playing with her hair – it would be pink one week, blue the next, red on Saturday night, back to basic white on Sunday – and she ate it all up. She had the thickest Cockney accent imaginable, and she did far too many reds and other downs, to stay low and cool in the face of the scene's vicissitudes and her boyfriend's spectacular wildness. She loved that Freddi boy with a great abiding passion, and although both of them seemed to roam far and free around the Sombrero's sexual arena, they called each other 'my girlfriend' and 'my boyfriend' and were very much a couple. I loved Daniella, who was adorable, and I loved Freddi too.

I didn't love him physically – in those days I approached sex as a game of conquest, which ruled out my friends as bed partners, and Freddi was fast becoming my best friend – and neither, I believe, did David, although he might well have wanted to; I don't think Freddi fancied him. No, with Freddi it was all hard work, hard play, and good business.

There came a time, after we had watched enough of his grand entrances into the Sombrero and fully grasped the depth of his style, when David began wanting the kind of attention-riveting glamor he created, and the light bulb went on in my head: If Freddi were ours – that is, on our payroll, in our house, right there on daily/nightly call – we might benefit enormously. I wouldn't have to shop for David's and the boys' clothes and fabrics anymore, or labor over a hot sewing machine; we wouldn't have to depend on the styles available in the stores but would have exclusive use of a fabulous designer, thereby raising the communal creativity level by several significant degrees and getting a lock on a style all our own; we'd have custom-tailored clothes that fit better than anything we could find on the open market; we'd get them quickly made, altered, and repaired; and so on.

This wonderful idea was to work out perfectly as David's success and image grew together. Freddi was the key to so much.

As was the whole Sombrero Club experience. For David it was crucial. He'd connected with a new world of listeners/subjects, who, when they weren't getting far out at the Sombrero, worked for a living in nonprofessional, nonelite jobs. They were wilder than college kids, and more direct, and they cared a lot more about dancing and looking hot and flaunting their sex, and – the bottom line – they were the majority.

I don't think David saw the opportunity immediately, or at least I don't think he saw it in marketing terms, but he certainly *did* see the themes and the stories staring him in the face, and he learned the language very fast (it wasn't, after all, very far from his own).

The Sombrero people began supplying the fuel very quickly; the material on *Hunky Dory*, the album he was working on in early and middle 1971, came directly from their lives and attitudes, and went straight back to them after its trip through his consciousness. I was the first person he played those songs to, and Mick Ronson most often the second, but Freddi, Daniella, Wendy, Antonello, Mickey King, and the rest of the Sombrero core, partying at Haddon Hall when they weren't at their club or their jobs, were next. Their opinions mattered a lot; if Freddi had given thumbs-down on a song (which never actually happened, as far as I remember), I doubt whether David would have recorded it.

It was a natural process, all this: David finding voices that called to him, getting turned on, responding, and feeding inspiration back, making a loop of it. His creative focus sharpened, and his career course changed: not so much in its ultimate destination – pop idolatry was still the goal, then as always – but in its method. He quit being so concerned about whether the BBC would play his new single, whether Radio Caroline would stay on the air long enough to put him into the big time, whether his tunes were catchy enough for *Top of the Pops*; and he began concentrating on giving his newfound soulmates a real, live show for their money – a show unlike that anyone else could give them – and trusting the buzz. He was doing what the Who had done for the mods and the Grateful Dead had done for the hippies (and what, after him, the Sex Pistols would do for the punks): plugging into a growing community, earning its love, giving it its anthems, popularizing its values, and riding it to the top. *All the young dudes... carry the news...*

The key to his career wasn't all David brought home from the Sombrero. One night, I remember a tad too clearly, we came back to Haddon Hall with a lovely young Spanish boy (the Sombrero being full of Continentals) and proceeded to fall into bed and frolic.

David was completely drunk, so he was having a fine old time, but I wasn't enjoying myself very much. I'd distrusted the whole idea from the start – bringing home a boy who didn't have his own transportation, who would have to be navigated or actually transported back to work in town the next morning – but David fancied him and his pretty, *tiny* bottom (really: it can't have been more than twenty inches around!), and being barley-wine blotto, he was totally impervious to any tour director or transport officer wisdom I had to offer.

There we were, then, going at it – with me somewhat unsure about what to do, since I'd never been to bed with two men at once before and therefore wasn't exactly lost in the throes of sexual transport – and *damn*, wouldn't you know it! Those drunk, sloppy, clumsy boys had a bottle of whiskey in bed with them, and someone, somehow or other, caused it to spill all over my stomach, thighs, pubis, and... well, you can imagine. It felt like a million fire ants.

My fun having being spoiled all too spectacularly, I went off to sleep in the living room and left David with his boy. What sort of a time they had together, God only knows. I'm sure David doesn't.

The Sombrero didn't do quite as much for me as it did for David, but I did find some very close friends there, and my horizons did broaden.

I learned, for one thing, about some of the grimmer aspects of the gay underworld, about the realities of sex on the street, sex for money, sex and drugs, sex and violence. I learned that if you're a boy who's making his living selling blow jobs to strangers, or you're a girl taking it up the ass from whoever, it helps your denial mechanisms if the drugs you're on are strong. I learned too that that kind of work breeds a powerful rage in almost everyone who does it, and you'd better duck fast when a hustler's anger breaks loose among lovers and friends (as, freed by booze and drugs, it often does).

The rent-boys and call girls at the Sombrero had a fiery energy that could be appealing, but frightening, and I felt thankful that I personally didn't have to live with it, or cope with the odds of survival they faced. I also saw, among the gays who worked 'normal' jobs, an awful lot of people who could and should have been beautiful, both within themselves and in society, but who were turned ugly by their own paranoia, and society's.

This was heartbreaking, for these were my brothers and sisters, the people among whom I knew I was destined to spend my life. For what was true for David in a creative/commercial sense – that he had found his natural constituency – was true for me emotionally: I'd found a very personal sense of belonging at the Sombrero. There was a distinct hint of poison in the wine. All the same, though, it *was* wine, good wine, and it *was* intoxicating.

A louder sour note: David's night with the Spanish boy. That, I think, was the first time I understood something about things between David and me. I loved the work, I realized – the marketing challenge, the creative intimacy, the rightness and relevance of the message, the energy of a growing and going concern – but the sex was lousy.

# 7

# PEARLS IN THE OYSTER, POISON IN THE WINE

One item belongs chronologically with the first few months of our Sombrero period, but it demands its own treatment: We were pregnant. I had conceived one morning at Haddon Hall in late August 1970 – I remember having no doubt about what had just happened – and on May 30th 1971, I gave birth to Duncan Zowie Haywood Bowie, a healthy eight-and-a-half-pound boy, at Bromley Hospital.

People have children for all sorts of reasons, and I was no exception: I had all sorts of reasons.

It was the natural thing to do. My mother's influence, my Catholic upbringing, and the earth-mothering ethos of the times conspired with something purely personal to persuade me that I was ripe for early motherhood. To have a child, I thought, was to follow the biological function of my body, and great benefits would result from such alignment with the natural order: I would feel better, my body would work better, what should be would be. And of course, if I had my children young, in the first years of my twenties, I would still be young as they grew, and still in the prime of life when they were grown and gone. We'd have each other for a good long time.

David too would benefit. I'd seen him with other people's kids – Mary Finnegan's, his Notting Hill hippie friends' – and I'd noted with more than passing interest how he was at such moments: kind, warm, relaxed, playful, happy; a natural daddy. His spirit was so lightened in the company of children, and they touched him so easily in places over which he'd layered many protective coats of coldness and cynicism, that I got big ideas immediately. Fatherhood might well be his redemption. With a child of his own, his frigidity might thaw; his fear of emotionalism might fade; he might feel a whole lot better.

The examples around us were encouraging too. We knew several people who had kids but weren't at all straight in their approach to life in general and child-rearing in particular, and it was good to see evidence that parenthood didn't mean the end of freedom or creative life. I remember too how appealing those people were to me. Wild, creative free spirits who were also parents had a very *substantial* kind of glamour.

These things were cooking around in my head when I first broached the subject to David – 'You're always playing with other people's kids, you know. Maybe *we* should have a child' – but the oldest motivation in the book was perhaps also an ingredient. Perhaps I could feel a distance growing between us, and thought parenthood would bring us closer together. I don't know. It sounds a bit like the wisdom of hindsight, but it has a ring to it.

David's reaction was interesting. 'Yeah... but you're so busy. Having a child, you know, that's a lot of work.'

Your typical male chauvinist. I can hear the thought processes. *Having babies means Angie's Becoming a Mother, disappearing into diaper world, giving up career aspirations, quitting work... which means* my losing my door-kicker!

It was okay, though. I reassured him, reminding him that such things as nannies existed in this world – the entire ruling class of his country had been raised by them, for God's sake – and telling him that in the industrialized Western Hemisphere in the third quarter of the twentieth century, he could get the best of both worlds from his wife. If that was what he wanted.

It was indeed, he said, and so we decided to have a baby. I quit taking the Pill and left the rest to nature, and sure enough, nature came through. Not that there was ever any real doubt about that, since I'm Polish on my mother's side, and therefore your basic fertility bomb. I get pregnant if you even *look* at me funny.

I believe the moment of conception was just after David woke up one morning in the all-white room that would later be painted blue and turned into the music room. Our lovemaking had been exceptionally pleasurable. It was in fact the orgasm I had, a deep internal body-quake, that convinced me we'd just made a child.

Looking back with a little more knowledge than I had then, I'm not as sure today. I might in fact have conceived two days previously, or three days later. We were making love about every other day around that time, so who really knows? All the same, it certainly *felt* like the magic moment.

Which, poor reader, you may find confusing after my telling you in chapter four that it would be several years 'before I met a man capable of taking me over the sexual top' and in chapter six that sex with David was 'lousy.'

First, I should clarify that our night with that Spanish boy, and my realization that there was something missing in the sex between David and me, happened well into 1972, after Zowie had been born and after things had changed between us. So while 'lousy' may be somewhat strong a term, it's in the neighborhood. Our sex life in late 1972 wasn't what it had been.

Second, I don't mean to write David off as a lover, even if he didn't do for me what other men would in later years. You have to remember that David and I were both very young and quite ignorant in sexual matters. Which was natural, and commonplace; the great majority of people in their early twenties in the early 1970s (and maybe even today, for all I know) had very little idea of how to pleasure their sexual partners fully; we had, after all, only just learned how to pleasure ourselves. Only later in life, as you gain experience and lose the intense ego-consciousness of youth, do you begin to realize how your own enjoyment is enhanced by giving as much pleasure as you get. And I'm sure that's been as true for David as it's been for me. I'm sure that with some people at some times throughout his life he's been a wonderful lover.

We weren't any different from most young couples, then. All he really knew how to do was pump, and all I really knew how to do was take it. I mean, in those days I'd *heard* about things like fellatio (what girl hadn't?), but the very idea of actually taking that thing in my mouth and playing with it was disgusting. He peed out of it, for God's sake! And I'm sure David felt the same way about my apparatus. So you get the picture.

\*

I can't continue talking about sex between David and me without telling you the piece of the puzzle I've been holding back. I thought I could keep the secret; in fact, it's been my intention all along to write this whole book without revealing it. But the deeper into evasion I get, the harder and more pointless it becomes to lie by omission.

There's no pretty way to present this particular fact. One day David said to me, 'I've got this problem. Sometimes I get this rash, and it hurts too much to fuck.' And he showed me, and I must admit, his cock looked as if it had been massaged with sandpaper.

I wasn't alarmed. He explained that the rash came and went on an unpredictable, irregular schedule, and that when it wasn't flaring up, he was just fine and could make love as much as he liked. And since he was fine a lot more than he wasn't, that meant the whole thing really wasn't much of a problem.

I assimilated that and thought, Well, it's *not* much of a problem. We'll just abstain when we have to, and otherwise we can carry on with this new love of ours exactly the way we want to. His opening up to me even helped; it deepened my feeling of trust and intimacy, and bonded me even more firmly into a sense of us, Light Person and guide, against the world (love really *is* blind).

The bleak aspects of the situation revealed themselves a few weeks later, when David presented me with a complication. There seemed to be something about me, he said, that made the rash flare up. When he and I made love, he got his rash.

Ever the reasonable codependent, I took myself to my gynecologist, who examined me, told me that I had a minor yeast infection but no sign of any other problem, and explained the facts of life to me, such as they were. He said that the primary known trigger for flare-ups of rashes like this was stress of one sort or another; therefore the most promising way to minimize episodes was to get enough sleep, eat healthily, and not worry.

Okay, I said, but what about the question at issue: Could there be something about me, that is, my particular vaginal chemistry, that triggered attacks in David?

The million-dollar answer came back hedged, ambiguous, and maddeningly inconclusive: *Conceivably*, said the doctor. While there was nothing unusual about me, gynecologically speaking, and besides, no research of his acquaintance pointed to vaginal chemistry as a medium for rash flare-ups or even indicated any potential in that line of inquiry, nothing could really be ruled out. Maybe I ate too much garlic, or not enough. Anything was possible.

I went back to David and told him the no-news, and we carried on. I did my best to take care of myself and to create a nonstressful environment for him, but none of that had any significant effect on the central problem. Whenever David and I made love, he got his rash. Or at least he *said* he got his rash.

The problem didn't go away, even though I spent considerable time and energy trying to find a solution to it – visiting various doctors, looking for new research or treatments. I'm sure you can figure out its implications just as easily as (much more easily, in fact) I can describe them.

Painful though it may be, I have to make the heart of the matter as clear, and as confusing, as living through it was. In a nutshell: I never knew, and I still don't know, whether David was telling the truth when he said that sex with me brought on the episodes.

Maybe, maybe, maybe... Maybe the rash stratagem was his way, conscious or unconscious, of repelling a person who had come as close to his scared-little-boy core as I had... Maybe he was telling the honest truth, and I really *did* play host to some biochemical wild card that activated his rash... Maybe, and I'm not kidding, it *was* the amount of garlic I consumed... Maybe other sex partners also triggered David's rash, and his sex life away from me was as difficult as it was at home, or maybe he could bed whomever he pleased and it was all just fine (he didn't tell me)... Maybe his strong preference for women of African extraction had something to do with some racially determined biochemical benevolence on their part (I wondered about that, as tacky as it sounds, I really did)... Maybe, maybe, maybe, maybe.

That's all conjecture, and it *was* all conjecture; you can well imagine, I suppose, how much mental and emotional energy such speculation consumed during my years with David. But then and now, all I know for a fact is that he said what he said, and we had to live with it, and events took their course. Sex between David and others flourished, as did sex between me and others, but sex between him and me slowly withered and died. It would come back to life only briefly, and flare for a while like some damned rash attack.

My pregnancy proceeded, and for the most part I enjoyed it. The National Health Service took wonderful care of me – it was quaint and socialistic, getting that much tax-subsidized attention – and I ate like a horse; my nesting instinct activated with a vengeance. The later months of my pregnancy featured a daily flurry of activity industrious enough to go down forever in the Queen Bee Hall of Fame: redecorating Haddon Hall; shopping for baby things; going with my friend Susie Frost, who lived in the basement apartment of Haddon Hall, to the East End markets for material, then coming back, firing up the sewing machines, and making clothes for the new Bowie – and then figuring, Well, why not? and turning out a whole line of cute, hip kids' outfits for sale. For a while there we had a little clothing factory humming along at Haddon Hall. It was great fun.

Oncoming motherhood wasn't, of course, my only theme. I remember dancing the night away at the Sombrero with my belly the size of the Goodyear blimp, and I remember plenty of business too. I was pregnant when we found Mr Fish's dresses; while *The Man Who Sold the World* was made and marketed and *Hunky Dory* was begun; while an endless flow of gigs, recording sessions, and deals and projects of all sorts came my way, demanding attention; and while David left England, Haddon Hall, and me for his month-long promotional debauch across the United States. I spent much of that month, I recall, up a ladder with a paintbrush, secretly preparing our palace for its returning king. David would walk through the front door into a whole new world, a showplace crisply and elegantly ready for his own final touches. Ah yes, so nice.

And David was so sweet with me, the typical devoted hippie husband and father-to-be, all concern and involvement. When he wasn't out on the road or adventuring in America he even came with me to the clinic for my checkups.

We had a frightening incident before I came to term. David got the starting handle for the Riley (a delightful but terribly unreliable car) impaled in his thigh, just missing an artery and his studly three piece suit. That stopped my heart, flipped me out, and made me think for a moment that I might be losing *both* of my babies. I wasn't, though. David spent a week in the hospital, and survived with only a scar to show for it all, and I carried Zowie to term. And *then* it hit the fan.

I can't describe fully how awful it was. The bare facts are that I was in labor for thirty hours, fully conscious (with an epidural anesthetic), until I finally managed to squeeze my eight-and-a-half-pound boy out between my very narrow hips, cracking my pelvis in the process. David told me afterward that I was screaming constantly and cursing everyone who came near me, in language he'd never imagined I knew. The claustrophobia I felt was ghastly.

I ended up in real trouble: physically torn and broken (with thirty-eight stitches as well as a cracked pelvis); ravaged emotionally by withdrawal from the painkillers and the guilt of having not 'coped' better with the whole experience; isolated in my suffering as everyone around me rejoiced and goo-gooed over the new baby; scared witless by the fear that I might have hurt him in childbirth, and might still hurt him by dropping him or otherwise mishandling him (babies had suffered from adults' carelessness in my father's family, and I had an awful phobia about that); and more than anything, utterly exhausted. I was strained and beaten half to death, heading blindly and helplessly down the age-old female path into chronic postpartum depression.

Poor you. You buy this book for the celebrity scoops and rock-and-roll blow jobs, and here you are, stuck in boring old real-life problems such as the complications of childbirth.

I survived the first two weeks somehow and finally could get out of bed and walk around the house without half killing myself physically, but emotionally I was getting worse rather than better: feeling more depressed, more guilty, and more and more isolated. And nobody – not David, and certainly not his mother, who would show up now and then – seemed to care.

Dana Gillespie did, though. The first time she laid eyes on me after the birth she barely paused to express her shock – 'God, Angie,.

you're white as a sheet. You look like *death*!' – before coming up with a typically healthy, straightforward solution: 'You need *sunshine*, girl!'

She was planning a brief vacation at her father's villa on Lake Maggiore in Italy, and she was unequivocal about it: She wouldn't even *think* of going without me.

She was right. I had to go. To be away from the pressure and the claustrophobia, to be in the sunshine and breathe fresh air, to have people around me who were caring and accepting rather than demanding and judgmental, to have some good plain fun ... Those five or six days gave me enough sanity to go back to Haddon Hall and handle it. They were my salvation.

They may, however, have been the opposite for my marriage. David, I think, was appalled by what I'd done, horrified that I could get up and leave my baby boy the way I had, gadding off (to his way of thinking) for fun in the sun with my friend.

He didn't express that, of course; honesty of that kind wasn't within his emotional range. Perhaps he arched an eyebrow when I first told him I wanted to go, but I can't vouch that he did even that. He raised no objections, going along with everything I did to ensure Zowie's welfare while I was away (chiefly, hiring Susie Frost as a nanny) and, as far as I knew, accepting my decision and understanding its urgent necessity.

That was just his front. Beneath it that good old non-confrontational, passive-aggressive machine was engaging gears, activating its clandestine weaponry, and going to work on our love.

Why? Well, I believe it came from the most common and powerful source of sickness in a man's relationship with a wife: his relationship with his mother. For David, I think, my flight conjured up images – not just images, but *memories* – of his mother's rejecting and abandoning his half brother. And for him, unfortunately, that was the big time in bad juju. So right there, somewhere during or just before or after my few days in Lake Maggiore, he scared himself into seeing me through the veil of distrust and resentment originally designed for Peggy Burns.

And in some ways, that was that: the beginning of the end of it all between him and me. I'd gained a son, but I'd begun the process of losing a husband.

Life goes on. We had oodles and oodles of distractions. This was a very intense time in David's career, the period in which we did the work that would make him a star.

On the business front, Tony Defries – embracing his new job by zooming around in a raccoon coat and growing his hair into a pomade-free freak frizz – was hard at work looking for a new, better recording deal with a new, bigger label than Mercury. On the image front, Freddi had signed on with us and brought Daniella as a girl Friday for our organization, and the overall sartorial effect of David and the boys was getting to be quite something. And on the creative front, David was working well, productively, and happily.

Not all the time, of course. As with many another professional writer in history, writing was something he avoided for as long as he could. He would get down to work only when it became obvious that delaying any longer would make very bad things happen very soon in his immediate vicinity.

He had an original way of forcing himself into action. When it became apparent that songs for an album needed writing posthaste, he would look around the scenery until his consciousness settled on a likely target, then make his decision and announce the result to me.

'Ah, you know, dear, I think I'll rebuild the Riley. I could take the engine out and work on it in the living room, couldn't I?'

I'd react in the way you'd expect – tactfully – but David, not to be deterred from his primary purpose, would simply come up with another project. So instead of filling the living room with the million or so tiny, oily components of the average 1960s English engine compartment (a Riley's engineering being no less complex, unreliable, and incomprehensible a squirrel cage than that of a classic MG or Jaguar), he'd decide to redecorate it. Which would result, naturally, in chaos: mess and disorder beginning in whatever corner he started to work, then spreading to the rest of the room, then out into the hallway, and so on until in one way or another the entire household was disrupted.

At a certain point, which I grew able to predict quite accurately, the mess would achieve a critical mass within David's consciousness, and he'd freak.

'God, I've got an album to do!' he'd say. 'Honey, I've got to go!' And off he'd run.

That's how it went for all the albums he made while we were together: *Hunky Dory* and *Ziggy Stardust* at Haddon Hall, and the rest at other places. It was as if the mess was the midwife for the work. Eventually I could tell, from the degree of chaos or order around him, just where a song was in its birthing cycle.

When he had finally come to grips with his muse and was ready to write, the signals would be clear. Rather than let me get him into his bath after I woke him for his coffee and orange juice around eleven-thirty or noon, as he usually did when he planned to go out and about, he would sneak himself into his clothes without bathing, then get back into bed with his guitar (the Harptone twelve-string he always played as an eleven-string) and stay there, reemerging only when he got to the end of a work cycle. Then he'd discover he was hungry and come poking into the kitchen. I'd usually fix him something, and after he'd eaten he would play me what he'd just written. If I liked it – well, even if I didn't, even if I judged it too dark or twisted or melodramatic, as I did 'All the Madmen' and 'Cygnet Committee' – he'd polish it up, then take it to Ronno and the boys, and they'd disappear downstairs to the little studio Tony Visconti, the son of a carpenter, had built in the old wine cellar. There they'd work it up until they liked it enough to make a demo tape, and since they usually didn't begin that process until late in the evening, after dinner, they'd often stay down there well into the wee hours, sometimes until dawn or later.

And that was the routine. The only significant variation during our Haddon Hall days came after David started writing on the piano instead of his Harptone ('Changes,' as I recall, was one of his first piano songs). Then, instead of going back to bed to write, he'd make his way to the piano bench in the music room and sit there cross-legged, totally absorbed, and from the look of him, very happy.

David was capable of extraordinary concentration when he hooked into the creative process, and at those times you could see clearly this was the work he'd been born for.

He looked transported, almost entranced, and watching him, I felt peaceful and sure of my own course. Things got simple when the work flowed, and all the subjects of our talk and experience and observation emerged from his mind skillfully distilled. They were proud and certain moments, those. A great deal of David's inspiration came from the United States. You can say that about many twentieth-century popular artists around the world, of course, but here we're talking biography, not cultural anthropology. What I mean is that David picked up all kinds of tricks, techniques, and attitudes when he went to the States, and when they came to him.

He returned from his radio tour, in February 1971, with the usual English boy's culturally-superior-kid-in-a-candy-store mix of arrogance and wonder: Ugh, the commercialism! The corruption! The crudity, the crime, the lack of control! Oh my, the *speed*, the *size*, the *food*, the *riches*, the *freedom*! And there were more individual impressions too. His antennae had been extended to their fullest in the cutting-edge circles to which he was introduced in New York and Hollywood, and he'd homed in directly on the most happening of happening themes in American pop culture, which at the time meant one simple name: Warhol.

Andy, as pop culturists will no doubt be explaining for the next couple of centuries, had managed in 1971 to position himself in the center of a giant spider web of avant allure and multisexual chic, from which location (actually his Factory on Union Square, just around the corner from Max's Kansas City) he fed, in his many-times-removed, deep-comatose way, on the most adventurous young things the USA had to offer him. He'd confer on them the top-of-the-hip credentials, which were his alone to give, and they'd give him – well, what? Polaroids? company? immortality? Why would the already dead seek eternal life, even if it did come only in reproduction?

Obviously enough, I have my problems with the Warhol mystique; I am not and never was impressed. But I can't deny its power, and only a fool would argue that it didn't greatly benefit David's cause and therefore mine.

In England in 1971, for instance, there was a very powerful curiosity about Warhol and anything and anybody in any way connected with his scene – Factory un-filmmakers and un-film stars such as Paul Morrissey, Viva, and Ultra Violet; musicians such as Lou Reed and John Cale in New York, and Iggy Pop emerging from Detroit – and David, with his usual ultra-keen eye for a hot-breaking trend, worked very consciously to link himself with that demand. He made sure to mention Iggy and Lou and anyone else he thought might do him some good in every interview he gave at the time, and I'm sure it worked. Both British and American tastemakers attuned to the trend frequencies soon got the idea that David Bowie was a close cultural ally of the Warhol axis. And of course, the way the media work, if you say something that sounds good, it becomes true (as Andy knew, preached, and demonstrated), and that's what happened with David and the Warhol gang.

He and they might have had some fleeting contact during his first American trip, for all I know, but the first solid contact came in London in the summer of 1971, when the show *Pork* played a long, dazzling run at the Round House.

It was a total hoot, that show – a fake Andy and his fake friends sitting around on an eye-popping white PVC set, exchanging the sleaziest possible too-bored hip-mutant New York gossip over the phone, about skin-popping and speedballing and club-hopping and cum-guzzling and everything in between, and all of it the real thing, actual dialogue taken from actual phone conversations with Andy taped by Brigid Polk (hence *Pork*) – and it just blew them away in London. It really was very wild, vicious, cheap, perverted, boring, all those Warholian things. The newspaper ads ensured success with a simple statement: 'This play has explicit sexual content and offensive language. If you are likely to be disturbed, do not attend.'

Who could resist? Very few. I know I was floored by the show, which defined everything to which I aspired in modern theater, and so was David. You could see it lighting the fuses of all sorts of ideas in his head as he sat there watching those people, every one of them as sharp as you could want a performance artist to be: Cherry

Vanilla doing her groupie role, eating chocolate cake and flashing her tits at every opportunity; Jayne County (then Wayne, before the surgery) stopping the show; Tony Zanetta, his hair bleached, doing Andy better than Andy could do himself.

We went backstage after the show (not my first encounter; Cherry, Wayne, and Leee Black Childers had come to a show of David's at the Country Club in north London, drawn by curiosity about 'that guy in the dress'), and a few days later we met at the Sombrero (I remember pinching Tony Zanetta's very cute bottom, and Cherry flashing Ronno for all she was worth – a hot one, that Cherry; I fancied her *beaucoup*). A little while after that we had them down to Haddon Hall and got to know everybody better.

A lot of fellow feeling was experienced, and lasting bonds formed. Leee, Cherry, and Tony Zanetta would become key figures in Main Man, the management/production company Tony Defries set up to handle David and other acts, and despite the ravages of time and fortune, they're all still very good friends of mine.

David, I think, was emboldened by it all. The fact that the Americans all lived together in a rented Notting Hill house, which the (horrified, delighted) tabloid writers promptly christened 'Pig Mansion,' made him feel extra good about his own semicommunal scene at Haddon Hall, and the shocking, utterly un-English openness of the *Pork* cast gave him some very good ideas. Lying in bed beside him in our lovely rose-colored room at Haddon Hall, I could hear the wheels turning in his head, the springs flexing and the gears clicking in, and when we talked I was pleased to hear him gaining yet greater faith in the value of shock, style, and statement.

It was a few months after we first saw Tony Zanetta as Andy that Tony Zanetta as himself arranged for us to meet Andy as himself, or at least as close to himself as Andy was capable of getting. It was at the Factory, during our trip to New York for the signing of David's new recording contract with RCA.

I remember a space done in aluminum foil and a bunch of incredibly pale people lounging around in various states approaching coma, squeezing out the occasional nihilistic statement or existentialist non sequitur or meaningless triviality (the closer to coma and meaninglessness, the hipper). I remember nobody paying even the slightest attention to me – I might as well have been wood, or nonreflective wallpaper – and I recall many moments of silent, relatively acute social discomfort before David took the initiative and played a tape of his new song 'Andy Warhol' to its subject.

That broke the silence, but only temporarily. Andy got up and left the room without a word just after the last note.

There was some doubt, unexpressed of course, as to whether or not that signaled the end of our encounter, but Andy returned after a few minutes, said, 'That was great, thank you,' in that little windup-toy-faggot voice of his, and then applied himself, in silence, to the task of taking Polaroids of David, peeling them off one by one, and laying them out before him on a coffee table.

So far so good. Nobody had jumped out the window, choked on his own vomit, or OD'd to the point of actual fatality while we'd been there, and while our host was certainly very low-key, so to speak, there was a clear inference that that was, well, normal. Andy *looked* dead, all right – his face was the grim gray-white plastic color of an hours-dead battlefield corpse, and that dreadful hairpiece of his looked as if some gang of drunken revelers at his wake had been, well, *using* it – but that was plainly an illusion. He was plainly alive and well enough to do his thing.

I have no idea how it all might have ended had things gone on the way they were going (we'd been there an hour or more already; how long could those people have sustained that kind of nonbeing?), but suddenly it all changed. Andy noticed David's shoes -bright yellow patent-leather, as I recall, one of my image-enhancing fashion finds – and evidently that spurred a sequence of neurological reactions resulting in, of all things, volubility. At once he became just as chatty as could be.

Things were fine from that point. An amazingly trivial conversation got started, and everybody relaxed. You could tell because their eyeballs twitched more slowly.

At the time I ascribed Andy's abrupt sea change to some sort of accelerated movement along the biochemical continuum or other random cortical event, but I misjudged the man. David pegged it for me later: Before he'd become the Campbell's Soup Can man, Andy had been a shoe designer! So we'd been able to come up with something that *interested* him. Now wasn't that lucky, and weren't we blessed?

So yes, David had a new contract with RCA. Tony Defries had struck while the iron was hot and the gate was wide open over on Forty-fourth and Sixth: RCA, having suddenly bestirred its corporate self and recognized the existence of a youth market, was in a mood to part with significant currency at the slightest reasonable-sounding excuse. And there we were, all expenses paid, quartered in high style and great comfort at the Plaza Hotel, single-handedly holding aloft the banner of RCA's new contemporary consciousness (they'd signed the Kinks and Lou Reed too, but Lou wasn't British and the Kinks weren't new).

Not that we cared about all that. Tony had secured complete creative control for David as well as lots more money (or rather, credit: everything was an advance against future royalties) than Mercury could or would have offered him, so David was happy – no more album cover hassles and so on – and I was happy that he was happy. We were all happy, really. RCA was treating us like stars, throwing parties for us and limo'ing us around the hot spots (we met Lou Reed *and* Iggy Pop at one party, and saw Elvis perform and Colonel Tom market at Madison Square Garden), and that stuff was just *wonderful*.

God, it's so nice when they bend over and smooch your tootsies like that, especially the first time around. When we walked into our room at the Plaza, an impressive enough experience itself, and saw what the record company people had done for us, it half killed me with kindness. Piled on the bed, and all around it, were wrapped presents: all David's RCA promotional material; the whole RCA album catalogue for that year, plus the entire Elvis catalogue; and personal welcome-aboard and welcome-to-New York gifts from all sorts of people in the music business. It was bigger and better than any Christmas I'd ever had, and all the more wonderful because it was so unexpected.

David and I looked at each other like little kids and grinned all over.

'This is it, isn't it?' he said.

I looked around me, drinking it all in, experiencing the same delightful impression as my man's. 'Yeah, babe, I think you're right. It's *happened*!'

And by God, it had. If they treat you like a star, it means you are one. So we'd done it – we'd arrived.

# 8

# THE BISEXUAL BOOGIE

*A*part from a good number of great rock records, my ex-husband gave two pretty significant gifts to the world we've known these past twenty years. He very publicly asked a question our generation was very obviously begging – Well, what sex *are* we? – and he almost single-handedly initiated some two decades' worth of dress sense and hairstyle. Popes and presidents have accomplished less, many of them much less.

It's interesting, you know, comparing the trends back when David made his first big difference, with the latest in looks today. As I write, in late 1992, the hot youth fashion statement of the moment happens to be an exact visual duplication of the guys in Blue Cheer – or Iron Butterfly, or Vanilla Fudge, or any other hard-core late-psychedelic rock band doing its thing circa late 1968 – all the way down to the split ends and pimples, the earth tones, baggy-bottomed jeans, and ugly open-toed footwear. The way these things go, it's quite possible that soon, perhaps as early as late '93, we'll see a reprise of (you guessed it) the David Bowie/Ziggy Stardust Glitter-critter look. The hippest of all young dudes of tomorrow, in all probability, will have cast off their grunge, slicked themselves *way* up and out there, and begun appearing on the scene in exotic see-through bodystockings, interestingly colored atomic-rooster buzz cuts, and Elizabeth Arden.

This may or may not come to pass, but I retain my opinion that David's Ziggy Stardust haircut was the single most reverberant fashion statement of the seventies.

It started one morning at Haddon Hall during the making of *The*

*Rise and Fall of Ziggy Stardust and the Spiders from Mars*, when, after his orange juice and coffee and his bath, David said, 'I want to cut my hair, and I want it to look different. What if I dye it red?'

I considered that for a moment, thinking about attractive redheads – Lulu, the pint-size Scottish bombshell with whom David had been working on her recording of *The Man Who Sold the World*, came immediately to mind – and I started liking the idea.

'Sure, babe. Why not? What kind of style do you want?'

He didn't have a very precise idea, so we went off to the newsstand and bought an armful of magazines, *Vogue* and its various clones and competitors, and sat down and started leafing through them. It didn't take David long to hit on a look he liked, a puffball-with-a-tail affair on some svelte young high-fashion stunner in a very becoming black evening gown. That ended the research part of the operation; now we needed a hairdresser.

This was in our social circles sort of a joke. Hairdressers weren't exactly in short supply around the Sombrero and related places. As we thought about it, though, a problem revealed itself. If we went to *Jacques*, then how would *Roger* feel? If we chose Joanna, might that not offend the panties off Claude?

I solved the dilemma by staying away from our regular circles entirely, beating the bushes of suburban Beckenham until I found a hairdresser who could do the job: Susie Fussey, a very pretty girl who impressed me when she did my hair. There was something about her – in retrospect I know it was her intelligence, adventurousness, and creativity – which seemed right.

And sure enough, she did a lovely job on David, as you can see on the cover of the *Ziggy Stardust* album. When the final lock had fallen and the last cloud of hairspray dispersed, and she stepped back from her work, it was another of those strange, exciting, revelatory moments: Oh my, David, look at *you*. Aren't you *something*?

It was an odd feeling, but I liked it. He looked just as ambivalently enticing as he had with his long blond hippie hair – just as powerful and vulnerable, just as delicately manly – but this new, streamlined red puffball upped the ante. Now he looked stronger and wilder;

just as fuckable, but a lot stranger and, well, more sluttish. Maybe even dangerous. Hmmmmm...

It had a definite effect on the way David saw himself too. The simple fact that the new hairstyle required regular maintenance forced him into an even keener, more constant self-consciousness. A puffball doesn't spring back into shape after a night's sleep the way a freestyle hippie fall does; a certain amount of fussing in front of a mirror is required; and a mirror can be a very productive place for a market-oriented narcissist of David's caliber.

And so the new hairstyle triggered new experiments with makeup, and greater interest in clothes, and it wasn't long at all before young David Jones had transformed himself into a figure that was pure, one-hundred-percent, head-to-toe Ziggy: a lithe, redheaded, face-painted, very revealingly and *very* originally clothed polysexual stardust alien.

Which of course did the trick, imagewise. There would never again be any doubt about which one David Bowie was, even if *who* he was immediately became a mystery that has persisted to this day, most entertainingly and quite rewardingly for almost everybody involved – particularly David, for whom the creation of Ziggy was the first emphatic act in a great liberation. It's somewhat trite, but it's true: By creating Ziggy to go out and front for him, David never had to act like himself in public if he didn't want to, which in turn meant that he could pursue art and applause without having to deal with his 'lack of self-esteem,' as the shrinks put it, or more accurately, his frigid self-loathing.

And of course, as the cultural historians have noted, David-as-Ziggy was one of the great social catalysts of the times. He was the flash that ignited a worldwide explosion of sex-role experimentation, Glitter competition, and narcissistic self-absorption. He was the traffic light at the turning point; he stopped the poor tired broken-down bus of hippie communalism and gave the green light to the Me Decade's millions of smaller, sleeker, markedly separate and unequal personal vehicles. So he really *was* something.

And as Ziggy began his conquest of the world's imagination, it became clear to me that, fortunately, I'd done my end of the job quite well. The team I'd marshaled was talented, spirited, and remarkably effective. David now had behind him a very fine full-fledged rock band, a marvelously cunning manager, a greatly gifted personal designer, a creative and dedicated stylist/wardrobe mistress, a hell-on-wheels wife to run everyone for him, and a full-time nanny to make it possible for her to do so. Which seemed like (and was) everything he needed. Ziggy was ready to rock and roll.

It's true that a single picture can make a deeper impression than words beyond number, but it's also true that a few of the right words in the right place at the right time can move more mountains than images ever could.

Such was the case with one section of an interview with David published on January 22 1972, in *Melody Maker*. The words were brief and simple – 'I'm gay and I always have been, even when I was David Jones' – but their effect was enormous.

The interview took place at the Gem office (Main Man hadn't fired up yet), rock journalist Michael Watt doing the honors and David feeding him the line dressed in three-quarter (street) Ziggy style. At that time, as I recall, he hadn't plunged as fully into Ziggy as he would a little later, when the *Ziggy Stardust* album was available for purchase, but he was at least halfway there; he was speaking at least half of his lines from the persona of his hype-spawned sacrificial-alien rock star. The 'I'm gay' admission was honest personal stuff, though, and I remember David's case of nerves when he emerged from the interview.

I had no qualms whatsoever about reassuring him to the fullest possible degree. I was so thrilled, in fact, that I hooted. I could hardly contain myself.

'David! You realize what you've done? You've fucking *made* it! There's gonna be no stopping us now, babe!'

He relaxed a little and explained that until the very moment he said it, he hadn't known he was going to. He hadn't made up his mind one way or the other, even after all the talking he and I had done, all the sex liberation philosophy and politics I'd been gently pushing on him. But the moment came, he said, and his instinct told him to do it, and he let it rip.

'You did the right thing, babe, you really did,' I told him. 'Just wait and see. It was the right thing to do, and the right time to do it. Marketing-wise, it was just perfect.'

He agreed – he's no dummy – but still he was worried. 'I don't know how Tony's going to take this,' he said. 'You think he'll be okay with it?'

'That's irrelevant, babe,' I told him. 'What you said is the truth, and you should be able to tell the truth whenever you want. You shouldn't have to be like Ken Pitt and his friends, sneaking around hiding yourself, keeping it in the closet. If Tony thinks that way too, then he's not going to be able to market you effectively, and we'll get rid of him and get someone else. But he'll be okay, I bet you. He sees you as an industry, or a building, and he knows a building can't have false foundations.'

As it happened, I think Tony Defries was profoundly shocked when he picked up *Melody Maker* and saw David's admission right there in bold type on the front page. But as I'd guessed he would, he proceeded immediately to point B, fully understanding the implications of the situation: If David's bisexuality was an item deemed worthy of front-page treatment by Britain's leading music business newspaper, then it was also an item more than likely to sell tickets. So damn the torpedoes. Tony was shocked, but for the first time, I think, he realized the full commercial potential of David's sex-role games.

The *Melody Maker* article itself, by the way, wasn't quite the study in black and white it was reported to be in the many reactions it provoked in the general Fleet Street press. Michael Watts had given his treatment of David a nicely perceptive spin.

'David's present image is to come on like a swishy queen, a gorgeously effeminate boy,' he wrote. 'He looks camp as a row of tents with his limp hands and trolling vocabulary. "I'm gay," he says, "and I always have been, even when I was David Jones." But there's a sly jollity about him as he says it, a secret smile at the corners of his mouth. He knows that in these times it's permissible to act like a male tart, and that to shock and outrage, which pop has always striven to do throughout its history, is a ball-breaking business.'

I for one appreciated the ambiguities bouncing around inside that paragraph, and I imagine that the gay/bi/multi community did too.

It was the simple printed admission that hooked the Fleet Street reporters, however, and they really went to town on it. It was wonderful. In those late January days I would pick up the newspapers and just giggle, loving every legend-building word. I could just *feel* all those kids out there perking up and taking notice, all those mums and dads sitting around the kitchen fire with their pots of char and Walls pork sausages, scratching their heads and wondering: *Hmmmmm... gay, he says... a fairy... hmmmmm... married... wears a dress... hmmmm... got a kid... hmmmmm...*

David's public response to the press's reaction was appropriate: the mild distaste of the cultured person confronted by philistines at work. He told another interviewer that 'as soon as the article came out in *Melody Maker*, people called up and said, "Don't buy the paper. You know what you've gone and done? You've just ruined yourself!" Well, I bought the paper and [the comments] looked all right, but from then on, the way the other papers picked up on [the interview] and just tore at it like dogs at meat, they made this enormous thing out of it.'

They did indeed. It was quite some brouhaha, and the phone at Haddon Hall did get busy. I didn't mind one bit, of course; my only real regret was the anxiety of poor dear Mrs Ronson, who called from Hull looking for reassurance that her beloved Mick hadn't *really* fallen into the den of iniquity her morning newspaper was describing in large and lurid terms.

'No, no, no, Mrs Ronson,' said I. 'It's not that way at all. Don't worry. David just chose a dramatic way of saying we think gay people are cool, that's all.'

I didn't, of course, tell her that no matter how odd his friends might be, Ronno *wasn't* in danger. Far from being corrupted by queers, in fact, he was plowing a purely heterosexual furrow through the young womanhood of London and the nation with a vigor I found admirable, if amazing.

Neither did I tell her that David's admission, combined with the imminent release of *The Rise and Fall of Ziggy Stardust and the*

*Spiders from Mars* and the very high-voltage buzz already running wild through the rock world in response to the public unveiling of the Glitter critter in concert, was about to enlarge dear Ronno's pool of potential sex partners by hundreds of thousands. And neither, for that matter, did I alert her to Mick Rock's infamous photograph of David/Ziggy bent over backward between her son's legs, going down on his guitar in mid-set at a concert in Aylesbury.

That might well have done to her what it did to everyone else – piqued her curiosity to no end – but I doubt that it would have excited her in quite the same way it lit up the kids.

That was some picture. *That* was an image worth a thousand words.

In the depth of the winter of 1971–2 you could actually buy a ticket to see David do his thing with Ronno's instrument (and invent rock theater while he was at it). That was when Ziggy and the Spiders went out into the world for the first time, and conquered it.

It was wonderful, that first UK tour. It wasn't a sellout all the way through – in some of the cities the halls were only half full – but everywhere David and the boys went, the reaction was delirious. I went to four or five of the gigs myself, and I'll never forget them, particularly the moment when I found myself in a box at the Queen's Playhouse in Glasgow, watching with my heart in my mouth as the fans started climbing up the wall of the theater to get to me. My mother was with me, and to this day I don't know who was more amazed, scared, and delighted all at once, she or I. When the show returned to London and played Imperial College, I remember, the crowd rushed the stage during David's encore and carried him out of the hall in triumph on their shoulders, like some great hero of ancient Rome.

It was wild: wonder and delirium from city to city to city. It might have been the costumes that did it – David changed his three times each show – or the spectacular sound system, a setup we'd ensured was far superior to prevailing industry standards, or perhaps the strobes that began pulsing when the Spiders launched into the

Velvet Underground's 'White Light/White Heat,' and kept flashing until the whole crowd was tripped-out crazy.

All those staging elements were new to the rock arena – but then, so was Ziggy Stardust, and so were the wonderful Ziggy songs, and so was my Light Person in all his charismatic glory. After trying for so long, he was finally claiming his place center stage.

The critics certainly thought so. When he played a Save the Whales concert at the Royal Festival Hall, a big benefit organized by the Friends of the Earth, the press seemed to have gone as crazy as the fans.

'David will soon become the greatest entertainer Britain has ever known,' declared *Music Week*, usually a greatly more circumspect organ.

'Anyone still unconvinced that David Bowie will sweep all before him should have witnessed the end of his remarkable concert last Saturday,' quoth none other than *The Times* of London, which, in a very flatteringly highbrow aside, characterized David, as 'T.S. Eliot with a rock and roll beat.'

*Disk*'s comment was succinct, but perhaps more *relevantly* flattering: 'Bowie saved the whale *and* rock.'

Gracious. Talk about arriving. This was heady stuff. Personally, I enjoyed *Melody Maker*'s comments the most; then as before they were a little savvier than the rest.

Writing under an accurate if corny headline – 'A Star Is Born!' – Ray Coleman noted that 'when a shooting star is heading for the peak there is usually one concert at which it is possible to declare, "That's it. He's made it." The show was a triumph. David varied the pace, even slowing down to do a slow version of Jacques Brel's "Amsterdam." At the end of the set he brought Lou Reed on stage to perform "White Light/White Heat," "I'm Waiting for My Man," and "Sweet Jane." It was Reed's first ever British appearance, but even that didn't stop it [from] being Bowie's night.'

It was all magic, much better than sex and drugs and those other common pleasures, and indeed the dynamic of those first months of real stardom *was* transcendent in that way. We were all high on work, action, applause, and more work. We didn't have time for getting thoroughly stoned or even properly laid – not on any regular basis, at least, although I can't speak for David when he was on the road without me, deluged with offers. Even if there *had* been reasonably lengthy gaps in the daily schedule of business, media stroking, writing, rehearsing, recording, traveling, and performing, which there weren't, most of us would have used the time either to sleep or be creative; to develop or hone or perfect something – a song, a guitar overdub, a costume, a deal, a set of logistics; or even to plan a new direction for the thrilling journey we were on.

I *loved* those first months of David's stardom, and so did he, and so did everyone else in our little troupe of players. We felt fine, famous, and fully appreciated; we felt extraspecial, intensely alive, incredibly alert; we felt like successful grown-ups, but also like boys and girls at play, as is the great gift of the performer's life. We felt like friends, and we felt like a family.

It was beautiful, it really was. When we finally got a break, what did we do? We rented a villa in Rome, and we all went on holiday together. We loved each other; it didn't even occur to us to go our separate ways.


Communality and creativity, no matter how happily intense, do not necessarily banish cold calculation. Or at least in the case of David Bowie in 1972 they didn't. This isn't really surprising; I don't think David has ever known how to get really carried away, except of course by booze and drugs.

Take, for instance, his approach to Lou Reed, who, as Ray Coleman mentioned in his *Melody Maker* review of the Save the Whales concert, made his first British appearance as a guest on David's stage. David, you see, was very smart. Since his first trip to the States – before that, actually – he'd been evaluating the market for his work, calculating his moves, and monitoring his competition. And the only really serious competition in his market niche, he'd concluded, consisted of Lou Reed and (maybe) Iggy Pop.

So what did David do? He co-opted them. He brought them into his circle. He talked them up in interviews, spreading their legend in Britain, and then, in the summer of '72, he personally chaperoned their introduction to British audiences. He held a very amusing day of press interviews with them at the Dorchester Hotel ('Any society that allows people like Lou Reed and I [*sic*] to become rampant is pretty well lost,' quoth he, very quotably), appearing as their ally and benefactor and getting at least as much attention as they, if not more. He connected Iggy and his group, the Stooges, with Tony Defries and Main Man, and achieved a situation in which he and Iggy had the same manager, but he'd had him first. He went to work, with Mick Ronson, producing Lou's *Transformer* album, a cooperative venture between RCA labelmates that (oh, that pleasant smell of roses all around!) gave artist and company the only major pop hit of Lou's career, 'Walk on the Wild Side.' Later in 1972 he stepped into the breach for CBS, Iggy's label, and salvaged what was felt to be an unacceptable production job on an Iggy and the Stooges album.

Everybody made out pretty well in all this action, and everybody ended up beholden to David Bowie in one way or another. That was some smooth operating, I thought, admiring David's moves and helping out with counsel and logistic support.

One aspect of logistics was housing, specifically the question of where Warholian Americans might find suitable accommodations during their working visits to Mother London, and I took care of that. Sometimes it was fun. Lou Reed's house-hunting, for example, was a stitch: not so much in the nature of events, which went along smoothly, as in the nature of Lou himself.

My first clear impression of him, which may or may not have coincided with the first time I actually met him (the impression is from London in '72, but I may have encountered him briefly in New York in '71) was of a man honor-bound to act as fey as a human could. He was wearing heavy mascara and jet-black lipstick with matching nail polish, plus a tight little Errol Flynn-as-Robin Hood bodyshirt that must have lit up every queen for acres around him, and he looked as if he would jump higher than the Post Office Tower if you so much as whispered 'Boo!' in his well-turned little ear.

David introduced us and we shook hands, kind of – Lou's greeting was a rather odd cross between a dead trout and a paranoid butterfly, while mine impersonated a half-drunk stevedore – and after the usual pleasantries we got down to business.

'Well,' David said before drifting off elsewhere, 'Angie will help sort you out a place to live.'

'I'd be glad to,' said I, looking Lou over one more time and thinking, *Hmmmm, Richmond*. Quiet, semi-arty, relatively cheap, well removed from the urban-cosmopolitan hubbub around the studio, and pretty.

I described Richmond to him and laid out a few alternatives, including a couple of likely neighborhoods deep in the heart of the scene, but he didn't bite on anything specific. 'Well, whatever *you* think is best,' was his decision. So I made a date with him for a couple of days later, thinking I'd line up a few prospects and take him around until he found something he liked.

Which is exactly what I did. I didn't drive at the time, so come the appointed hour I showed up with a minicab and a driver, expecting Lou to make it three.

Except that he brought his friends with him, and that made it five. And his friends, let me tell you, were amazing. My interest in Lou, and my respect for his strangeness, escalated immensely at my first sight of those two: both very young; both utterly, almost astonishingly gorgeous, with ash-blond curls and heart-shaped faces, their eyebrows and eyelashes as dark as if they'd been dyed, their bodies slight, sweet, and slender; different in that one was a boy and one a girl, and similar in that they were brother and sister.

'Angie, I'd like you to meet my boyfriend and my girlfriend,' Lou said very matter-of-factly, and I thought: *My* goodness. *How fabulous! What a rock-and-roller!*

'Well,' I said, 'I'm so pleased to meet you both,' and decided on the spot that the way to play this one was very cool, very ladylike; hospitable and accepting, without even one tiny hint of overintrusive curiosity. (England and my parents had taught me well: When in doubt, act properly brought up.) So we all squeezed into the minicab for a perfectly normal day, just another trot around the housing market with just another nice young *ménage à trois*.

I did very well, I think, but it was difficult. Those three were fascinating, holding hands (in pairs or all together), exchanging sweetnesses and kisses (ditto), and bless them, being very happy and healthy. They all seemed excited to be in London, and I enjoyed their enthusiasm. I warm quickly to a person who loves my own lover-city, but this was more than that, baby; Lou and his kids appeared to be having a genuinely good and happy time together, and it was infectious.

They made their housing choice – not Richmond, I recall, but something almost as civilized a little closer to town – and moved in, and things went along fine just the way they were. Sometimes David sent me to fetch Lou for rehearsals and sessions at Trident, and it got to be a private little game of mine: Who would be holding hands today? What dynamic decided? Who had been doing what with whom before I arrived, and how was it, and what strange separate paths had those three people's lives traveled to their present togetherness?

I never found out, but I certainly had an interesting time imagining, as I did during and after later encounters with Lou.

One intriguing item, a couple of years after the *Transformer* sessions, was Rachel/Ricky, the transvestite (or sex change, I never got it straight) with whom Lou was hooked up when he came back to play London. She/he was really something: cream-white skin, jet-black hair, very tall, very gothic – I think she was Puerto Rican or South American originally – and just drop-your-panties *stunning*. She was very amusing in a camp, clever way, and of course ultra-extroverted. Definitely the center of attention.

There we were once in Lou's hotel room after his show, with him the talk of the town in all the wild places, and what was the sole topic of conversation? This character's shopping! Where she'd spent Lou's money today, where she was going to spend it tomorrow, what treasures she secured, what got away, the whole experience in vivid detail! Lou hardly spoke.

But that was okay with him, I think. He was in love; what's-her/his-name was his world. It can't have been easy on Lou when they broke up and, as I heard it, she/he quit drinking and drugging, went straight (as an arrow, they say), and married a nice girl from his/her hometown. Poor Lou. More grist for that monstrous, superindustrial-strength angst mill of his.

Yeah, poor Lou. You hear such stories about him, particularly about his paranoia and his temper, and I have no trouble believing them. I've never seen him lose it completely – that is, I've never seen him physically violent – but I've been there when he's come close. He blew up at David and Ronno in the studio one day during the *Transformer* sessions; I made a beeline for the door as soon as he exploded, and went shoe-shopping on Carnaby Street for an hour or two. The last time I saw him, in New York, we had dinner together one night. I ate well, but he didn't eat a bite, and I watched with growing concern as he swung through his changes and then went thataway: from real pleasure to see me, to a venomous but more or less rational attack on David, to a state of bugged-out, all-inclusive paranoia which struck me as truly insane. He was stoned, so his mood was affected by however his pharmaceutical cycles of choice were intersecting during that particular hour or two, but even so . . .

You might get a better sense of Lou if I tell you something he told me during dinner.

'You have to get stoned in the city,' he said in absolute seriousness. 'It's a necessity. The atmosphere is so polluted that you have to put chemicals in your body to counteract it.'

I don't know where he got that idea, whether he picked it out of *Naked Lunch* or his own head, but oh well, whatever. He's never dull, that man.

And I must admit that I'm indebted to him for raising my self-consciousness. When I first saw him with his brother-sister combo, that just fascinated me. It seemed so weird, so exotic. But then one afternoon after I'd dropped him off at Trident for a session, and I was walking in Soho, marveling again at how odd it all was, I caught myself. *Wait a minute, Angie,* I thought. *Lou's scene is weird, but it's no more outrageous than your own, is it?*

The fact that I didn't fool around much during the cyclone of David's early stardom doesn't mean I was any kind of good girl or conventional wife. Hell, no!

I didn't fool around much, but I did fool around. Let me tell you, for instance, just what I meant when, writing about my healing days with Dana at Lago Maggiore after Zowie's birth, I said that I got the chance to have some good plain fun.

The Gillespie villa was a three-story affair built into the steeply sloping bank of the lake itself. You entered through a veranda running from the lakeside road to the top floor of the house, and found yourself in a large living room with, at its far end, picture windows offering a magnificent view of the lake. The bedrooms were on the lower floors, and in front of the house were huge, glacially smooth rocks where you could lounge in the sun and, when the fancy took you, slip off into the cooling waters of the crystal lake. A speedboat was available for our transport and entertainment, as were various other amenities.

The day I'm talking about, Dana and I had gone across the lake in the speedboat to the local outdoor market, a fabulous place. We'd come back, smoked a nice big English-style hash joint, sunbathed all afternoon, eaten dinner with the senior Gillespies, and retired to the bedroom we shared to smoke another spliff.

That's where we were when bad weather started brewing on the lake, one of those sudden, often spectacularly violent alpine summer storms. The wind started rattling our windows fiercely, so I got up and threw them open, then hopped into bed with Dana. We lay there in the dark in the storm-filled room, stoned out of our minds, holding on to each other and enjoying ourselves immensely. And then of course I proceeded to do what came naturally, and started making love to my gorgeous friend. It wasn't a novelty – Dana and I had dallied before, both just us two and with others, including David and her boyfriend, and she'd taken to introducing me in her most intimate circles as 'my perfect gentleman' and 'Angie the creamy slit' – but to be enjoying her again was a wonderful and welcome change from the strain of my previous few weeks. It felt great to really let it rip.

We were well into it, losing ourselves, tangled up like a couple of Kama Sutra yogis – Dana so lusciously voluptuous, me so grey-hound lithe – when one of life's shocking nanoseconds exploded somewhere behind me and – Holy *shit*! – there in the doorway was Mrs Gillespie.

You have never seen a human being move so fast, or two people so intricately entwined so suddenly straightened and separated. I was up and across the floor to the window, and gazing raptly at the storm on the lake, in the blink of an eye. I'd already stopped moving while Mrs Gillespie was still trying to focus on the wild erotic image she may or may not have seen on the bed.

You couldn't tell from her expression, but there was an odd tone in her voice as she spoke the words that had been on her lips when she opened the bedroom door: 'Ah . . . There's a big storm coming, girls.'

Angie the finishing school prefect answered: 'Oh yes, Mrs Gillespie, don't worry. We'll be all right. I was just closing the windows.'

I didn't know if the poor lady had rumbled us or not, and I still don't, but both Dana and I would swear that the next day at breakfast, when we announced that we were going to a rock concert that evening in Como, a look of relief flitted across her face. *Oh, thank God*, I bet she was thinking, *they're going off to chase boys*.

That wasn't strictly accurate, but then again, it wasn't strictly *in*accurate. We were in fact going to see a popular Italian band, I Giganti ('the Giants'), who had scored a big hit with an Italian-language version of 'Space Oddity.' They were playing one of those big outdoor evening events the Italians love, with fireworks and children's acts as well as rock and roll, and we thought it would be a gas no matter how bad the band turned out to be.

It was indeed a gas – a zillion teenagers dancing their buns off on a huge temporary dance floor, the whole town kicking up its heels – and moreover, the band wasn't even vaguely bad. They were a hoot, in fact: hot rockers, great singers and showmen, and handsome as they come in the dark, distinctly non-effeminate manner of Italian rock-and-roll gladiators.

We went backstage after the show, and my oh my, it was nice to be appreciated so deeply. Those guys were *thrilled*. Dana was enough of a treat all by herself – she'd already had a couple of hit records in Britain at that point in her career, and she was staggeringly beautiful – but also to meet the wife of the great David Bowie himself . . . well, you can probably imagine.

We all got very stoned and social, and ended up piling into

someone's sports car and roaring (and howling and yelling) back to the Gillespies' for further socialization. I say 'we all,' but in fact I mean Dana and the band member she'd liked best, a very comely bearded fellow, and me and (who else?) the drummer. We made ourselves comfortable in that lovely living room overlooking the lake, and worked happily at getting even more stoned. In my case that meant smoking joints; Dana, I think, had found some acid, and she and her beau had started tripping.

Dana was definitely the wild one that night. I was still pretty badly damaged from Zowie's difficult birth, so I wasn't available either emotionally or physically for sex with a man. Besides, I was a married woman and these were Italians; to them, marriage was sacred and married women off-limits. So my drummer and I held hands and conversed pleasantly if inefficiently (across the language barrier), while Dana and her fellow squirmed and slurped and squished along obliviously, laughing and chattering madly with each other between clinches.

Eventually my drummer realized it was late (about three-thirty in the morning, if memory serves); the band had a gig the next day. We started trying to lever the lovers out the door.

Tough as it was, we made it with them onto the veranda next to the road; but then we paused for parting remarks, and that was a mistake. I was answering my drummer's queries about possible plans for a David Bowie Italian tour (he had none, as far as I knew), when I happened to look over his shoulder, out toward the road, and there they were.

That dude had Dana hitched up around his waist, supporting her whole weight, and was thrusting happily into her, but starting to lose it. The coitally coupled unit of which his component alone had contact with terra firma was heading very unsteadily out into the middle of the road, and as I watched in amazement – half terror, half hilarity – it began to topple, his back leading the way. Dana wasn't big or heavy, but she had huge 44-D's, and as I knew from my own experience with her, you encounter certain weight distribution problems with breasts that big. If you don't watch out, that high center of gravity will do you in.

He went all the way down onto his back with her still straddling

*An early picture of me, taken in Cyprus, where I grew up.*
*(author's collection)*

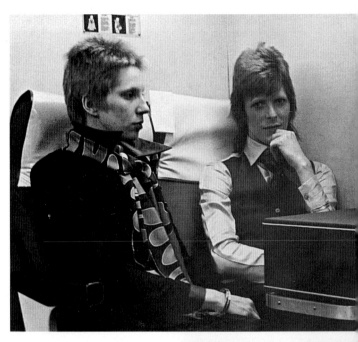

*David and me, married,
heading for the Continent.*
(Leee Black Childers/
Neal Peters)

*Our beautiful baby, Zowie,
once he got some hair.*
(Author's collection)

*David, in one of the five jackets I bought for him on Sloane Street.* (Mick Rock)

*A great stage shot of the Great One at New York's Radio City Music Hall in 1973, during his Ziggy period—long before the "insane" period.* (Dagmar)

*Well, well . . . look who we have here: Ian Hunter, Mick Ronson, photographer Leee Black Childers, and a friend.* (Dagmar)

*The very gorgeous, sexy Mick Ronson. Now you see why the girls couldn't keep their hands off him, and why the boys wanted him too. The girls won. The boys always lost.* (Dagmar)

*Two shots of David and me posing at a showing of the Paris collections. (Terry O'Neill)*

*My darling son, Zowie, with Rose, the daughter of David's designer Kansai Yamamoto. (Dagmar)*

*For my first photo session with the Sun Newspapers, I was made up by Pierre La Roche and photographed by Terry O'Neill. (Terry O'Neill)*

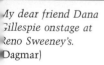

Marianne Faithfull (above). Stoned or not, she always pulled it together when it came time to perform. (Stephanie Chernikowski)

*My dear friend Dana Gillespie onstage at Reno Sweeney's. (Dagmar)*

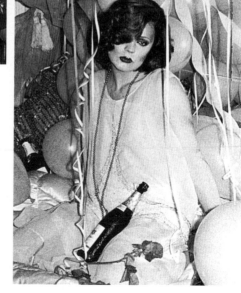

*Cherry Vanilla in the boudoir. What fun! (Author's collection)*

*Terry O'Neill's famous shot that convinced David he was being attacked by demons. His dark hand on my waist was the omen.* (Terry O'Neill)

*Back to a version of sanity at Radio City Music Hall in 1973, when David was with the Spiders from Mars.* (Dagmar)

Kansai Yamamoto with me in Japan, cheering the boys on, hours before he had to save me from the Japanese police. (Dagmar)

David and Tony Visconti in Philadelphia, listening to mixes for the David Live album. (Dagmar)

*Iggy Pop, whose virtues include being cute as a button and raunchy as hell.* (Stephanie Chernikowski)

*Lou Reed (left) in concert, years after his brother-sister ménage à trois.* (Stephanie Chernikowski)

*John Entwistle, Pete Townshend, Keith Moon. Boy, did they know how to party!* (Dagmar)

*Wonderful, sweet Elton John.*
(Dagmar)

*Mr. Goat's Head Soup
himself, Mick Jagger.*
(Stephanie Chernikowski)

*Michael Jackson, as he looked when I knew him, which is very different
from what he looks like now.* (Dagmar)

The Thin White Duke. (Dagmar)

The divine Ava Cherry, who was spending more time with my husban than I was . . . and not by my choice either. (Dagmar)

The Thin White Duke with Art Garfunkel, Paul Simon, Yoko Ono, John Lennon, and Roberta Flack at the Grammys in 1975. (Dagmar)

*Andy Warhol, about as excited as he ever got. Doesn't his face look like rice pudding? (Stephanie Chernikowski)*

*My audition for Wonder Woman, the role Lynda Carter already had in the bag. (Terry O'Neill)*

*Rod Stewart and David in 1975, after Rod's Madison Square Garden concert. Two mods who had graduated to high times and big money. (Dagmar)*

*David on his revolutionary* Diamond Dogs *tour.* (Dagmar)

*David on the set of* The Man Who Fell to Earth, *which was the beginning of the end for us.* (Springer/ Bettmann Film Archive)

*Two shots of my ex-husband. Left, during the Serious Moonlight tour, and above, in a recent incarnation in Switzerland. (Left: Stephanie Chernikowski; above: R. Konow)*

*Joan Rivers, Howard Stern, and me shortly after the gag order expired. Boy, did my appearance on Joan's show make headlines! (Tina Paul)*

*Angie today. Happy — and alive.* (© Rick Gillette)

him, but it didn't faze either of them. They stayed stuck together, God bless them, and kept at it. Dead in the center of the highway, astride the yellow line, doing it in the road.

My drummer and I thought on our feet, then used them. He ran up the road in one direction and I ran in the other, ready to stop traffic. None came, but I'll always be proud of having done the right thing.

Another fun little fling was my happy dalliance with Anton Jones on David's first US tour, which began late in the fall of 1972. Anton, a tall, athletic, witty, talented, gorgeously green-eyed Jamaican – black, handsome, built like an ox, and funny: what a combination! – had first joined our troupe as the chef on a Roman holiday; now he was traveling with us across North America as a bodyguard. He was a wonderful man, and for me he was far and away the high point of the tour.

Not that he had much competition. We weren't exactly seeing America from superstar level yet. We traveled by bus, for God's sake (not a modern Silver Eagle, with beds and everything, but some ordinary chartered bus), and stayed at Marriotts and Sheratons (not the upgraded, semi-civilized spots they are today, but the tacky plasterboard palaces of yesteryear), and played an awful lot of halls where the sound (if you could call it that) echoed around an awful lot of empty seats. I remember that a whole batch of West Coast dates were canceled, and that in Florida, Ronno's hair turned green from the chlorine in the pool as we sat waiting for news of the next date and living on room service because there wasn't any cash.

There wasn't much I could do to help matters, since the crucial action was all happening (or at least was supposed to be happening) between Tony Defries and RCA. I found that frustrating, but I kept my mouth shut. With nothing to be done, there didn't seem much point in dwelling on depressing truths or raising irritating subjects.

Besides, David's ear was occupied otherwise most of the time. He was in constant conference and/or coitus with a shifting parade of somebodies-or-other – local record company promo men, disc jockeys, and promoters; straight and bent and underground press people, publicists, groupies, and press person/publicist/groupies (those trades, then as now, being somewhat interchangeable) – and so he and I went through the experience separately. We were more like partners in a very busy business than like man and wife. We didn't even share a room most of the time, as I recall, and actually, it would have been awkward if we had. Threesomes and foursomes and other varieties of multiparty sex are of course very fine in their place, but David's coital conferencing was more a motivational maneuver than a recreational act, and best performed one on one.

Thank God for Anton, then. He was a great distraction. We'd fool around together on the bus and bounce around together in the motels, and generally just enjoy each other in every way.

That should have been fine with David, according to the stated terms between us, but I guess it wasn't. The crunch came one night in Memphis or Louisville, or somewhere else southern, when, seeking escape from a broiling-humid motel room, Anton and I went swimming in the motel pool.

As far as we were concerned, we were perfectly right and proper; the pool was lit, and it wasn't even midnight yet. Motel management didn't see it that way, though. We were splashing happily, laughing and whooping and having tons of naughty fun – who knows who had what in whose mouth? – when all of a sudden it seemed we had every uptight redneck desk clerk and assistant deputy night administrator in the south central United States in our face. Those people were seriously annoyed. They ordered us out of the pool immediately – they were *shrieking* – and proceeded to scold us as if we were delinquent five-year-olds.

Anton made the error of talking back to them too, and that made them even crazier: some great big bold Mandingo warrior with a weird foreign accent taking an attitude like *he* thought *they* were the subhumans, and *he* might just stop *their* clocks if *they* didn't start acting right. You could feel their lynching fingers twitching, baby!

David saved the day (for once). He showed up in the lobby and charmed things down very efficiently – and saved Anton, but he didn't save me. He got rid of me as quickly as he could, in fact, setting in motion events that very rapidly produced plane tickets and sayonaras. I was on my way to New York the next day, and back to London very soon after that.

The effect was lasting. From that point on I was never invited along on tour. I'd go on the road for brief periods now and then, either when I insisted or when David grew lonely or felt that he needed my mothering or door-kicking services, but usually those times would end just the way my first tour ended: I'd start having too much fun, David would start feeling threatened, and home I'd go. So as far as my being a core member of the traveling troupe, that was it: I was banished.

In a way, it was okay with me. Touring is a hassle, far too much hard work, with too many of the stresses of 'normal' travel and none of the benefits; nobody but a born gypsy or a person running from something really likes it.

In other ways, though, my banishment wasn't good at all. I'd already lost some of my intimacy with David by working myself out of a job – by finding and hiring Tony Defries, by getting Freddi and Daniella and Susie on board to take care of the roles I'd once performed – and now I was losing contact and influence in yet another area of his life. Furthermore, I had the distinct feeling that that was fine with him, and even finer with Tony.

I was a little paranoid about that, but then I realized it was appropriate for me to be disengaging from David's career. The energy I had been pouring into him needed to go elsewhere now.

Now, you see, it was *my* turn. Together we had made David a star – 'T.S. Eliot with a rock-and-roll beat,' no less – and now, according to the pact we had made that turning-point day in the upstairs back bedroom at Plaistow Grove, we would do the same for me. With the resources now at our disposal, I thought, that shouldn't be hard at all.

# 9

# SAYONARA, SPIDERS FROM MARS

*I* may have wanted my own career, but that didn't mean I was free to pursue it. David and Tony may have been edging me out of the center of things, but that didn't mean I was free to disengage from David's business. Those boys kept me pretty busy.

Not that I disliked the work. For one thing, it had become almost second nature for me to promote and protect David and the ideas he stood for; my role had its own great internal momentum. For another, the job very definitely had its moments. I mean, really: If you had to work for anyone but yourself between 1972 and 1974, could you have done any better than David Bowie? He *was* where the action was, and some of the action *was* so much fun.

In April 1973, for example, I had a wonderful working vacation in Japan, an utterly fascinating place (far superior, as former Axis nations go, to the Fatherland) and the home of many a dedicated David Bowie fan. Something about David – perhaps his almost formal, mime- and dance-based approach to theatricality – struck a powerful chord in those ancient-cultured islanders, and the more contemporary Japanese cultural consciousness, ga-ga as it was about its own marvelous B-movie monsters and trashy alien oddities, took to the strange new English Glitter critter as if he'd popped up out of some fiery anomaly only miles off the wharfs of Nagasaki. So great was the enthusiasm, in fact, that *The Rise and Fall of Ziggy Stardust and the Spiders from Mars* stayed on the Japanese charts for more than two years. It was selling very healthily indeed when we showed up, kicking off pleasantly proportioned sales booms among the earlier albums and attracting audiences that packed every hall the band played in.

This was great, and went some way toward compensating for the basic riskiness of the enterprise. In those days the Japanese circuit wasn't set up for Westerners or rockers, and so we faced various surprises and hazards. A Japanese promoter could still welsh on a deal, legally and honorably, by saying that his father had withdrawn his approval at the last minute. A Japanese cop, never a model of restraint at the best of times then or now, was still apt to approach a crowd of harmlessly boogying teenagers as if they were a horde of invading Mongolian infantry.

More often than not, however, our novel Japanese experiences were very stimulating. One of my most vivid memories of the trip is of going with Leee Black Childers to the Imperial Theater in Tokyo, right behind the hotel where we were staying.

The title of the show has eluded me for some time now, perhaps because almost immediately after seeing it, Leee and I christened it 'The All-Dyke Review' and left it at that. This was an apt title, if not strictly accurate; the participants weren't all dykes, I don't think, but all the boys' parts, as well as the girls', were played by women – in a cast of thousands, almost, on a huge stage with aprons and catwalks and props and pyrotechnics elaborate enough to blow the socks off even a hardcore staging junkie like me. And that's not all. The combined efforts of this legion of players and supporting personnel were turned not to traditional imperial art or even Western grand opera, but to Broadway. They were staging a 'Greatest Hits of Every Musical You Could Ever Have Heard on the Great White Way.' In Japanese.

We couldn't believe it. It was stunning, and not just as the ultimate in bizarre theatrical experiences. No. What really grabbed Leee and me was that every man-played-by-woman on that stage was the most gorgeous hunk of polysexual Oriental humanity you could ever in your wildest fantasies begin to imagine. We are talking one-in-a-billion *knockouts* here, one after another.

It took a great deal of effort, but after a while I was able to decide that the one among all those beauties who encouraged my love light to its most incandescent was a character by the name of Reisami.

No sooner had this determination been reached than I started making plans.

It was difficult. What were the rules? They have so many of them in Japan, and the Japanese are so keen on them. Were four orchids acceptable, or insulting? How about a dozen? How about a single flower with a simple handwritten poem? How about a gift-wrapped Gucci purse stuffed with hundred-dollar bills, the keys to a brand new Porsche, and a wad of explicitly enticing Polaroids?

I settled on flowers, I forget how many, and tickets to David's concert, and crossed my legs.

A note came back. Yow. Bingo! Reisami was, unfortunately, unable to attend the concert because of schedule conflicts, but she would be pleased to meet me.

She arrived at my suite at the Imperial Hotel at the appointed hour, with an interpreter ('Oh yes, she is very pleased you like the show,' et cetera, et cetera) and lovely gifts, and she was so charming and gracious and *pristine* in her formal poise and incredible beauty that I couldn't carry through. It would, I thought at the time and still believe, have been the very height of Ugly Americanism to pounce on that luscious lovely and ravish her right then and there, interpreter be damned. Imperial edicts might well have resulted.

And so, with almost painful ardor as her amazing face etched itself into my erotic memory, I realized that this kind of thing had probably happened before, probably often, particularly to men like my father and his comrades in arms. Reisami and I exchanged pleasantries through the interpreter for a while, and then I bestowed on her an appropriate package of Bowie paraphernalia and bade her a most regretful but decorous farewell.

Nothing else in Japan quite matched Reisami in terms of erotic titillation, but that was okay. Compared with the other human forces at work during our Japanese trip, eroticism was insignificant.

The audiences there, for instance, were incredible. Young and fresh and almost childlike in their exuberance, worlds away from the older, infinitely less innocent crowds David was drawing in Europe and the United States, they gave us so much. Their sheer happiness when David appeared before them was wonderful, a mass delirious feeling.

They showered us with gifts, literally and figuratively. I remember sitting with David cross-legged in our hotel suite in our lovely new kimonos, sorting through treasures – an exquisite little doll some kid had made for him, or a magnificent functional samurai sword, or a spare haiku written in his honor – while Zowie slept sweetly only feet away. A cocoon of wonder and happiness came down around us. David and I hadn't made love together in months, but we did in Japan, several times.

We felt like a family too. Having Zowie with us on tour was a first-time experience, and it gave a new flavor to the scene. When we traveled on the bullet train to Hiroshima, Zowie went roaming around the car, as two-year-olds will, and the other passengers were so sweet to him. By the time the train ride was over – oh, the Japanese are wonderful with children! – he was friends with everybody. One woman picked him up and sat him on her knee and started feeding him with her chopsticks. He was delighted, and she smiled at us so tenderly that tears almost welled up in my eyes. When I saw David's face shining with pride and love for his boy, they did. David could be so kind, so gentle; I loved him so much, I really did.

He was at his very best on that Japanese tour: creatively vital, stimulated by his work and his surroundings, and happy and comfortable among the people who loved him. Japan had engaged his interest for years – there had been Japanese prints in the room at Mary Finnegan's where we first made real love together – and he was thrilled to be there. He was fascinated mostly by the fact that all around him was a society founded on Buddhist precepts; this was not the small, fringe collection of individuals with whom he'd studied Buddhism in Britain. While he was far too popular to observe Japanese society outside the well-protected confines of hotels and limos, he did what he could to learn. A Japanese photographer and his assistant accompanied the tour from start to finish, and David spent hours with them, questioning and absorbing with that soft, intensely focused energy of his. He was that way too with Kansai Yamamoto, the brilliant designer to whom he'd been connected by the (very) live wires at RCA's Japanese office. Quite apart from Kansai's stunning outfits, which were to impress the cotton socks off millions of Europeans and Americans on the

*Aladdin Sane* tour and provoke Japanese fans to ecstasies of inter-cultural appreciation (the great Bowie, a real Western rock star, digging *them*! They almost couldn't stand it), our visits with the designer and his family gave David, and me, a deeper feeling for the roots of Japanese culture. And the vision of Zowie with Kansai's three-year-old daughter, Rosie, he a bright little curly-headed blond, she a perfect straight-black-haired doll, both of them in kimonos (Zowie wore his over his usual clothes for the entire tour), was one of the prettiest I've ever seen.

It was another of those moments. Right then and there, with my husband and son beside me in harmony, all the discord of the recent past faded away and I felt more strongly than ever that I was doing the right thing. My Light Person and I were moving forward on our destined path, and we were going to be all right.

The tour went on in a happy rush, show after wildly successful show, moment after sweet moment. Wearing Kansai's strange and beautiful Spring Rain costume, David was appreciated ecstatically at every show: wonderful for him but very hard on the costume, which had to be rushed back to Kansai's shop and painstakingly repaired after each mobbed performance. Getting into the spirit of things, the Spiders too adopted local color, particularly Trevor Bolder; dark and shortish, in platform shoes and with his long hair pulled up into a funky topknot, he made a perfect rock-and-roll samurai, and the audience loved him for it. They loved the whole stage-front lineup, in fact, and those boys were quite a sight: David the light-shedding hero, looking like a wild mythic doll of some possible Kabuki future; Ronno all Western, blond and bare-chested and beautiful; Trevor the Kurosawa homeboy. Woody Wood-mansey, hidden behind the drum kit, didn't figure in the picture – the drummer's lot.

All three of the lads from Hull were happy on that tour, and they were great, good, down-to-earth company.... *Eh, Angie, this fried fish is luvly. Almost as good as the Gainsborough, innit? Where's the vinegar?* (Woody on first tasting shark tempura.) ... *Cor, would you look at that? I wonder if it glows in the dark?* (Ronno at the picture window of our hotel suite in Hiroshima overlooking the Peace Park, formed around the crater where the bomb exploded in 1945 – David and I standing by his side in mute wonder, not quite believing first, that someone would build a hotel in that precise spot and, second, that someone would place us in a suite with that particular view. David appreciated the gesture, though. 'That,' he said quietly, with a slow shake of his head and a grin of knowing pleasure, 'is *soooo* Japanese.'

All in all, then, the Japanese experience was a gas. It got a little nasty right at the end, in Tokyo, when the damned cops did their heavy-handed thing on a crowd of worshipful teens who'd rushed the stage, causing several rows of seats to collapse. Those jerks' one and only priority was restoring order and disciplining the unorderly, to the point that Leee Black Childers and Tony Zanetta and I had to fight our way through club-swinging goons to help kids trapped under the seats, some of them hurt quite badly. But a country's policemen, jailers, and other officially sanctioned thugs don't own its soul, and so I can say without reservation that I loved Japan and the Japanese. It didn't even bother me much when, as I was on my way out, I was informed that I wouldn't be welcomed back. I guess foreigners aren't supposed to manhandle the local storm troopers.

David's exit from the island nation was more auspicious than mine. He took a ferry from Yokohama to Nakhodka on the Asian mainland, then a train to Vladivostok, and then the legendary Trans-Siberian Railroad into the heart of Mother Russia – to Moscow itself – and thence southwest through Soviet, Polish, and German territory into France. We would rendezvous in Paris.

It was an amazing trip, and a great accomplishment. No Western artist of David's stature, let alone a major rock-and-roll star, had ever attempted or been granted permission for such a journey in the cold war era.

I was sorry to see him go, of course, because the intimacy between us in Japan had been so welcome and so hopeful, but I couldn't feel bad about it. I was proud of him for embarking on such a trip, and proud of myself too, because the odyssey had been my idea. It had emerged from a lunchtime brainstorming session in London between me and Bob Musel, the head of United Press International's

British office. Yes: Veteran straight journalist; Glitter critter singer/songwriter/superstar of the moment; and Warholian-American photographer (Leee) penetrate the heart of the Soviet darkness ...

What a coup. I was really doing my job, wasn't I?

*Aladdin Sane*, the new set of songs and new character to sing them that David had created while on tour in the States, was released in Britain while we were still in Japan. Advance orders exceeded 100,000 units; this had not happened since the heyday of the Beatles, and the album went gold on the day it was released. The word 'Bowiemania' appeared in the language, and when we alighted at Charing Cross Station from the train bringing us home from Paris, screaming teens by the hundreds swooned and swarmed.

That kind of thing can get your blood going, and it certainly gave *me* a case of the happies. While David and the boys and girls of our troupe went zooming off on a triumphant sold-out British tour in the spring and early summer of 1973, I zoomed around London taking care of business in a state of positivity and enthusiasm.

As the final dates of the tour approached, David called to talk about a party to cap it all off. What did I think?

What I thought was that our house wasn't big enough and wasn't appropriate anyway. The swank Café Royal in Regent Street seemed the right place to celebrate the triumph of Britain's foremost rock star, and a menu of strawberries and champagne, exclusively, seemed the right refreshment.

He liked that idea (who wouldn't?), and we settled on the date – July 4, the day after the last show of the tour, at the Hammersmith Odeon in London – and I set about assembling a guest list. There came to mind, among others, Paul and Linda, Mick and Bianca, Peter Cook and Dudley Moore, Elliott Gould and Ryan O'Neal and Tony Curtis (all working in England at the time), Rod Stewart, Keith Moon, Lou Reed, Jeff Beck, Cat Stevens, Lulu, Barbra Streisand, Sonny Bono (without Cher), Maggie Abbott, the agent who could corral all these people, and D.A. Pennebaker, who was to film the concert at the Odeon. With several dozen others filling out the bill, I thought, that ought to be a reasonably interesting cast of characters for a happy little bash. David thought so too, and I set the gears in motion.

What I didn't know – what nobody knew, except David and Tony Defries – was what the theme of the party was going to be; that is, what David was going to say from the stage of the Odeon at the end of the July 3 concert. And *that*, and I quote, was: 'Not only is this the last show of the tour, but it is the last show we'll ever do. Bye-bye. We love you.'

I was surprised, of course, but I wasn't exactly stunned, or flabbergasted, or moved to any particular extreme of emotion. It was more than obvious to me that David was simply executing some well-conceived career ploy and using the magic of the moment to amplify it to maximum effect. No way in hell, not unless he was handed an absolute guarantee of fame, adulation, and lavish living expenses forever without having to lift another finger, would David 'retire.' So I hardly gave it another thought.

Until, that is, I spoke to Ronno and Trevor backstage and learned that they and Woody had been completely surprised by David's announcement and, moreover, were beginning to grasp its implications. As Trevor put it, 'We're out of a job, Angie. He's giving us the fucking sack!'

That figured, I realized, recalling an incident on the last American tour. I have forgotten where it happened exactly, but I remember David's telling me about it.

It started when Tony and David hired a keyboard player, Mike Garson, for the tour. The guy was a Scientologist – which should have stopped them from hiring him, but didn't – and he of course proceeded to execute his primary mission: to recruit new Scientologists, in this case Trevor and Woody (Ronno wasn't buying) and then reroute their personal finances in the general direction of the church. This in turn led to increased financial expectations on Trevor's and Woody's part (long overdue, since they'd never been paid half of what they earned or a quarter of what they were worth).

The whole process culminated, disastrously, in a confrontation somewhere on the road in Big Rock Candyland. Woody and Trevor, or maybe even the whole four-man band (I'm fuzzy on the details here) refused to perform until Tony and David sat down with them and struck a new deal.

David was furious, just *furious*. 'That's it,' he told me. 'They can't hold me up like that. I don't care who they are, I simply won't have that kind of disloyalty.' And from then on, his passive-aggressive machinery engaged gears, and the lads' days were numbered.

What is freaky – chilling – is the fact that he kept them on through the Japanese tour, then through the British tour, without even hinting at his decision, and only then, once they'd given him their best and were enjoying their most triumphal moment, did he let them have it – full bore, all at once, in the most public, humiliating manner possible. That's what you could call exceptionally cool, intelligent self-interest – but you'd be a lot closer to the truth, I think, if you called it ruthlessness, nonconfrontational cowardice, and cruelty.

The Café Royal party the next night was a great success, with David at the very top of his form; he was pure charm and gentle friendliness, open and happy and gay. And, I must say, I had a wonderful time too. The mood was light, the Glitter dazzling, the night bright and beautiful with stars and success and serendipity.

I sailed over the undertones, then, and to be frank, I probably wanted to. I wasn't interested in examining bad vibes or perceiving negative omens.

I can make that observation because there exists a record of the moment, Pennebaker's film of the Hammersmith concert. If, as I did recently, you watch the backstage scenes where David and I are talking, you can see what I didn't want to: David's smiling face when it's turned toward me is a mask. The fire rekindled in Japan had gone out.

I continued to be useful as Mr Big Shot got bigger. David and the other artists assembled under the Main Man banner needed care and attention of all sorts, and I was after all *very* good at care and attention. I did get done what needed doing.

Take the Stooges, for instance, Iggy Pop's band. My mission in the fall of 1973 was to take the Stooges. Tony Defries had grown weary of them for some reason (I suspect their chronic, incorrigible drug use) and had decided that while the very best place for Iggy was still London, the Stooges belonged elsewhere, preferably another country. I was dispatched to escort them to Heathrow, their plane tickets in my hand (to forestall their conversion into drug money), and then accompany them into the air and all the way back to Ann Arbor, Michigan, where they, the MC5, and many other practitioners of raw, heavy, doped-out radical pre-punk/metal rock had made themselves a home. I'd heard so much about the scene there from Iggy and the lads that I wasn't displeased with my assignment.

I had myself an interesting time too. I had a fling with James Williamson, the lead guitar Stooge, followed by a fling with Ron Asheton, the bass-playing Stooge, and then Ron introduced me to Scott Richardson, the owner of a magnificent white-blues voice who played bass and sang for SRC, a wonderful hard-rock-and-blues band who were heavy local heroes but never made it to the national or international scene, and I fell for *him*.

He was bold and blond and very attractive, and besides, he wasn't a junkie (that is, then; or more accurately, yet). Being with him, therefore, wasn't the kind of waiting-for-Godot experience I'd had with James and Ron: lots of motel rooms with the TV on, lots of great slow sex, lots of interminable interludes while they disappeared into the bathroom to cook and shoot and nod and dream.

Those were my first intimate experiences of Junkieworld, as a matter of fact, and I didn't really like it much. For one thing, junkies can't be very spontaneous. When you say, 'I've got an idea! Let's go to Paris for the weekend!' the first thing that comes into *their* mind isn't 'Oh, how wonderful! Where's my passport?' No. It's, *Oh shit, I don't have a French connection.* I think that's the big reason the Stooges weren't too upset about being sent back to Ann Arbor: Home was where the best dope and the most dealers were. Which was sad, and a real drawback for a world-traveling, experience-hungry, active character like me.

So Scott Richardson's scene wasn't that way, and that was fine with me. He and the guys in the band *were* into cocaine, though, and so my Ann Arbor visit was notable in that way too. Fancy that: coke and smack all in one trip.

I didn't get into either substance, as it happened. I'd rather have fought barehanded to the death with a dozen switchblade-swinging diesel dykes than stuck a needle in my arm, and my first experience of snorting cocaine was (for quite a while, anyway) my last. Just like Woody Allen in *Annie Hall*, I was the idiot who took her first snort, experienced a terrible tickling sensation, and proceeded to sneeze those oh-so-expensive little white lines all over the carpet.

It was so unhip. Very uncool. Scott forgave me (he'd have forgiven *anything* for a shot at getting close to David Bowie), but I'm not so sure about the guys in the band. The dealer, I know, was disgusted. His look was all disdain and judgment: I'd been so uncool he almost got up and left right then and there.

And of course he *was* the final arbiter of the communal cool, for at that particular time in our cultural history, your average cocaine dealer was anything but the predatory scumbag he's perceived to be today, his wares nothing like the societal scourge of contemporary reality. Cocaine in 1973 was very elite and reputedly harmless: a happy-time, nonaddictive, very hip-superior lift; such a status-enriching commodity, in fact, that in the trendiest circles its conspicuous consumption was becoming virtually de rigueur. Only pedestrians, it seemed, didn't do it, or worse yet still smoked pot.

Personally, I hated the stuff right from the start. It was far too close to home. The third quarter of 1973, you see, is when David and cocaine began to work on a serious relationship.


Before we approach the sorry saga of David's drug addiction, though, I should map out the lay of the land between David and me regarding boyfriends, girlfriends, and boy/girl friends during this period.

It was simple: I wanted what David was getting, so I went and got it, sometimes literally. As time went on I made a point, whenever possible, of seducing David's sex mates myself, ideally before he'd bedded them. It was never hard to mark them; I knew his type, and I could see the charm-your-pants-off light in his eyes when he turned toward a likely prospect.

I was interested, of course, only in talented and significant people:

Cherry Vanilla, Marianne Faithfull, individuals of *that* caliber. The passing trade, David's parade of groupies and business lubes, didn't interest me at all. My attitude was that while they might be the ones doing the bunny with the great Bowie, I was The Wife! I had the rank and the privileges.

And yes, I did let *that* be known, honey. When I came into the room, you'd better jump up and salute, girl (boy), and *then* get back down on your knees (or back, or stomach). Otherwise your big day would start going wrong rather quickly. Or if you answered the phone by the bed in the hotel room in Manchester or Milwaukee or Mannheim or wherever, and didn't comply promptly when I said, very pleasantly, 'Hello, dear. This is Angela. Please pass the phone to David,' you were going to get an earful.

Usually it all worked out fine. Sometimes it got a little difficult, discussing rock-and-roll logistics with your husband while some star-struck little West Berlin hermaphrodite or round-heeled New York publicist was stripping his chrome; David's ability to maintain career focus under pressure was indeed exceptional, but everybody's human ('What was that, babe? I missed it. Did you say Mylar *side*pieces, or Mylar *cod*pieces?'). Most of the time, though, we could conclude our business with reasonable success.

Amusing, yes – but David hurt me. In the third quarter of 1973 he began breaking our unspoken rules. He began making his conquests and maintaining his mistresses close to home, in my circle, in my face. He started sleeping with a big (two-hundred-pound), beautiful black woman who was *my* friend. He imported Ava Cherry, a blonde black singer he'd met in Chicago, and set her up in a Main Man-funded career and a Main Man-financed apartment right around the corner from *my* house. Those pieces of business left me feeling – what's the word? – unloved, I guess.

## IO

# WONDER WOMAN AND THE COCAINE KID

$D$avid's 'retirement' did nothing to slow the wildfire spread of Bowiemania (how surprising!). Three weeks after the Hammersmith Odeon show, in late July 1973, five of his albums were in the British top ten, and three months later his star still shone from the pinnacle of the pop party tree. He was number one, and he was getting even bigger.

This suggested, again, among other things, that it might be time for him and the Main Man organization to turn at least some of their attention toward his side of our bargain. It was, very plainly, career start-up time for Angie.

On the other hand, it was also *1980 Floor Show* time for David. Approached by Burt Sugarman to create something for the American TV rock series *The Midnight Special*, he'd come up with the concept of a highly theatrical cabaret extravaganza, a Bowie-twisted *Sonny and Cher Show* set in the future (1980) and featuring acts from various rock-pop yesteryears – Marianne Faithfull and the Troggs from the sixties, David Bowie from the seventies. And now, as usual, he needed someone to pull it all together for him. And as usual, that someone was I.

A location had to be found. Burt Sugarman had wisely refused David's first suggestion, that he perform the time- and money-gobbling miracle of shooting a live, full-scale David Bowie road show, and opted instead for my idea: a special production in a smallish, easily lit and managed three-camera space such as a club – such as the Marquee Club.

So the club had to be booked and set up and dressed as a

nightclub of the future. The main players had to be found and secured, as did the supporting cast of dancers and backup singers. Natasha Korniloff had to be roped in to design costumes, and relations with Burt Sugarman had to be handled, and a few dozen other matters had to be attended to. It was hard, and it was fun.

And of course, this being show biz, I got to associate with some interesting people.

Ava Cherry wasn't exactly interesting, but it was educational to observe her in action. She looked great, wonderfully eccentric and exotic in her bowling-ball fuzz of tight bleached-blond curls – just the item to dress up a Bowie stage show – but after studying her performance as a (backup) singer, I had to conclude that her primary talents must lie in other areas. She could, I'm told, do extraordinary things with apparatuses very close to, though not actually in, her vocal cords, but I'm not so sure about that. Her singing voice certainly didn't suggest the presence of anything interesting in its vicinity.

I wouldn't go so far as to call Ava a coke whore, however. Bigger, better benefits came with the job of being David's mistress than a healthy share of the daily white powder. David, after all, *had* told her, 'You could be the next Josephine Baker! You could be a star!' when he'd run into her in France during the recording of the *Pin-Ups* album, and until that happy day (which of course never arrived) he had Main Man maintain her in an apartment, fund her singing and dancing lessons and her wardrobe, commit to financing a solo album, and pay her a weekly allowance generous enough for a girl with no living expenses.

Someone wrote that 'she was overwhelmed with her good fortune and traveled in a cloud of amazement.' Right.

To my mind, Amanda Lear was much more interesting. Introduced to David by Brian Ferry of Roxy Music (that's her on the first Roxy Music album cover), she was recruited into *The 1980 Floor Show* as mistress of ceremonies, a role she played in the character of a future Marlene Dietrich. She was really fascinating. I had her pegged as a genuine hermaphrodite, rather than the sex-change everyone said she was; she was exceptionally beautiful, in a particularly delicate, feminine way you don't see in straightforward sex-changes.

Amanda, unlike Ava Cherry, was mysterious and elusive – part Vietnamese and part European, I believe, but that's all I can say with any degree of authority whatsoever – and, again unlike dear Ava, she was hot stuff as a singer and performer. She too was David's mistress and a Main Man artist, signed at David's insistence, and she too would soon occupy an apartment a stone's throw from our front door. She would pay her rent out of her own pocket, though, and that was another thing I liked about her.

Last in order but first in importance among the *1980 Floor Show* trinity was the wonderful Marianne Faithfull. She shouldn't need any introduction, but perhaps she does in some circles, particularly mass-market American ones.

There are three brief, relevant facts about Marianne. She was Brian Jones's girlfriend, then Mick Jagger's, in the Stones' early star days; she had one and only one hit around that time, 'As Tears Go By'; and many years later, when everyone seemed to have forgotten her, she made *Broken English*, an album rightly regarded by critics as one of the most powerful, incisive, and generally brilliant works of our musical time. Since then she has continued to enliven the recording scene quite wonderfully.

This year, 1973, was one of deepest obscurity for her, however, and David's motives in putting her on the show may have been somewhat short of altruistic. He had her figured as a prime candidate for the rock nostalgia wave then flooding the American (*Midnight Special*) market – an unsettling 'dredge 'em up before they die on us' phenomenon – and then too, he wanted to get in her pants. She'd been Mick's, so he as well had to have her.

The coital connection worked out, at least to the extent that he had her, but the career revival aspect of things got a little out of hand. Marianne didn't just show up for one last halfhearted hurrah or long day's journey into the twilight of the golden-oldie circuit; she got out there and summoned up all her craft and soul and plain slaughtered 'em. She was riveting, magnificent. And her performance triggered the chain of creative events that would produce *Broken English*.

Marianne's act was all the more startling because she was so stoned. She's been in recovery for several years as I write, but at the time of the show, and for quite a while thereafter, she was a full-fledged junkie.

I don't know if she was actually shooting up, or doing bigtime downs to try kicking the horse that rode her (I think the latter), but whatever, the effect was extreme. That was one slow lady – until, that is, she had to hit her mark and perform, at which point she emerged from her cloud and flat-out nailed it, whatever it was.

You hear that kind of story a lot in the theater, usually starring some hairy old half-dead whiskey sot with Celtic roots and Shake-spearean leanings, but until I watched Marianne work so brilliantly, then simply pass out until it was time to work again or go home (usually with my help), I'd thought it was all just thespian hooey. But there she was: amazing.

I didn't get very close with her personally during that show, but I did later, after David and I split up, and then it was *she* (that monkey!) who seduced *me*. Got me stoned as a silly schoolgirl on pills and great big hash joints, then slipped up on me when I wasn't looking. She's wild, that woman. I love her and admire her.


While we worked on *The 1980 Floor Show* we were in new digs. We'd sublet Diana Rigg's place in Maida Vale, a large but still somewhat cramped apartment in a mildly bohemian, pleasantly anonymous section of north-central London.

Anonymity was what we needed. Bowiemania was nice in its way, but having a few dozen star-struck young teenagers to whom you haven't been introduced camping out on your front doorstep, day and night, seven days a week – very well behaved and respectful, waiting quietly with worshipful eyes and trembling autograph books – is strange. Seeing a few more added to their number every time you look out your window is even stranger.

At Haddon Hall, I adapted as best I could, remembering not to go naked near the front door or windows and taking pots of tea out to the poor young things, but it still felt strange, and then it felt threatening. Some guy got into the house and grabbed some cash –

not much, and I grabbed it right back from him – and that brought it all to a head. I went to David and laid out the new facts of life.

'This is just going to get worse, babe,' I told him. 'You're just going to go on getting bigger, and so are those crowds of teenagers, and what's more, if one criminal knows where we live, others do too. Things could get weird if we stay here.'

He hated to face it, because he'd grown very fond of Haddon Hall, as had I, but he had to admit the inevitable. 'Okay, we've got to leave,' he said. 'We should move up into town, don't you think?'

Yes, that's what I thought, and so I went looking for a house. I found a wonderful prospect in Chelsea, a townhouse on one of the streets running from King's Road down to Cheyne Walk and the river, but I ran into opposition from Tony Defries. 'You simply can't afford such extravagance, Angie,' he told me. 'Maybe you can live like royalty when David's record sales earn back his advances from RCA, but until then you have to be reasonable.' And he refused to make the lease money available. Since all our money came through Main Man, he could do that.

I went to David, but it didn't do any good. 'He's got a point, babe,' David said. 'I think you should find something cheaper.'

Tony had tapped into a good thing here, I thought. While he spent David's money (or RCA credit, or whatever it really was) like water, whatever projects, promotions, and personnel he wanted Main Man to finance, including limos and lunches – really, the gall and grandiosity of it all was amazing! – he'd connected with David's own lower-middle-class reluctance to live beyond the family means and his father's old Yorkshire frugality, and had locked him up in a box. You don't need to keep your goose in a palace, after all, or even a decent townhouse; it'll keep laying those golden eggs just fine in a nice cheap chicken coop. Tony's notion of ideal accommodations for the Bowies, I'd guess, would have been a nice cozy Soho garret for David and perhaps a modest farmhouse in the north of Scotland, or better yet Siberia, for me. But he compromised somewhat, and we ended up at Diana Rigg's sublet.

It was okay, but it was hardly perfect: one of those typical actor's homes, cluttered with charming *objets*, souvenirs from every town she'd ever strode the boards in, collector's items of this and that, of almost every conceivable genre, and paintings, lots of paintings (her husband was an artist).

The place very plainly wasn't ours, then, and it was cramped. There were a lot of us – David, me, Zowie, Scott Richardson, Daniella when she was there to care for Zowie, and whoever else slept over: Marianne passed out or playing naughty with David, Ava, or some combination thereof (also passed out or playing naughty with David), and whatever new blood resulted from individual and communal forays into London nightlife.

I wasn't much involved in the games. I had quit sleeping with Scott after I'd brought him back from Ann Arbor and he and David had become the best of friends (their shared interest in cocaine helped forge the bond), and in fact I don't remember spending many of my nights at Maida Vale at all. If I recall correctly, I was off with Mickey Finn much of the time.

Mickey, T. Rex's drummer and a wild and wonderful lad, was the only really enjoyable thing to come out of my adventures with Wonder Woman.


Wonder Woman the comic-book character, that is: lush black hair, projectile mammaries, super powers, the works. She first entered my life courtesy of Michael Lippman, an agent, in a scheme he brought to Tony Defries; it involved getting me a screen test for the Wonder Woman part in the television series, then in development, so that I could be on *The Tonight Show* (hosted by Johnny Carson, of course), so that I could promote David's *1980 Floor Show* edition of *The Midnight Special*.

If that sounds convoluted, it was, and in fact it was even more convoluted than it sounds or I knew. To run it past you again, though, the deal as I understood it went as follows:

First, the *Midnight Special* show needed promoting as cheaply and effectively as possible. Second, *The Tonight Show* was carried on NBC, and was available, under the right conditions, as a promotional vehicle for other NBC shows such as *The Midnight Special*. Third, David was, to put it bluntly, your basic talk-show host's worst-nightmare guest: monosyllabic, elitist, paranoid, defensive, sarcastic, and very probably stoned out of his mind. Fourth, I was the opposite: alert, talkative, confident, aggressive when need be, ladylike when that would play best – an actress, in other words. Fifth, unfortunately, *The Tonight Show*'s policy was that Johnny's guests had to have a legitimate-sounding reason for sitting there on network television, and being the wife of a rock star with a show to promote didn't cut it.

All this led to the final piece of the puzzle, which was that *Wonder Woman* happened to be looking for its Wonder Woman at the time, and Michael Lippman could arrange for an audition. The fact that the wife of a major British rock star was in Hollywood to try out for the starring role in an American TV series was a good enough hook for Carson's people – just dandy, in fact – and so the deal was done.

Such was the arrangement described to me by Tony Defries one pleasant day in London, and I must say it improved my mood considerably. Wonder Woman sounded like a great part, and a marvelous opportunity for me. And how nice that it had come through a Main Man – sponsored initiative, rather than my own! That's exactly how things should be working, I thought. There are a million ways to skin a cat, and if this one had an extra curve or two, so much the better: I would get a significant shot at what could be a career-breaking part, *and* advance an ongoing Bowie project.

I went at it seriously. I bought Wonder Woman comics and felt out the character, I developed a logic for how to play her, and I got myself a costume. I had Natasha Korniloff make one that came right out of the comic-book pages, and it was a gas. Man, did I look good: a tiny wasp waist, legs going on forever, lustrous long black hair, even artfully padded, projectile-pointy Wonderbreasts! And to make the illusion more than complete, I had the marvelous Terry O'Neill do a photo session.

And off to Hollywood I went, in an energized cloud of creative enthusiasm and superheroine spunk.

Well, what a joke. First I showed them the photographs, which totally flabbergasted the director – things were going well so far – but then, before I went to my dressing room to don the stipulated turtleneck, some woman from the studio came up to me.

'I see you're not wearing a bra,' she said. 'You have to wear one for the screen test. It's mandatory.'

I couldn't believe it. I hadn't worn a bra for *years*. 'Well, if that's what you want, okay,' I said. 'But I think you're going to have a problem finding one small enough.'

She didn't like *that* very much, but she walked off, and I went to the dressing room.

I was slipping into the turtleneck when someone knocked on the door and then opened it without waiting for a response. It wasn't the woman I expected; it was some nondescript, mildly unattractive man. He came in and introduced himself, then started making small talk, and *then* started touching me. The scumbag was coming on to me, virtually feeling me up!

I couldn't believe it. I just looked at him. 'What are you *doing*? Who on earth do you think you *are*?'

'I'm a writer,' he said, as if that information would immediately convince me to lie back and spread 'em.

It didn't. 'So what?'

That seemed to take him aback. He paused, perplexed – this must have been a precedent-breaking turn of events for him, requiring unfamiliar responses. 'You *do* know I wrote the script for——, don't you?'

I thought about that for a moment, examining my memory of the movie, a famous black exploitation film.

'You're *proud* of that?' I asked in my very best finishing-school-prefect manner. 'I'm supposed to be impressed? Don't you know, you awful little man, that script was truly wretched, and moreover it was the only bad element of an otherwise wonderful production? Now take yourself out of my dressing room before I fucking kill you!'

He left, and needless to say, I considered myself out of the running for the part from that moment on. I decided to go through the motions, though, but I also decided I needed protection, so I got Michael Lippman to come and sit with me in the dressing room.

That's when I got the really bad news. Michael listened to my tale of woe and outrage, then told me.

'Angie, it's okay,' he said. 'You were never going to get the part anyway. You weren't even in the running; nobody auditioning is. Lynda Carter's already got the part, you see. All this is just a performance to satisfy the unions, and we're taking advantage of it to get you on Johnny Carson. So really, don't worry about it.'

Don't *worry* about it? You mean, Don't rip your dick off and stick it in your ear, Michael, and then hop a first-class flight back to London and do the same to Tony Defries? Or more to the point, don't blow this pop stand right now, bolt out of here and not even *consider* showing up on Carson? Don't blow you guys' cozy little job sky-high and let *you* crawl around for the pieces?

None of that was actually said, mind you, although sometimes I wish it had been, and even that it had been done. Maybe not to Michael, whom I like and actually respect, but certainly to old Big-Nose Defries, as we called him.

Cooler counsel from Michael prevailed, however, and I saw some vile pragmatic logic in the whole arrangement. I assimilated Tony's dishonesty – and I decided that I would never trust him again and left it at that. I was still very angry, of course, and I must admit that vengeful schemes, dreams, and fantasies occurred to me from time to time, but I didn't act on them. I attached myself to the philosophy of the Sicilians – revenge is a dish best served cold – and postponed gratification until whenever the best opportunity presented itself.

In the meantime, back to work. I set about preparing myself to go on *The Tonight Show* to promote the hell out of the family business, and consoled myself with the thought that television exposure, especially on Carson's show, never really hurt a girl looking for acting work.

I found the experience pretty queer, and I guess I'm not alone in that perception. Rock and roll and TV were worlds apart in those days, and hippies and post-hippies throughout TV-land tuned Carson in just to freak on how abominably unhip his whole trip was. And while Johnny may have been doing the trendy drugs – gossip said that he was snorting quite a bit of coke as well as drinking pretty heavily, which among other things gave rise to much pencil-breaking and object-tossing on the set – neither he nor his people were even fuzzily tuned in to what was happening.

When the staff saw my dress, which showed a lot of skin, they freaked. They were getting ready to tell me flat-out I couldn't wear it, when I put my foot down. 'Look,' I said. 'I'm in rock and roll, not the Mormon Tabernacle Choir! I'm going to wear this dress. Either that or you can go find yourselves another guest. Okay?'

Evidently it was okay, because I stayed on the show. At one point I overheard Michael Lippman and a man from NBC talking in the corridor. 'I hope Angela is good tonight,' the NBC guy was saying, 'because if she's not, we're gonna lose thirty percent of our audience for *The Midnight Special*.' Not exactly what you need to hear when you're about to walk out into the lights. I almost had a coronary.

Johnny settled me down, though. He was a good line-feeder and perfect gentleman all around, very nice, even if he did seem a trifle tense.

Dinah Shore, also a guest on the show, on the other hand, was being a bitch *that* day. I think she must have gotten a bug up her posterior about my dress or something, because she took my presence as a cue to keep harping on the royal wedding of the week/year/decade (Princess Anne and Mark Phillips, I think it was) in a condescending way that assumed I was both English by birth and royalist by inclination.

I had to straighten her out, and did so quite politely: 'You seem to be under the misconception that I am English. I'm not. I'm American, and I do not cleave to royalty.' Yet she just kept coming at me.

I started to lose it. Even though I really didn't want to get low with an older woman on network television (an awful breach of finishing-school etiquette), I was primed to let her have it – *Look, you provincial prune, get out of my face! What do I care how some mob of inbred, horse-faced foreigners spend their taxpayers' money?* – but Joan Rivers, also on the show, stepped in and saved me. She started into one of those wonderful routines she does about the royals, and all was well that ended well. She had to rescue me from Dinah again, however, several times. That woman was relentless.

Oh, well. We came out on top of *her* (although not in the sexual sense – the very thought is nauseating). When she got her own talk show and wanted David and me on it, I was able to refuse point-blank, with no hesitation whatever, and that worked pretty well. She begged us, so we told her exactly who we wanted on the show with us, got them, and had it all our way. And actually, she ran a pretty good program: smart questions, gracious hosting, and nary a hint of that shrew on the Carson show.

Our *1980 Floor Show* was one of the highest-rated editions of the entire *Midnight Special* series. And as far as *Wonder Woman* was concerned, my vision of the title character hadn't been too far off the money. When I first saw the show on TV, I was mildly sickened, if not exactly surprised, to note that the script had veered sharply away from its Ms Wholegrain angle. Now it featured the classic cartoon approach, and Lynda Carter was running around in an exact duplicate of my costume.

And that's how I started learning about show biz in the real world. David wasn't at all surprised when I told him about the whole mess, but he *was* angry.

'That's outrageous!' he said. 'I'm glad I wasn't there, babe. I'd have had a hard time not decking that screenwriter. Those fucking TV people are just so *low*. So are the music business people, for that matter. I mean, I can hardly stand them, and I've been around this business a lot longer than you have.'

He had a point, and now I was in a position to hear it. Before, when he'd warned me away from projects I wanted to take on, for instance the first role I might have gotten, in a low-budget film called, self-explanatorily, *Groupies*, I'd reacted with frustration and resentment. I thought he was stifling my career just because he had a double standard – he said he believed in women's rights and sexual liberation but balked at letting his own wife work, especially if it meant her showing her skin on screen – but now I realized he had other motives. He may have been a chauvinist (let's not be ambivalent: he *was* a chauvinist), but he was also someone who'd been down the show business road ahead of me. He knew where the potholes were, and where the trolls lurked, and he wanted to protect me.

But he hadn't seen this one coming. As far as he knew, the Wonder Woman audition was on the up-and-up. 'Tony didn't tell me either,' he said. 'I'd *never* have let you be put in that situation if I'd known, babe. Huh. I suppose Tony knew that, didn't he?'

'Yeah, I'm sure he did,' I replied. 'So he manipulated me, and he manipulated you too. And for nothing! I'd have *gladly* gone and done the audition just to get on the Carson show and push our *Midnight Special.* I'd have played along with the whole charade from start to finish, and done it smiling, if Tony had told me the truth. So I don't know, babe. He's playing games. I don't like it.'

'Neither do I. I'll talk to him about it,' David said.

I don't know if he ever did, but I know several other things. I know that a little further down the line, Tony began trying to talk David into divorcing me, painting a picture of me as an extravagant spender and cash-bleeding liability and showing him how much better off he would be without me, and I know David didn't buy that line. I know that as 1973 turned into 1974 and Tony's extravagance mounted, David grew increasingly uneasy; his tone when he talked about Tony began to echo his frustration with Ken Pitt.

I know too that Tony's problem with me wasn't, strictly speaking, personal. In a way he couldn't help himself. He was such a thorough-going, incurable misogynist that he had only one option when any woman of talent, intelligence, and ambition appeared within his sphere of influence: he had to banish her as quickly and absolutely as he could, by whatever means were at hand.

Perceiving this about him was not, as you might imagine, pleasant. The wretched fellow didn't seem able to handle the fact that I'd slept with his long-time girlfriend (Dana, of all people!) before he had.

But anyway, Tony is a tiresome subject and I've had enough of him now.

An unsettling development: After my Wonder Woman debacle (successful as it was in promotional terms), David and Tony concocted a character bearing a superficial resemblance to Wonder Woman physically, and owing everything to her in terms of idea genesis. This was Octobriana, a sci-fi super-priestess of high Bowie camp and magic, and she was a pretty cool customer. I rather liked her. My only problem with her, in fact – and it was quite a large problem – was that she was designed from the ground up as a vehicle for Main Man – managed, David Bowie – financed Amanda Lear. Not, that is, for me.

I know that this is a subject almost as tiresome to you readers as Tony Defries is to me, but what did that piece of business tell me about David's commitment to the career deal between us? You can figure that answer out for yourselves, so I'll proceed to the next question: What exactly did David want from me, that is, from our marriage?

He didn't want things between us the way I wanted them, obviously enough: creatively and professionally coequal, sexually and emotionally free, but intimate and trusting with each other. So what *did* he want? Did he want things as they were: distant sexually, close emotionally and creatively only when he needed my services? Or did he want them warmer, with me under his wing in a much more conventionally male-chauvinistic model of marriage? Did he, as I strongly suspect, want the basic good old-fashioned English rockstar marriage in which hubby lances his way boldly and beautifully around the globe, free as an eagle, while wifey stays happily home on the nice suburban Home Counties estate, studying macrobiotics and macramé and raising babies in perfect post-Woodstock Victorian virtue? Or did he simply want me out of his hair?

The answer to these questions, I regret to say, is: *How the hell would I know?*

For one thing, David was unapproachable on the clear, direct level where the all-important nitty-gritty like this can be discussed. Most people share that shortcoming to one degree or another, of course, but David's whole character was built on evasion, illusion, and manipulation. He was incapable of telling me what he wanted; it probably never even occurred to him that he could; sad to say but true, he probably didn't have an honest bone in his whole emotional body. Now and again he'd reveal his true feelings in a song lyric – but how are you supposed to love and honor somebody when you have to wait for album deadlines before you hear his new songs, and *then* find out that you hurt him, or that he yearned for you, back whenever the song was written?

And I played right into a setup like that. My job in our relationship, I (mis)understood instinctively, was to be the interpreter and effectuator of his unspoken desires. I was tuned to figure out what he wanted, and to do it (or not do it, or do the opposite, depending);

I was *not* tuned to come right out and ask, or not to give a damn one way or the other about whatever he so secretly wanted. There are names for these roles played in relationships, and truckloads of literature and phone books full of people and programs to explain and modify them, but back when it mattered I had no idea what was going on in the hidden programming, David's or mine.

Let's return to basics, though. David didn't and wouldn't tell me what he wanted of me, no matter how deviously I might try to get him to make it clear. And besides, everything sexual between us was hopelessly complicated – ruined, rather – by his (supposedly) Angie-allergic rash. None of it mattered anyway, because he was getting deeper and deeper into cocaine, the great leveler of absolutely everything. Trying to have a relationship with a coke freak is like trying to eat an aircraft carrier.

And me? Well, for me it was a fog, murk, a dance in the dark. I wanted him back. I wanted him to leave me alone. I knew what was happening. I believed it really wasn't. I cared too much to let myself think about it. I was having too good a time to give a damn. Take your pick, it's all true.

## II

# BROWN SUGAR AND BULLSHIT

You can't really be rock-and-roll royalty without a rock-and-roll palace. We didn't have one. We needed one.

I got us one, insisting that David make Tony cut loose the funds for the roomy, stylish, thoroughly fitting accommodations I had already found for us in Chelsea. David was ready – he too was tired of our cramped quarters in Maida Vale – and so he leaned on Tony, and we made our move. Now we could expand back up from our bare-bones family unit to our proper operating size, assume our rightful place in the rockpopsocial scheme of things, and start having the serious fun our status demanded.

Chelsea was the perfect neighborhood. Chic, hip, rich, arty, permissive, exclusive only of the disinclined and insufficiently funded, it was the home of the rightest of the right people, the film and fashion and music elite who'd made it out of less lustrous breeding grounds – Notting Hill, Earl's Court, the various slightly less acceptable northern and western neighborhoods, and even eastern and south-of-the-river London – or for that matter, the traditional domains of establishment and aristocracy: Mayfair, Belgravia, a kingdom's worth of stately country homes.

Chelsea was informal style epitomized, an unpretentious and charming melting pot. The gardened Georgian squares, the little mews houses, the gracious and well-proportioned streets running down to the sweetly civilized northern bank of the Thames: these were superior digs, London life at its casually elegant finest.

Living in Chelsea, a person of style and substance had easy access to a wonderful array of social pleasures; not just one's friends' private houses or the welcome-all daily fashion parade along boutique-studded King's Road, but some very good, fun, semi-exclusive clubs, restaurants, and other mingling spots.

Laurita's, for example, was wonderful. On Fulham Road, it was the creation of Laurita and her gorgeous and exciting Puerto Rican husband, Cosmo (only the couple's exquisite children were more comely than they). They ran a friendly, happy, insanely popular place that was as good for your spirit as its menu, classic fat-drenched soul food, was bad for your cardiovascular system. Everyone ate at Laurita's, and everyone loved Laurita.

The Last Resort, a bar and restaurant right across the street, was another kind of thrill. It didn't last long, but while it did, it could be exciting. It had a dance floor small enough to get packed and hot rather quickly, and as well as the usual mix of art/fashion/theater/film/music people, it attracted a faster, slicker contingent: advertising executives, shadily wealthy importer/exporter types, and outright gangsters. You hit the Last Resort when you wanted a bit more of a charge than usual, anything from a good hard dance sweat to a one-night stand with a guy packing a gun.

You hit the Speakeasy, on the other hand, when you wanted flat-out rock and roll. That was the destination of choice when you felt like dressing to kill, hopping on your motorcycle, and heading off to hurt your ears.

If dinner was your primary desire, however, and you were in the mood for magnificence, you went to Thierry's, and there you ate as well as the luckiest man in France. If on the other hand you found yourself awake and hungry enough for lunch, you traveled the short distance into Knightsbridge and took a table at San Lorenzo on Beauchamp Place. Likely as not you'd bump into Mick and/or Bianca there, or any of your other rock royalty and film/theater/fashion/art running mates – Brian Ferry, Lionel Bart, Mary Quant, whoever – and also, unfortunately, persons whose royalty came with their birth certificates. Yes, the horse faces haunted San Lorenzo too.

Otherwise, the newly opened Hard Rock Café was always available when someone else wanted to go there (I didn't mind it, but it wasn't really my style), and Peter Morton's other place, the more exclusive Morton's, was another option. He had a very tasteful piano bar there, and he offered all sorts of drinks with which your rich and successful rock-and-roll yobbos could sit around at two in the morning having a lovely time of it, sipping alcoholic concoctions native to humanity far remote from their ken: southern California surf worshippers, Japanese shipbuilding tycoons, Malaysian rubber planters, Mexican cattle barons, whoever had really learned how to mix a good one.

Not that Morton's was all rock-and-roll yobbos. Like most of the more exclusive places on my circuit, all were welcome – diplomats, criminals, politicians, even bankers and chairmen of the board – as long as they had wealth and, crucially, style. A ton of money by itself wouldn't get you in, but a ton of money and the right suit would.

Probably I'm forgetting some other significant fun spots, but as far as I can remember, my only other regular hangout was Tramp's. And basically, I hung out there more than anywhere else. That fine host, Johnny Gold – so relaxed, often to be found somewhere skiing or sailing or sunbathing, but on the premises just enough – treated David and me with infinite graciousness, and the whole scene was just right.

Tramp's stayed open later than other places, for a start, and had the best people, the cream of the usual rockers-to-bankers set, plus whoever was in town doing something interesting: French film directors, Broadway stars, Italian race car drivers, you name 'em. And as if that weren't enough, Johnny ran the place with such good humor. You'd be sitting there feeling a bit peckish, and the chef would appear at your table with a little something: a nice pork sausage protruding from two balls of mashed potatoes in the manner of your husband's three-piece suit, perhaps, with your name written around the base in garden peas. Tramp's really was *the* place, then and for a long time afterward. It was exactly right.

The house I'd found for us was also perfect. A large, gracious, five-story terraced structure on Oakley Street, it was smart and white and simple externally, its clear Georgian lines a pleasant and appropriate contrast, I thought, to the gothic red-brick fancies of

Haddon Hall. Internally it was all modern and all stunning. It had been gutted and remodeled into an exquisitely white and sensuous showplace, its airy new beauty suggesting the Mediterranean (my style) a good deal more strongly than it did the Thames, and I decorated it accordingly with sudden splashes of very bright primal color, Kevin Whitney's wonderful paintings and the like.

The look was a little ahead of its time, and it impressed our guests: Mick Jagger visiting from the Viennese-aristocratically elegant decor (courtesy of Marianne Faithfull) of his house on Cheyne Walk; that dear man Ron Wood dropping in from his Danish-modern manse in Putney; that dear girl Twiggy and her consort, Justin de Villeneuve, visiting from the fabulous Art Nouveau grotto they'd created in an East End warehouse; musicians many and various accustomed to the rock-and-roll norm of a very large and comfortable couch, a very large and accessible bed, a very powerful and wonderful sound system, and to hell with the rest of it.

Our house was spacious and well laid out, offering all the amenities. It had a self-contained apartment where Freddi Buretti and Daniella could live, and work on costumes, party clothes, and Main Man tasks of the moment; a kitchen and dining floor equipped to cater to as many guests as any sane host or hostess might wish to accommodate; another floor devoted entirely to a living/partying space and starring a luxurious white leather sunken seating area and a state-of-the-art sound system; and two top floors of bedrooms, one serving as guest quarters and the other featuring Zowie's room and, right next door, the master suite with wardrobe closet and sunken, satin-sheeted king-size bed. Elegant, well-appointed bathrooms were located where they were needed.

It was a great house for a party, of course, and it had to be, because Chelsea in 1974 was one of those places at one of those times. London was still a first-class energy magnet in the early seventies, drawing to itself the most adventurous artists, designers, writers, musicians, and creative souls of all sorts from all over Europe, Australia, America – everywhere, really – and Chelsea was where those people grouped and mingled and partied.

The party, moreover, was most definitely *on*. The pop arts were at the peak of their power, the money was still there, the vibe was confident, the good times felt permanent.

You could say, looking back, that collectively we were just about to hit the crest of the pop energy wave first set in motion by the Beatles a decade before. Soon the wave would break, and we'd be foundering or even drowning – in punk, coke, smack, disco, decadence, disillusion, degradation (and mass unemployment, urban warfare, and all the other consequences of bloody Margaret Thatcher's eat-the-poor governance) – but right then and there, around the streets of Chelsea in '74, it felt as if our party would just go on getting bigger, richer, sweeter, and wilder forever. It may have been Nero fiddling, but he was playing us a hell of a tune.

When I say 'us,' I mean everyone from us, the hip, arty residents of Chelsea, to us, the generation born immediately after World War II – the second generation of rock and roll – and also us, the British rock royalty of the day: the still vital Stones/Who/Kinks/ex-Beatles axis; newer stars such as Roxy Music, Yes, and Emerson, Lake, and Palmer; neophytes Queen, Slade, and Gary Glitter, among others; and such perennials as Rod Stewart, Elton John, Marc Bolan, and of course Mr David Bowie, named Britain's number-one male singer, best producer, and best composer by *Melody Maker* in January 1974. Yes, in that year David was *still* number one and getting bigger.

You could tell it from the newspapers and magazines, and from the instant hospitality we received in all the hip places, but you certainly couldn't tell it from the money. The situation was ridiculous. In some ways things were relatively convenient; we could instruct the people on our regular circuit, club owners and the like, to bill the Main Man office, and they'd do so, and that would be that as far as we were concerned. When we needed cash for nonchargeable expenses, though, it was a bloody nightmare.

The routine, as I recall, went something like this, give or take a variation or two either pleasant or irritating, usually irritating:

First, call the office and tell them to cut the check.

Next, call again when you find out they haven't done it, and tell them again.

Next, call yet again and get the explanation of why they haven't done it *this* time. When you receive no clear response, demand to speak to Tony.

Wait for Tony to call back.

Get tired of waiting and call again. React pleasantly to the news that Tony has disappeared in the limo and won't be back until tomorrow.

Call the next day and demand to speak to Tony.

Do it again.

Do it again, and succeed this time. Listen to Tony's assurances.

Wait for the check to emerge.

Get tired of waiting and call again, screaming now.

Go pick up the check, take it to the bank, and react pleasantly when you're told it isn't signed.

Take the check back to the office and wait for Tony to return from his business lunch. When he strolls in, make him sign the check.

The bank being closed by now, wait until it opens again the next day, and call.

React pleasantly to the bad news about the insufficient funds.

Call the office and tell them to make the check good and to call you once they've done so.

Wait.

Get tired of waiting and call again. Scream. Receive assurances.

Go to the bank *immediately*, and if the gods are smiling today, cash the check. If they're not, begin again.

This routine wore on me and *wore* on me until I simply couldn't take it anymore, and before I pulled the pin on the grenade and stuffed it down Tony's trousers, I went through David to force a new routine. Henceforth I would receive a regular payment from the office, £2,000 a month I believe it was, to cover all my expenses. Which was fine and dandy until Tony started working on it. I'd receive my money and figure out my budget and go about my business, and then I'd discover – Surprise, darling! – that it was now my responsibility to pay the household phone bill, which with calls all over the world at all hours of the day and David's cocaine-addled night could be more significant than I care to remember. And so on. Chisel and scam and dodge and hedge, chisel and scam and dodge and hedge: Tony's game.

It wore on David as well as me. He'd started hanging out with Mick Jagger, for one thing, and he didn't like the disparity between their life-styles.

'Mick seems to own half the bloody world, and I don't own anything!' he'd say. 'I go to Tony, and he just keeps telling me I'm not making enough to pay back RCA. My record sales just aren't big enough. But there's certainly enough bloody money for Main Man to afford any projects *he* wants to do, isn't there?'

He had a point. During our first months at Oakley Street, Tony was moving Main Man's head office from Chelsea to a suite on Park Avenue and Fifty-fourth Street in New York and expanding its staff to no fewer than twenty-six full-time employees.

The extravagance was truly impressive, as was the largesse raining from Tony's hands on all manner of Main Man employees, artistes, and associates; the word in New York on Main Man was that it was manna from heaven, the best new candy store in town. Do whatever Tony told you to do, and your worries were over. Main Man's top people had expense accounts at The Four Seasons and Max's Kansas City and carried charge cards from Harrods and Bloomingdale's, as well as American Express, and Main Man paid all the bills.

David, the sole source of the spendfest, didn't get it. 'Everything I've got is leased, or borrowed, or Main Man owns it, and I've never got any cash!' he'd tell me. 'I dunno, babe. It sure seems to *me* that I'm making it. What's happening? Were all those people getting into all those concerts for nothing? I can't fucking stand it! Where's my money?'

'Well, darling, I don't know,' I'd reply sweetly. 'Maybe you should ask Mick how *he* operates. You know, get some tips. He's a pretty good businessman, I think. Maybe there are better ways of doing things than the way you're doing them.'

That, of course, was something of an understatement. The average performing flea had a more advantageous arrangement with its trainer than David had with Big-Nose. Tony's approach to David emulated that of his hero Colonel Tom Parker to poor Elvis.

I don't know whether he ever got up the nerve to tell Mick, and if so, whether Mick was able to keep a straight face while listening. Maybe he was; he's a pretty decent bloke when he doesn't have his eye on your purse or your pussy, and he certainly seemed to like David a lot – but more on that later. Whenever David wasn't off around the corner at Ava's or Amanda's, he was off around the corner at Mick's.

Or off around the corner, or the world, somewhere. David wasn't much in evidence at Oakley Street at all.

It was the cocaine, I think. When you're into cocaine, you don't want to endure friends, family, festive dinner parties, wonderful meals, those kinds of things. No. You want to get together with another cocaine addict or two or three, and do cocaine: talk your heads off, stay up forever, obsess yourselves crazy. And anyone who doesn't want to do that, who doesn't think that's exactly how human beings are born to spend their gifts and energies, is irrelevant and irksome.

David's whole way of life changed, then, everything from his daily schedule to his choice of companions. He started living largely in the dark, in the company of other coke freaks. He visited home only when he needed to or could be assured that his nearest and dearest, or other non-cocaine people, wouldn't bother him.

I saw less and less of him, and I just hated that. I couldn't stand watching the David I knew vanishing from his own life, and I couldn't believe there was nothing I could do to bring him back.

Powerlessness was a terrible, bitter pill for me. It went down hard. I couldn't accept the reality that David was fading inexorably away into the grip of a disease all his own, that *he* was sick and *he* was abusing our bond, so I turned my rage on myself. A lot of the time I felt just how he wanted me to feel: like a drag on him, a stone around his neck. Our relationship was that of hostage and captor in which the captive begins protecting the captor, then taking on the captor's guilt.

But that wasn't the whole story. There was room in that fog of feelings for some sharp contrasts, and so I fought for myself as well as beating myself up. In my own way I survived, took what I needed, and even hit back.

David didn't get away with his mistresses scot-free, for instance, or at least his mistresses didn't get away with *him* scot-free. During the time he was involved with both Ava Cherry and Ava Clark, a beautiful West Indian actress (I'm surprised he wasn't fucking Ava Gardner too), I had some fun. Whenever I knew he'd be attending some public or semi-public function, an opening or a party or whatever, I'd make sure that invitations were issued via Main Man to both Avas, and then I'd go along myself and watch those two collide. They didn't have a very permissive attitude about each other, you might say, so their encounters could be funny.

I'd have them both come over to the house too, and that was even funnier. One night, I remember, I got Daniella to toss out the bait, and sure enough, both of them hustled immediately to Oakley Street, expecting David to be there waiting for them. He wasn't; there were just Angie and Daniella relaxing on the gorgeous white leather sofa, sipping a fine chilled Chablis, with no idea where David might be. Maybe he would show up at any moment, maybe he was off with Mick somewhere, who could say? We know how David is, now don't we?

The two Avas circled each other for a while, trying to restrain themselves and Daniella and I found this enormously amusing. But then Ava Cherry exploded and stormed off with a string of expletives, leaving Ava Clark alone with us, still waiting.

There wasn't any doubt about how to proceed in *that* situation. I looked at Daniella, and she looked at me, and the thought passed wordlessly between us: *Ava's up for it, isn't she?* And she was indeed. I had Ava, and she was tasty, that one, and it was a great night's naughty-girl pleasure.

Perhaps it was childish behavior, but it served its purposes. For a start, my need for security demanded it. On a very instinctive level I felt that if I'd bedded people, if I'd seen them stripped naked and taken them, I'd robbed them of their power to compete with me; they weren't serious opposition anymore.

My ego demanded it too: David needed to know that he wasn't the only tomcat in the Bowie family. And so did my lust for life. I needed to know that I wasn't missing out on the goodies.

*

And oh my, I surely wasn't. Roy Martin was his name.

I'd seen him once at Dana's place, 'the Bunker,' but I first connected with him one late night when Daniella and I, afflicted by a severe case of the munchies at Oakley Street, made a late-night sortie to Tramp's for some of its wonderful raspberry chocolate cake à la mode.

He was sitting with Mick Taylor, a Stones guitarist at the time, and Mick's wife, Rose (of whom more anon), and I noticed him immediately: lush dark hair, wonderful turquoise eyes in a lean, muscular, aquiline face – great strength and sensitivity there, and not a little danger too – and as I noted when he stood up, among the slimmest, most elegantly formed hips I've seen on a man. He was wearing a denim jacket bedecked with pins and patches and all kinds of other funky decorations, and that's where I made my mark. Even though this was my first meeting with the Taylors, I simply couldn't make my farewells and leave the place without walking up to him and saying, 'I'm not going to say good-bye to *you*,' and writing my telephone number on his jacket with a marker. 'I expect you to call me,' I added.

He called, eventually, and even more eventually (Daniella having forgotten to relay his message to me: an oversight for which she almost lost her life) we got together. He was an actor and director, and he invited me to the show he was in, the very advanced satire *Remember the Truth Dentist* at the Royal Court Theatre. I'll never forget it: He walked out into the lights, delivered his speech (marvelously), did four complete, effortless handsprings across the stage, sat himself down at an organ, and started singing like an angel and playing like a master. Well. I fell in love right there and then: *bam*, that was it.

Roy was a challenge, as I found out the first time he and I tried out his huge Victorian bed in his room at 63 Cromwell Road. We were relaxing afterward and I was thinking we'd just had a wonderful time, but evidently he wasn't.

'How old are you?' he asked.

I was a taken aback a touch, but I answered him. I was twenty-five, I said.

'Well, what a shame,' he said. 'So young, and just look at you. No muscle tone, no stamina. You've let yourself go to hell, haven't you? You've got the body structure of an athlete, a dancer, but you're a mess. Do you ever get any exercise?'

I couldn't believe it. Who the hell did he think he was? 'How can you talk to me like that when we've just made love?' I was really hurt and angry.

'You call that making love?' He laughed. 'Well, Angie, if you really think *that* is what sex is about, all I can say is, you've got a lot to learn.'

I stared at him, speechless. Then I found my voice and started mumbling something about what gave him the right... He cut me short.

'Look, I'll tell you what gives me the right, and I'm never going to say this again, okay? I'm falling in love with you.'

'What did you say?'

'I'm falling in love with you.'

'Oh. Okay.'

And it was okay. I was still smarting from the critique of my lovemaking, but a position statement as clear as the one Roy had just delivered made up for a lot, as did his promise to teach me what I needed to know. I had every confidence that he could come through on that promise too. He was ten years older than I, but he was in infinitely better shape, much stronger and suppler, with much more stamina and control, and he was a wonderful, *wonderful* lover. I'd never experienced anyone like him.

He and I started a sexual relationship that would last three full years, and from the very beginning he taught me so much. I learned that I couldn't be physically tuned if I lived on red meat and sugar and all that other crap, and that if I exercised properly, my body both felt better and performed better. I learned how to deepen my pleasure in many ways: how to smoke a joint for maximum effect, how to eat sensually, and of course how to really make love. I learned how to let myself go all the way into orgasms the likes of which I'd never even dreamed. I learned how to prolong my pleasure almost indefinitely, and how to do the same for my partner. I learned about vibrators and other tools, and games and fantasies; I learned how to get tied up and enjoy being restrained long enough to come. I learned that I could really act out the scripts running in my sexual imagination. Together Roy and I dismantled my inhibitions, one by one.

Life with him was an adventure. One morning (well, about three a.m., the middle of the night, really) I awoke suddenly in his bed, and there beside me was a gorgeous naked girl. I had a vague idea who she might be – one of the top models in Europe – but I didn't stop to check her ID. We made love for an hour or so, and waited until the morning proper for formal introduction. Which was fun. 'What a lovely way to meet someone!' she said, and indeed it was. She and I got to be good friends.

Another time (there were all sorts of other times with him), Roy and I were lying in bed talking, and I happened to mention that I needed a car. 'I'm tired of paying for taxis everywhere I go,' I said. 'It's very expensive, and it really bothers David. He can't stand to see all that cash disappearing every day. I think he'd be much happier if I just spent the money once, on a car.'

'Well, how much do you have to spend?' Roy replied.

About a thousand pounds, I told him.

He grinned at me. 'You're in luck, Angie. I can get you something really good for that. I was a driver for years – driven for the best, I have – so just leave it to me. I'll get you a car.'

And he did: a very fast and luxurious dark blue Daimler worth *much* more than a thousand pounds.

Procuring elegant cars wasn't Roy's only field of expertise either. Once we happened to be talking about jewelry, and I mentioned my love of emeralds (this I'd inherited from my mother) and remarked in passing that nobody seemed to give me jewelry, and I wished someone would. I wasn't angling for a gift, I really wasn't; I was just telling him about myself.

'That doesn't surprise me, Angie,' he said. 'You're not quite the conventional girly-girl type, are you? People probably think you don't *like* jewelry.'

'Yeah, I guess you're right,' I said, and that was the extent of the discussion. But when my eyes opened the next morning, they focused on a new addition to my finger: a magnificent ring with three very big, beautiful emeralds. I had to wonder how Roy had gotten it.

He certainly had his uses, that man. As well as everything else, it was he who introduced me to the idea that material possessions are transitory and unimportant, that it's how you feel, not what you've got, that matters – and knowing now what I didn't know then about the events awaiting in my life, I'm glad I learned that when I did. It was also he who actually put me on the stage. He didn't talk about it; he took action. Someone left the cast of *Remember the Truth Dentist*, and Roy said simply, 'You're an actress, and there's room for you, so you should do it.' He coached me and helped me, giving me his craft and passing along his experience freely.

And of course (back to sex), he was terrifically useful in bed. He really knew what to do. His vibrator, for instance, was a marvel: not one of those silly plastic dildos, but a big, industrial-strength fifties item with a heavy-duty motor and a suction-cup head that put the vibes where they were needed. We used to joke about it: 'When we break up, Roy, I'm taking that thing with me!' 'Oh no, you're not. You do that, I'll hunt you to the end of the earth.'

In threesomes or larger aggregates he was also terrific, particularly when the basic scene consisted of me and another woman (or two). A big problem with pure lesbian sex, I've found, is fatigue. When all you've got to work with is your natural womanly assets, it often takes forever to get the poor dear(s) to come, especially when everyone's stoned, and a good, willing natural-born man with a good, hard natural asset of his own can, when called upon, bring that sort of situation to a most pleasantly rapid conclusion. I've often fallen away limp from my labors, my tongue almost ripped out by its roots, and watched in sweat-soaked erotic glee as Roy's power drove the other woman up, up, up, and finally away.

Roy was such a strong, sensitive, and powerful rider that it shouldn't come as any surprise that he loved motorcycles and handled them masterfully. And of course that's another thing I loved about him, because I too have a passion for good bikes, the leaner and meaner and faster and more ferocious the better. I got lots of kicks on Mickey Finn's Norton (I have forgotten which model, but it was a restored fifties racing bike, and it went like a beautiful black rocket), and when Roy came into possession of a brand-new bright red Honda 400 SX, I loved that too.

We howled around town (the Hyde Park underpass, on the way to Tramp's, was a favorite high-speed rush), but the best times were our runs out of London, where you could wind a bike up to a hundred miles an hour or more – 'doing a ton,' as the Brits say – on the gently winding, cop-free country roads.

Sometimes we just roared and roamed. Other times we had a destination in mind, usually one of the peaceful spots ringing London where the rock-and-roll royalty of the Scepter'd Isle had established the sleepy little fiefdoms from which, when the dollar or yen or whatever sounded its siren call, they sortied forth to take the wealth of the world.

Really, I often thought of those guys as the last inheritors of the great British tradition of country-squire world conquerors: nice, down-to-earth chaps equally comfortable sorting out the problems of their tenant farmers and, after a bracing ocean voyage, relieving inhabitants of whole tribes, villages, countries, and even continents of their tangible assets with enormous verve and frightening determination. In the old days, of course, the tools of choice were the Birmingham Brown Bess musket and the Sheffield steel saber, and a good deal of blood got spilled. Now the best equipment was itself foreign – Fender, Gibson, Rickenbacker – and the only real damage was a certain degree of hearing loss. But the end result was the same: amply financed comfort in the bucolic splendor of Britain's greenest and most pleasant land.

Every time I saw some drummer or bass player or lead-guitar god traipse into the kitchen of his lovely old Home Counties manor house in his gum boots, stinking of cow manure and mumbling happily about the progress of his radishes, I'd have sudden visions of his campaigns – a panty-strewn motel room here, a riot of cocaine-crazed concubines there; a massive auditorium somewhere out in the colonies, filled with smoke and stabbed by primal lightning, shaking to its very foundations with the wild, guitar-and-drum-driven dance of ten thousand ecstatically transported natives – and I'd get goofy with the sheer incongruity of everything. All those world-conquering rock-and-roll dervish-men (well, most of them) were just such normal, self-effacing, rose-gardening, shed-pottering *Englishmen*.

Eric Clapton was like that. All I remember about visiting his country house, in fact, is the impression of a really good, sweet, decent, everyday bloke; a thoroughly nice chap relaxing at home, offering cups of tea and hoping the rain would let up in time to walk the dog before dark. Eric has more controlled soul and sheer animal passion in his fingertips than any ten people, of course, and he's capable of creating beauty no one else is even capable of describing, but you'd never, ever know it.

Not so his old Cream-mate Jack Bruce – but then, Jack's a Scot, a wildfire Celt, exempt from the constrictions of Anglo-Saxon decorum. You know it as soon as you look in his eyes; *his* passion is all right there where you can see it, burning bright and ready to go.

Jack's an extraordinarily compelling person. Whenever Roy and I visited his house, a handsome tan brick place in the country about an hour north of London, he'd sit down at the grand piano, near a bay window in his living room, and play whatever he was working on at the time – always wonderful music, very intense, often classical in form – and I'd get the peculiar feeling that everything he was doing, every note and nuance, was aimed directly at *me*. It was almost as if he were casting a spell, or seducing me somehow. It felt peculiar, and after our second visit, I mentioned it to Roy.

No, sorry. I didn't mention it to Roy. I think he must have seen a look in my eyes he'd seen before, because he gave a little laugh and said, 'He's done it to you too, hasn't he?'

'Yes, he has,' I replied. 'I'd lie down and die for that man, I really would.'

That was an interesting realization, and it gave me a great respect for Jack's power, as well as a new appreciation of Cream's music. I began to perceive that Eric hadn't been the heart and fire of that band at all, despite much of the popular press and conventional legend. The drive and fury and passion of Cream at its best came from Jack. He was the powerhouse; it was he who pushed Eric to extremes of emotional improvisation he never achieved before or after Cream.

Visits with Jack were fascinating also because he was the first recovering drug addict I'd talked to. He was able to tell me just what it was like to shoot several hundred thousand pounds' worth of heroin up your arm and live to tell about it, and more to the point, to come back from that never-never land and be doing well in the real world without drugs; he had a beautiful wife and kids, and seemed very happy, and he was making fabulous music. It was from him, then, that I got the unvarnished bad news/good news vis-à-vis the drug problem in my own family: a full, graphic understanding of the destruction drug addiction wrought upon a person, and an appreciation of the fact that addiction didn't necessarily have to end in death or permanent insanity. Maybe David was lost from me, I thought, but maybe too, he didn't have to be lost forever.

For now, though, he wasn't quite lost at all; merely absent. He was elsewhere but Oakley Street most of the time, playing with Mick Jagger or working on his *Diamond Dogs* album, and then he was elsewhere but London. In April 1974, he boarded the SS *France* – David wouldn't fly; he'd had premonitions – and steamed away to take up residence in New York. That, he told me, was where the action was.

I couldn't argue about that, even if the idea of anyone's actually volunteering to live in an environment as savage as New York baffled me. But the city was, plainly, taking over London's luster as the action center of the world's music business, and just as obviously it was where David's money was being spent, so you could make a good case for the proposition that he belonged there.

The real clincher, however, wasn't any of that, or even other such surefire Gotham selling points as Broadway, twenty-four-hour nightlife, quaintly colorful garbage and graffiti, profoundly poisonous pigeons, Central Park squirrels more hazard-resistant than even the cockroaches of Beirut, and cockroaches capable of surviving thirty-kiloton thermonuclear explosions two feet away and *still* finding your eyelids in the middle of the night. No, for David none of this mattered, and neither did New York's real, no-kidding appeal, whatever it might be. For him the deal was simple:

cocaine. It just so happened that for David Bowie at that particular point in history, the best, most consistently and easily available cocaine was in Manhattan, supplied by a new friend and ever more frequent companion, the (sophisticated, witty, charming, wealthy) art dealer Norman Fisher. The Norman connection was so superior to any other, in fact, that there simply wasn't any question about where David belonged.

Main Man rented him what had been the Italian ambassador's suite at the Sherry-Netherland Hotel on Fifth Avenue, opposite Central Park, and his new life began.

He met my new beau before he left, and liked him a great deal. The affection was mutual; Roy thought a lot of David, enjoyed his company, and respected his position as my husband. The two became friends, in fact.

I liked that, and so did David. 'I feel better about leaving you here, now I know you're with Roy,' he said. 'I think Roy can take good care of you when I'm not around. I trust him.'

I liked that too. I felt good, less abandoned, more considered and cared for. David's trust in Roy seemed, at the time, an entirely benevolent phenomenon. And maybe it was, maybe it was.

# $S$TICKS AND $S$TONES

$H$aving raised the subject of David and Mr Michael Phillip Jagger, our Chelsea neighbor, it would be remiss of me to overlook it without further ado. Mick has been significant in David's story, after all, and you could certainly say that he's touched mine too. Herewith, then, some further ado.

First, let me make it plain that I like Mick, and in certain ways even admire him. I appreciate it, for instance, that you'll never find *him* following the script acted out by far too many of the yobbos who became English rock royalty – the gum boots, the golf, the lying around in the country, the monthlong Caribbean cruises, the generally idle self-satisfaction and creative torpor. No: Mick may be rich, but he's not idle. Whenever *he* sits down for a three-hour lunch at San Lorenzo, he's talking tours, films, ventures or deals of one sort or another, and he *never* picks up the bill. I like that.

Mick is also extremely witty, with that frank, fast London earthiness, and he's open and natural, very worldly, not at all impressed by anyone else's conceit and certainly not stuck up himself. A very intelligent and charming human being, altogether, and great fun.

I must admit too that I'm in awe of him as a business mind and a manager. He's kept the Stones more or less together and solvent for some thirty years – amazing when you think about it. Brian Jones died and Mick Taylor resigned, but those are the only personnel changes the Stones have had since they started recording. Incredible! That's like keeping the Flying Wallendas on top without having new generations come into the act. It's like doing what Frank Sinatra has done, but with five egos instead of one.

Mick's the ultimate team player. He knows what Charlie Watts wants, and what Bill Wyman wants, and he knows that if he makes sure they get it, he'll get what *he* wants, which is for the industry called the Rolling Stones to keep producing whatever he needs.

And then, of course, there's his thing with Keith Richards. What wonderful publicity! One month it's: *Oooh, Mick and Keith aren't talking!* Then it's: *Will they ever do another tour?* Then it's: *No! Never! Mick's mean, Keith's hurt!* Then, just as inquiring minds are losing interest, it's: *Scoop! They've made peace!* And to prove it, there's a nice photo of them having lunch together in Cannes or somewhere, Keith all bright-eyed and peppy after another of those refreshing total blood transfusions, Mick looking droll as can be. It's precious, it really is. I love it.

And of course I love Mick and Keith's music, and their whole thing – I'm a Stones fan, not a Beatles fan; the Stones always seemed *far* more dangerous, therefore infinitely more interesting. On the whole the Stones are very nice guys, give or take a little kink or two.

Bill Wyman, for instance, the Stone I know second to least (I don't know Charlie Watts at all, and not having known Brian doesn't count, since he's dead). I've never paid much attention to Bill – no people have, have they? – so it wasn't until a few years ago, when we were both shooting the movie *Eat the Rich*, that I got a clear glimpse of his character.

It blew me away. I'd seen men like him before, in the States mostly, older guys with lots of gold and chest hair sticking out of their shirtfronts, guys who hang around coffee shops near high schools. I just didn't know the type came in a model that's also a Rolling Stone.

He was amazing. He had two kids with him, who seemed to be personal assistants, a boy of twenty-two or so and the boy's girlfriend, and all three were on the same wavelength. They talked about a party they were going to that night. It was as if it were still 1962, and Bill Wyman was still about to go to Carnaby Street and down King's Road to get himself a new outfit, 'and then we'll go out and 'ave some dinner, and then we'll go to the party, right? Now, we've got to 'it a few pubs wiv dolly-birds in 'em. . . . '

He used those very words. I couldn't believe it – the man was around fifty years old! But maybe he was onto something. Maybe if you spend all your time thinking about dolly-birds and fab new gear, you really can hold back Father Time. Bill certainly looked wonderful, and his vibe wasn't by any means unsavory; his enthusiasm, a kind of mindless kid-in-a-candystore delight, seemed genuinely boyish. I sat there stunned at a world in which a real, live Rolling Stone, after everything he had seen and experienced, could remain a perpetual teenager.

Two other Stones I knew quite well in the early days were Ron Wood, the nicest man on the planet, when he was still with the Faces, and Mick Taylor, when he was married – but anyway, more on that (again) anon. For now, Mr Jagger.

David was thrilled when the mighty Mick first paid attention to him. The Stones were from his own middle-class suburban south London, and they'd been by far the most successful local heroes on the scene; they were the very top big boys, up to their necks in sex and drugs and money while the little boys, David and his friends, were still drawing allowances from their dads. Some of the seminal adventures of David's adolescence, as he told me when we traded our life stories, were played out to a sound track of Rolling Stones music, on record or live in person around their early stomping grounds: the Crawdaddy Club, Eel Pie Island, the Marquee.

David and Mick became very fast friends very quickly, and it was rather amusing for the rest of us. They were always yakking on the phone together like teenagers, or going to see each other at the studio, or inviting each other over to hear their mixes. 'Shall I meet you at Tramp's?' became the million-dollar question of many a day.

I wasn't much involved. I'd been to Mick and Bianca's house and tried to be friendly with Bianca, but she was very reserved, and nothing I did seemed to break the ice; I think she was uncomfortable because of my friendship with Marianne Faithfull. Oh well, I've endured worse disappointments.

My appearances *chez* Jagger were infrequent, therefore. I remember only two visits with any clarity: one when I was there on some sort of business for David, and Mick was working with Mick Taylor on the song that would become 'Angie,' and the other for Mick's birthday party: David was already off in New York then, and I ended up half carrying Brian Ferry home to the couch at Oakley Street.

There was a lot of that sort of thing in our circle, and indeed in London in general. Partly because the city is so spread out and difficult to negotiate in the middle of the night, and partly because the English have long been accustomed to intimately shared living quarters, our friends thought nothing of staying over at our house after a party or whatever, or of our crashing at their places. It was no big deal – you found somewhere to sleep and claimed it, not worrying much about other bodies scattered here and there – but to some people I suppose it seemed odd. Middle-class American visitors, representatives of the only society on earth rich enough to have grown accustomed to living one to a room (sometimes with their own *bathroom*), often tended to be shocked, thinking such arrangements unsanitary and probably even immoral.

Perhaps that's why such a furor of publicity erupted when, as a guest on Joan Rivers's talk show, I mentioned that one morning on Oakley Street I came upon David and Mick sharing a bed.

I had just flown back to London from New York. I entered the house and went into the kitchen, and Daniella told me, 'I think Mick and David are asleep upstairs.'

I said, 'Oh, okay,' and went and opened the bedroom door, and there indeed they were, asleep in our bed. I asked them if they wanted coffee, and they said yes. And that was that.

There are two ways of looking at that incident. One was that it was a thoroughly normal London scene: Best friends stagger home drunk or stoned from some night spot or party or whatever, strip off their clothes somehow, and fall into bed and pass out. Morning comes, wife arrives with wake-up beverage, hangover begins, life resumes.

But oh, no. Joan Rivers, and her studio and TV audience, and every gossip columnist in the world, leaped straight to the other obvious conclusion, which is that since Mick Jagger had been found in bed with David Bowie, Mick must be (gasp!) gay or, even worse (faint!), *bisexual!*

Well, leaving aside the question of why on earth that should have been news to anyone who'd paid any attention to the Stones' affairs, particularly the convoluted girlfriend-swapping and buddy-bonding among Mick, Keith, and Brian before Brian ended up in that swimming pool, I really don't like the automatic assumption that if two men are found in bed together, something sexual must be happening. That's so square, so typically American.

On the other hand, when I walked into that room and found Mick and David together, I felt absolutely dead certain that they'd been screwing. It was so obvious, in fact, that I never even considered the possibility that they *hadn't* been screwing. The way they'd been running around together and the way David made a virtual religion of slipping the Lance of Love into almost everyone around him, and then the fact that Mick had a perfectly good bed of his own just three hundred yards away from where he was passed out naked with David – it all added up inescapably in my head as well as my gut. I didn't have to look around for open jars of K-Y jelly.

Maybe I should have, because then my eyes would have seen the proof of what I knew in my heart. But I didn't, so I can't say conclusively that those two alley cats were actually going at it that night. While they were still awake together in my bed, I wasn't there.

But I *was* there another time Mick got his pecker up. It was in New York at the Sherry-Netherland suite, where I was staying with Dana. David, if I recall correctly, was on tour, or maybe not; maybe he was just off doing his cocaine thing somewhere.

Dana and Mick were having an affair at the time, as it happened, and while I looked a little askance at that (Mick was, after all, a monogamously married man, or at least that's how Bianca seemed to understand the arrangement), Dana certainly didn't mind. She was in pure fun mode.

On the evening in question, as the investigating officer would put it, she was in the bedroom of the suite sleeping off jet lag when Mick called. I told him she was still passed out, and he said, 'Oh. Who's that? Is that you, Angie? Yeah? Well, I'm going to come over and visit, all right?'

He was staying at the Plaza, just across from the Sherry-Netherland, so it didn't take him long. He arrived and we said hello and

I asked, 'Well, should I raise Dana? She should get up now anyway, or she'll screw up her body clock completely.'

'No, no, let her sleep,' he replied, and the way he said that was loaded: very coy and suggestive. I looked at him, and sure enough, there was a little leer on his face. I thought, *Jesus. He wants to make love with me. His best friend's wife!*

Playing for time, I offered him a drink. He asked for some kind of Courvoisier thing he and David were drinking at the time, and I went into the kitchen and made it for him, then took it back into the living room.

He came on strong then, suggesting quite bluntly that we get it on right then and there. I protested – 'I'm your best friend's wife, Mick! I'm married to David, remember?' – but he kept at it, and after a while I thought, *Oh, what the hell. Why fight it? Let him do his thing and let's see what happens.*

He went to it, then, and I cooperated, but I couldn't get into the spirit of the thing. All the time he was kissing me and feeling me up, an image that had hit me when he first came in the door kept flashing into my mind: Mick as a billy goat.

This was one of those peculiar moments when you suddenly see something in a person for the first time, and it's so vivid and obvious that it seems the most essential truth about them, and you wonder why on earth you've never seen it before. *That's it!* I kept thinking. *That mouth, that strut, that uppity way he has – he's a billy goat! And he behaves just like a billy goat! He's like David, he'll fuck anything!*

That perception wasn't very erotic, so I was beginning to have a problem taking Mick's attentions very seriously – frankly, it was all I could do not to burst out laughing – when Dana saved the day. She emerged from the bedroom and saw what was happening, and, being Dana, reacted appropriately. 'Oooooooh, good!' she laughed. 'Fun! Antics! Let me in!'

I didn't have to spend too long on that idea. 'No, I don't think so, Dana,' I said quickly. 'Why don't you just take him back into the bedroom for the second round?'

She laughed, and off they went together, and everything worked out fine for everyone (except Bianca, of course).

I don't know how I'd have handled Mick if Dana hadn't shown

up on cue. I'd have been forced to stop him one way or another, I think, because another anti-erotic theme was accompanying the billy goat refrain in my mind. I kept thinking of all the people I knew Mick had slept with in the previous three or four months, then imagining how many more there must have been, and calculating the odds.

Any way I figured it, I realized, he was the walking definition of an absolutely unacceptable risk. I liked Mick in his place; but he was such a slut.

I dismissed the whole affair as a silly ego- and hormone-driven incident, and almost forgot about it, but then the Stones released 'Angie,' with Mick singing that plaintive lyric at someone with my name, and I had to wonder: Did our brief, unconsummated encounter mean more to him than I'd ever imagined?

I thought about it more, and realized the answer to that question was no. Mick's pass at me was one thing, and 'Angie' was another. It was probably just the latest example of the legendary acumen of the Jagger-Richards songwriting and publishing team. Those boys used every trick in the book when it came to getting their songs noticed, and I'm sure they weren't above using my name for the sole and simple purpose of causing Stones fans, gossip columnists, and inquiring minds everywhere to wonder, just as I did: *What's this? Is Mick in love with David Bowie's wife?*


There are levels to this. Beyond Mick's goatishness, beyond the male bonding and rock star companionship between him and David, there was something else: competition.

David, you see, wasn't into respecting his elders, and he certainly wasn't into restraining his ego. He listened to that voice religiously, and in 1974 it was telling him, among other things, that he was the biggest, brightest, best rock star in the world. David Bowie not Mick Jagger, was The One. Mick was last year's rock star, a little long in the tooth, perhaps more suited to life in the pasture, and if there was a hidden theme underlying David's attitude toward him, it was: *Move over, old man. Young man coming through.*

David didn't have to be obvious about it, and he wasn't. Most of the time the charts and the headlines delivered the message for him; he simply added the occasional subtle reinforcement, such as his recording of 'Let's Spend the Night Together.' When you cut a new version of a song so firmly identified with the original artist, you're paying tribute, naturally, and that's good, you're flattering. But if you have the status David had, you're also staking your own claim to the song's glory and history. And in this case I have no doubt whatsoever that David was out to steal Stones thunder – or more to the point, Stones territory. He was tomcatting the turf, spraying young scent over the old cat's, as he had done with Marianne Faithfull.

All of which is just normal human stuff, the usual flak between ambitious people going for the same goals. It's no big deal. Business and personal relations, and even friendships, survive. It's not fatal.

But in this case it nearly was, and I was the near fatality.

Here Rose Taylor reenters my story: Rose... the wife of Mick Taylor, Stones guitarist and writer of the melody that became 'Angie' when the main Mick wrote the lyrics; Rose the lovely, blue-eyed, copper-haired, steel-souled Celt from the Notting Hill-Camden Town school of hippie hard-trading (antiques, whatever moved in the market); Rose the survivor; Rose the ruthless; Rose the familiar.

David wasn't involved with the Taylors; they were Roy's friends. He was more a friend of the family, just as he became with the Bowie family; that's how he liked things.

That was the social context of the visits he and I made *chez* Taylor: The geographical context was a picture-perfect old stone cottage, complete with rambling vines and rose trellises, south of London in the lush and gorgeous calm of rural Sussex. We motored down there, by bike or Daimler, for two or three weekends.

We did what one did on country weekends in those days: took long, rambling walks; cooked and ate big, hearty meals; played lots of very loud music; smoked enormous amounts of hashish; and visited with the neighbors. In this case the neighbors were a some-what older bohemian couple, in their late thirties at least. He was a manager, she was a witch. Mostly a white witch, I think, though what do I know? She and I got along well because we shared a Mediterranean upbringing; she was originally from Greece. We got stoned and talked about good magic, not so different from the kind of herbal-holistic healing, personal-power enhancement, and positive goal-visualization you read about in self-help books today, certainly nothing sinister.

During the Steel Wheels tour the Stones office received a request that, while not unheard of, was rather unusual. There was, it seemed, a young man in (location withheld) who was suffering from (name of disease withheld), an extremely rare condition that ages a person very rapidly long before his prime.

The disease was terminal, and the boy in question was well down the road. He already looked bizarre, with many of the features of a seventy-year-old imposed on his teenage self. He was bald, and he talked through a voice box in his larynx, and he was going to die. But before he did, he said, he had one great wish: to meet the Rolling Stones.

Management talked to the Stones about it, and the Stones agreed, and an invitation was sent out, along with plane tickets to a Stones concert in (location withheld).

Everything went according to plan, and on the appointed night the young man showed up backstage before the show.

Management had prepped Mick and the others as thoroughly as possible – 'Now look, Keith and Charlie, this kid is pretty far out. He doesn't look normal at *all*, so don't freak when you meet him, okay?' – but even so, the encounter was awkward. There was the very distinct feeling that the sooner it was over, the better. Looking that strange and sounding that strange, the kid seemed almost more alien than human.

The Stones shook hands with the boy, then were exchanging small talk with him, when someone, I don't know who, posed the question to the boy.

'Well, is there anything we can do for you?'

This was supposed to be the moment in which T-shirts or tour jackets or perhaps more extravagant gifts are forthcoming, and those items were of course close at hand, but such was not to be. The standard script took a sudden wild turn.

'Yes, there is something,' said the kid, in that weird, croaky voice. 'I want to get high, and I want a blow job.'

There was stunned silence until Keith (who else?) started laughing, then laughing harder, then laughing so hard that he had to fall down and convulse on the floor.

You should know the ending of this story already, but in case you can't figure it out for yourself, here it is. The kid got high and watched the show, and later a prepaid, well-briefed call girl came by his hotel room, and he got his blow job.

I like all kinds of stuff about this story, but what I most enjoy is thinking about what must have been a wonderful moment. Just imagine how that kid must have felt when, sitting there at home in his condition and wanting what he wanted before his disease ran its course, the light bulb went on and he finally figured out a virtually guaranteed, all-expenses-paid way of getting it. He must have known his Stones. He must have known there was no way they would even consider refusing him.

## 12

# *S*EX, *D*RUGS, AND *D*IAMOND *D*OGS

*D*avid had the United States, New York, and cocaine in the summer of 1974. I had the United Kingdom, London, and Pamela.

Pamela was my friend. She was a drug, and she was the best argument I've ever known for the proposition that not all drugs are destructive. She certainly proved that some drugs are better than others: Pamela took you as far as you can imagine from the stupor of smack or the mania of cocaine.

I never knew exactly what Pamela was, what chemical formula the letters PMA denoted; its designer told me recently that it was only one molecule away from the drug called ecstasy. Basically, it was essentially a limited-edition psychedelic that had all of the beneficent effects of the better mass-market products – the euphoria, the sensory glow – without the usual drawbacks – the wild hallucinations, the physical tension, the risky/edgy aspect of the psychedelic experience. Concocted by a London pharmacist for people like me and my circle, it came in the form of a white powder that we mixed into juice and tripped on for about six hours, perhaps with a little booster after a couple of hours. It was very powerful, but it was gentle too. Extraordinarily sensual, it enhanced physical experience so that whatever turned you on – dancing, bathing, dressing up in silks and satins – gave you almost orgasmic pleasure. Making love on PMA gave you orgasms that were out of this world.

PMA was a wonderfully pleasant part of my summer of '74, which, in retrospect, may have been both the highest and the last of my really high times. I was still a serious working woman, but I was also a full-fledged member of London's pop/arts royalty, and believe me, I sampled the pleasures of my status with gusto. The house on Oakley Street and the other two centers of my social circle, Dana's Bunker and Benny Carruthers's house in Earl's Court, were scenes of great high jinks. The party people I'm talking about included Dana and Daniella and Roy Martin and me, of course, the core unit, and then a circle of very close and wonderful friends.

My house in particular was a wonderful environment for psychedelic fun. On those sweet days when we decided to quit work and do Pamela, I loved to roam around and appreciate its attractions – to drift in the splendor of the amazing sound system, or play with the fortune's worth of clothes and costumes, or watch my friends' beautiful bodies bathing in the luxury of scented, candlelit bathrooms or heaving on the huge custom-built bed sunk into the floor of my bedroom suite – or even better, to take my pleasures more actively, joining the boys in lining up the trade we attracted and tipping them over on their round little heels. Oh, yes: goat fun in luxury. That was the life.

We had such a wonderful time. Among other things, I had a fabulous collection of lingerie – negligees, suspender belts, bustiers – and once we got some Pamela inside us, the girls and I might dress (or rather *un*dress) ourselves as provocatively as possible and see what happened next. And of course once *we* started, the boys joined in. They would raid our huge walk-in closets and come out in velvet suits, Moroccan silk caftans, Indian robes, whatever they could find. We would make ourselves and one another up too, and things could start looking rather wonderful.

The real sport, though, was fucking. Serious, all-out, no-holds-barred sex. The way my bed was sunk into the floor, you could sit around the sides and look down on whatever was going on, and we did that, and whoever felt like it would join in. I personally joined in a lot. Pamela made me very horny and very aggressive, even more so than I usually am (I like to say that sexually, I've always been something of a male chauvinist pig). I was hell on wheels. Those luscious girls, Long-Legged Liz and all the others whose names I've forgotten or never really knew, were ravished on my Pamela days.

Then there were others. There was a brilliant guitarist and record producer. He was our disc jockey at Oakley Street, playing us the best rock of the day mixed enchantingly with classical guitar pieces, Moroccan music, and whatever else appealed to his great good taste. He was and is a handsome man.

'Biffo,' an actor, was another of the boys. A character for whom the term 'colorful' is both appropriate and inadequate, Biffo possesses enormous talent, enormous wit, and an enormous cock – the biggest, in fact, that I and many other people have ever seen. He can hang three English-pint beer mugs off that thing!

He used to joke that while the genitals he'd been born with were impressive enough, he'd improved on nature with frequent and vigorous massages during his years in Her Majesty's Prisons, to which he'd been sentenced for inflicting grievous bodily harm (or GBH, as it's known in British penal circles). Biffo has an unusual biography. Born East London Irish, he had the blessing of a strictly religious upbringing before beginning his career as a 'minder,' or bodyguard/enforcer, for the local underworld hierarchy, including the notorious Kray brothers. Only after offending the law and enlarging his endowment in custody did he find his vocation on the stage.

His girlfriend in 1974, Vicki Hodge – Lady Victoria Hodge, that is, one of Europe's top models in the sixties and seventies, more recently notorious for her escapades with Prince Andrew – wasn't involved in the games at Oakley Street. I think Biffo just liked to screw around without her, however, and that the arrangement wasn't entirely acceptable from her point of view. She used to park her Mini across the street from my front door and sit there, waiting and watching, and at about six o'clock one morning she came looking for Biffo in a rage, wreaking havoc among the milk bottles on our steps. Yes – Lady Victoria, 27; milk bottles, 0. And *still* he wouldn't let her in. I wish he had, because then I'd have gotten to know her sooner than I did. Vicki's great; she and I became fast friends a little further down my road.

Biffo alone was more than enough on Oakley Street, though. He was a wild and wonderful man, and an inspired, often hilarious impromptu speaker; he had a fine tenor voice, eminently suited to the Irish airs and scurrilous drinking songs he fancied, and he was one of the main inspirations for my Parlor Poetry evenings – informal dinner parties of twenty or so, to which, if invited, a guest was expected to contribute some type of performance, live or on film or tape. Biffo was also, on other occasions, the instigator of a fair amount of spontaneous sex. I'd use the more familiar 'casual sex' in this context, but to me the term has always seemed inappropriate for any activity as wild, strenuous, and mind-blowing as the kind of sex *I'm* familiar with. (I mean, what *is* 'casual' sex? Copulation while you cruise the classifieds? Orgasm while opening the mail?) Anyway, no matter. Biffo was a very naughty boy indeed.

Another bad lad was Lesley Spitz, originally of Vienna, a wonderful lunatic whose vocation was wheeling and dealing; in '74 his specialty was antiques. He'd married the family au pair when he was seventeen, so he had two wonderful kids, Lana and Nicky, and he'd also been Dana's husband at one time (he's her type: short, dark, and handsome). He and I have the same birthday, which has always created a bond between us; sometimes I have felt as if we were joined at the hip.

In that summer of '74, one bad girl, Barbara, and I were joined more frontally.

You know, a great many of my sexual encounters have faded from my memory, or at least grown indistinct over time, but not my first taste of Barbara. I was at Dana's flat in Thurloe Square one afternoon, smoking a huge spliff, when suddenly a beautiful black-haired girl, a tiny thing with big breasts, came walking into the room as if she were family. And of course she was, as I learned when Dana introduced us. She was younger than Lesley, a student at a teacher training college at the time.

I couldn't believe her. I kept thinking, *God, she's gorgeous*! And the way she and Dana were behaving together, exchanging sexy-nurse jokes, was promising. You might say that my interest was piqued. You might in fact say that my libido was up and running like a freight train.

Dana and I were going out somewhere that evening, and according to the policy originally laid down by Tony Defries, we had to start planning Dana's outfit. She preferred a hippie look, but Tony had seen her make such an impact one night when I dressed her in high-fashion feminine that he insisted she do that whenever she went out on the town (and he was right, because she just slayed 'em; she was such a knockout that people hardly could stand it). So Dana, Barbara, and I went into the bedroom, nice and stoned, to start picking out Dana's glad rags.

Barbara was coming with us that evening, Dana said, so she needed an outfit too. Acknowledging the obvious, I told Barbara she should wear something as low-cut as possible to show off those lovely breasts of hers. 'For a little girl, you know, you've got huge tits.'

'I know, I know.' She laughed. 'It's unbelievable, isn't it? It drives me nuts.'

I didn't say what it did to me. I just took another long look at her, then nodded at Dana's 44-D's and laughed. 'Well, I guess that makes me odd man out, doesn't it?'

Dana picked up on that one quick as a whip. 'That's exactly right, darling. In fact, I think you're the only *man* here.'

She was right enough about that, and we all laughed, but the next thing I knew, Barbara was looking straight at me, and the next thing after that, her arms were around my neck and her tongue was deep in my mouth. What a wonderful moment, as hot as they come.

So were the next five or six days, which Barbara and I spent together holed up at Dana's, especially the third day, when she told me she'd never been with a woman before. I still get teased about that, both by other friends and by Barbara herself, but I don't mind. Turning Barbara on to the joys of love between women was one of my sweeter accomplishments. I can still get all hot and bothered just thinking about it.


Where was I? Right: my friends. My list of Chelsea players.

There were great writers, singers, and actors: Lionel Bart, Paul Jabara, Marianne Faithfull, Bryan Ferry, Simon Phillips, Simon Turner, Chris Jagger, and a dozen or two more. There were the Warholians now employed by Main Man who joined the games whenever they were in town: Leee Black Childers, Cherry Vanilla,

Wayne County, Tony Zanetta, and the rest of the gang. There were other actors, musicians, artists, models, middlemen, bit players, and strays moving through, a cast of hundreds ranging from unknown and innocuous to infamous and insane; and our circle at the time being the ground zero of trendy London, there were also royals scattered throughout. Frankly, though, I never paid them much attention. It never impressed me that this or that chick sticking a gram up her nose in the kitchen, or blowing some guitar god between studio takes, was the Marchioness of Someplace-or-other. They're a useless lot, those people, and they don't improve on close inspection.

Hollywood royalty wasn't very impressive at Oakley Street, either. At one point both Elliott Gould and Ryan O'Neal were in town and on the circuit, 'star-hopping,' as we called it (similar to bar-hopping, but more exclusive), and we got to see a little more of them than we really wanted to. Elliott Gould wasn't so bad, a touch bland and boring when he wasn't performing, but I didn't care for Ryan O'Neal at all. For one thing, he was sloppy drunk most of the time – once he passed out at Oakley Street and we had to board him overnight, choosing Leee's bed and thus giving Leee the chance at a cute little waking-up-with-Ryan-O'Neal-in-my-bed story he's been telling ever since – and then too, he spent a great deal of his energy in London trying to get Bianca Jagger into bed with him, which was a pitiful spectacle. Bianca was always so late for things – three or four hours here or there seemed to mean nothing to her – that, given the demands of his shooting schedule, I'd be surprised to learn that Ryan ever made it. More likely he spent a lot of time waiting; much moody lingering, I fear, over very long, lonely, and probably lugubrious lunches.

But I digress. Back to the lead roles at Oakley Street, and Ben Carruthers, unfortunately no longer among us; he died of colon cancer a few years ago.

Benny was beautiful in every way. Tall, slim, dark, and *very* handsome, he was the grandson of a president of Mexico. He had grown up in California, and was a marvelous actor and writer. He was also a major catalyst in the pop culture of our times. His home was, I think, *the* salon of the seventies in London, justly infamous throughout Kensington, Notting Hill, and all parts adjacent or farther flung, and he brought many worlds together there. Film and rock and video, largely unconnected fields in those days, began fusing via his hospitality, his ideas, and his friends: John Cassavetes, Stanley Kubrick, Eric Clapton, Keith Richards, and on and on. Benny, who was too busy acting as the spark plug for other people's careers and projects to get much of his own work down on film or tape (although his role in Cassavetes' *Shadows* will always endure) has never been given credit for his role. That's why I'm making a point of it here: He was too important to be left out of any history of our cultural times.

Benny and I wrote and worked together later, touring theatrically with *Krisis Kabaret* in 1976, but in 1974 our connection was mostly social, recreational, and connective. He and I (and Dana too, for that matter) were just as interested in exposing brilliant people's work to other brilliant people as we were in more primal mutual exposure – more so, in fact. Sex was fun, but art was special.

There was no sex between Benny and me. He was beautiful, but the way I was wired, I wasn't attracted to people who were already my friends and whom I therefore considered my equals. What I liked was conquest and role reversal, so my stance wasn't the usual trip: *Oh yes, big kind sir, I'll come along with you.* It was: *Come with me, little boy [or girl], I like the look of you.*

And as I've said, there was plenty of conquest at Oakley Street, a steady supply of fresh blood that either showed up somehow of its own accord or, on occasion, was secured by more active means.

One time, I remember, Biffo and I were on our exercise run over Albert Bridge into Battersea Park when we spotted an attractive young thing of sixteen or seventeen, with long straight brown hair, still in her school uniform – knee socks and field hockey shorts and all, God bless her! – and we simply couldn't resist.

'Excuse me, dear,' said Biffo, ever so pleasantly. 'Are you wearing stockings under your shorts, by any chance?'

She looked startled, but then Biffo added his line – 'because if you're not, you should be' – and praise be, she smiled. A very good sign, I thought, getting that little tingle already.

'Well,' she said. 'As a matter of fact, I'm not.'

Biffo gave her his very best come-hither look. 'Well then, why don't you come with us, and we'll find you some. I'm sure we can find your size with no difficulty at all.'

As we walked back to Oakley Street, we got to know her a little and filled her in on who we were, and then we were good to our word. We gave her a nice cold drink and a good warm spliff, and introduced her to our hosiery collection, and she modeled a pair or two. Then Biffo did a little modeling of his own – 'showing the marrow,' we termed it, still impressed every time we set eyes on that magnificent implement – and when none of us could stand it anymore, Biffo and I ravished her until she had to go back off to school.

She didn't leave, however, before asking when she could come back and play again. That was pretty much the usual outcome. They all came back. In those days there was a spirit of adventure abroad in the land.


And so it went, not just the sex but the whole sensual, spontaneous, creative spell cast over the lives of me and those in my circle in that place and time.

It really was another time: the fine and beautiful clothes, the wonderful food, the brilliant music, the thrilling surprises of my Parlor Poetry evenings, which were really my best moments. It's not everyone who gets to experience her favorite artists, among the best in the world, debuting new works among their peers – perhaps the most stimulating performance environment possible – in her own home.

All was well at Oakley Street, then, but Chelsea wasn't the whole world. More to the point, it wasn't New York, and it wasn't David's domain. I was still in thrall to that domain, though, so from time to time I had to leave the London scene and go wherever David was (by airplane; I didn't share his fear, didn't think the boogeyman would get me if I took to the skies).

Wherever David was, it was cocaine chilly and often very strange, but being with him certainly had its moments. In his personal life he'd hollowed out a bleak little cavern of an existence, using an oppressively unfurnished, unattractive brownstone on West Seventeenth Street as a base for himself and his loyal band of sycophants, and that was plain sad; his life seemed full of lonely drugging and obsessive work, and that was about it. But of course, all the energy poured into his work was doing wonders for his professional life. The new music was wonderful. *Diamond Dogs*, the album and the tour, was by far his most ambitious work to date, and it succeeded magnificently.

The whole project, from the conception of the album to the refinements of David's choreography around Jules Fisher's breathtaking stage set for the tour, was a triumph. The basic notion, with its weave of sci-fi/shock/totalitarian/mutation themes, was a brilliant synthesis of Kafka, Dalí, Genet, Burroughs, Orwell, Huxley, and the other underground thinkers conversing in David's head; he did a great job of translating their ideas into ticket-selling, brain-bending rock-and-roll theater. The songs were tight and smart and effective, high-power rock at its rhythmic/melodic peak. The band, eight instrumentalists and two dancer/backup singers now, were fabulous. The costumes and the choreography were stunning. The set, and the lighting, props, and effects, were wild. Nobody in rock had ever considered going on the road with anything even remotely that ambitious; it was like going out with a state-of-the-art Broadway show, and setting it up and tearing it down every night. David wasn't performing a concert: he was starring in a full-scale dramatic production, the first rock opera to be produced and performed as such. When he took to the boards in Boston or Cleveland or wherever, he wasn't presenting songs from a stage; he was singing stories in a fantasy city in a time out of time.

This was new territory for rock fans – not entirely unexpected, given David's obviously escalating theatricality, but revolutionary all the same. Until the *Diamond Dogs* tour, fans had had to concoct their own visual fantasies from whatever stimuli were available in the average concert hall, namely, back projection and brain chemistry supplements. And before him, there was only the light show: the San Francisco psychedelic mob and Pink Floyd.

After David, of course, there was all kinds of stuff, everything up to the current benchmark of pop theatricality, the Michael Jackson road show, but I don't think there's ever been anything to match *Diamond Dogs*. Plenty of shows have been bigger, the expenditure of effort and funds more conspicuous by far, but none has been brighter. None has tried to mean as much or succeeded in communicating its meaning as effectively.

The show was a knockout, then, and a sellout; every single seat contained a bowled-over Bowie fan. David's performance, on the other hand, was erratic. Sometimes, when the coke was working for him, he was brilliant, almost as good as he could be when he was straight. Other times, when he wasn't up enough, or he'd been up too long, or he was beyond up, into mania, he missed cues and forgot moves and botched things in all kinds of ways. But surprisingly, his voice stayed strong – I can't conceive how that happened, what with the abuse from chemicals, cigarettes, and sleeplessness – and his cast did too (those people were *great*), and so the shows worked almost despite him. He'd done such a good job of creating and putting the whole production together that his personal performance on any given night could afford to be below par.

He had a way of coming through when it really mattered too. His two Madison Square Garden shows, very big deals indeed in the media center of the world and his own new hometown, were as good as he could make them. He was alert and energized and enthusiastic both nights, especially the second, when every star, critic, and Somebody in New York was on RCA's or Main Man's guest list.

There was a big party at the Plaza Hotel after that second concert. In those days, *nobody* worth his Marshalls played New York without a conspicuously consumptive bash at the Plaza at *least*; Glitter was good to the great hotels of Manhattan. I remember the event in terms of the festive mood and the lovely men there – Helmut Berger, Rudolf Nureyev, Hiram Keller – and I have only a passing recollection of what was perceived as the loudest social grace note of the occasion: David disappearing into a walk-in closet with Mick Jagger and Bette Midler, and staying there for a period somewhat more than thirty minutes and somewhat less than an hour.

People seemed to find that stylish, or intriguing, or something. Not I. To me, it was a simple instance of rudeness and egomania.

I wasn't surprised either. David, nicely balanced for the show, obviously needed to get all bent out of shape as quickly as possible afterward, and Mick was his male-bonding/bashing buddy, and Bette – well, manners were never exactly her strong suit, were they?

I can't really fathom the nature of an ego that would need a fix like that: to gather a good percentage of your worthiest peers around you, supplement them with your most vital business partners and the world's best gossip-spreaders, and then display your personal corruption in as flagrant and insulting a manner as possible.

Oh, well. I suppose they got what they wanted out of it. Once they finally emerged they all looked terrifically stoned and seemed to have great trouble talking without sawing their molars off. Which is how they liked it, I guess.

It was good to get out of New York. It always is, but during those diamond-doggy days it was especially relieving.

The open road, for instance, was most refreshing. Yes ... the limo purring along at a steady seventy-five, good old Brooklyn Tony Macia's bodyguarding bulk behind the wheel, Detroit back down the interstate unraveling behind us, Minneapolis-St Paul up ahead somewhere, the moonroof open, the powerful telescope surveying the summer night sky from its tripod mount, the aliens up there perhaps recognizing that we meant them no harm, that *we* were the ones who could be trusted ...

They had been having a bad time, after all. One of their craft had been intercepted somewhere north of Detroit, engaged by the United States Air Force and – well, we never found out what happened after that. We didn't know if the saucer had been forced to crash-land on earth, or blasted out of the sky so that it *fell* to earth, or what. We didn't know if its occupants – its crew? – were dead or alive or somewhere in between, although we did know that there were four of them.

We knew all this because while we were in our hotel room in Detroit, we saw an afternoon TV news flash to the effect that a

UFO had crashed in the area with four aliens aboard ... more news at six.

We tuned in again at six – of *course* we did, along with everybody in the state – and learned more, but not much more. The news crew confirmed the landing, yet avoided being specific about its location and presented what little information they had with great caution, as if doing their best to downplay the sensational and possibly panic-causing information they were supplying, straight-faced and soberly, to their public. These were the station's regular newscasters, reputable and popular, with everything to lose by creating a hoax and nothing but brief notoriety to gain.

That, however, is what we were told when the eleven-o'clock news came around: The prime-time news crew had perpetrated an irresponsible and inexcusable hoax, and had therefore been dismissed from their jobs. No UFOs had landed; no aliens were in custody, dead or alive; the United States Air Force had positively *not* engaged or intercepted any craft whatsoever in the skies above Michigan; and that, officially and absolutely, was that.

It was difficult to know what to make of this incident. At one extreme, it could have been just an overblown cosmic-hippie-cocaine dream, an instance of too much weirdness for too long crashing through into the perceived reality continuum. On the other hand, we had the videotape.

Yes, even in 1974. It so happened that the documentary filmmaker Alan Yentob was along with us on the trip, making the film that would become *Cracked Actor*, and he had his VCR hooked up to the television set in our hotel room when the afternoon news flash first caught our attention. So we'd taped the whole six-o'clock and eleven-o'clock news shows. There was no denying that the broadcasts had happened.

The broadcasts at *least*. In David's opinion, and mine too, what had just occurred was indeed a warp in the usual business of business-as-usual.

David believed very strongly that aliens were active above our planet, and so did (do) I. That's why we were so alert in the limo on the way to Minneapolis, watching intently for signs of further UFO activity in the bright night sky. It was mostly David who had his eye pressed to the telescope (purchased by Corinne Schwab, his personal assistant, during a lightning shopping spree in Detroit). He'd talked about the six-o'clock newscast during his show at Cobo Arena in Detroit, and he believed that the energy thus created might well have communicated itself to the beings monitoring from above us human reaction to their fallen (slain/captured/atomized?) fellows.

I don't know quite what David expected, because by now he'd moved beyond his manic-monologue mode into his silent, non-communication state, but I suspect he wouldn't have been surprised at all if the aliens had come right down to the limo and tractor-beamed him up for an exchange of ideas. He was feeling pretty much like the center of things here on Earth at the time, after all, and it probably seemed obvious to him that *some* right-thinking human should take on the job of Man's ambassador...

No aliens heeded the call, though, and after a while he disappeared into his coke, sheltered by Corinne, and I lost interest. I left the tour, and them, the next day.

There was a lot of that kind of stuff in those days. Some interesting, even mind-blowing things happened, events and signs and phenomena worthy of the deepest thought and most intensive investigation. But the necessary attention span wasn't there. The brain that was so good at amalgamating other people's ideas into stylish new forms – songs, shows, images – wasn't suited to serious study, and so, I suspect, David's serial preoccupations didn't gain him much insight or even real knowledge. He could send Corinne out for all the UFO books in print, and imagine himself to be tuned right in to the alien thing, but then he wouldn't read the books. He could get obsessed with Howard Hughes, but the nature of his obsession wasn't that of a serious student. It was that of a character vampire; he wanted to *be* Howard Hughes, or at least to be seen as a figure resembling his image of Howard Hughes. This wasn't surprising. Living off other people's energy was David's thing; he's been hopping from one to another, doing very nicely, all his life.

Oh yeah, one more thing: If the idea of a Hughes-like figure in the back of a limousine, riding through outland America with his mind on alien affairs, reminds you rather strongly of the man who fell to earth in *The Man Who Fell to Earth*, that's not surprising either. Nicolas Roeg's first vision of David on film was through Alan Yentob's *Cracked Actor* documentary, featuring plenty of back-of-the-limo footage from the *Diamond Dogs* days. So in several significant ways, David was playing himself in *The Man Who Fell*. So was Tony Masia, driving the limo and providing personal care and protection in the movie, the documentary, and life. It was even the same limo.

And speaking of aliens ...

Michael Jackson comes up at this point in the story because, like Oz and the Wizard, he was at the end of the yellow brick road when the *Diamond Dogs* show pulled into the western terminus of its tour, the City of the Angels.

Really, though, Michael's no alien. He had a strange childhood and adolescence, but to my mind he's turned out rather well. His heart's certainly in the right place – he's into love and brotherhood – and that's more than you can say for most people, child stars or not.

Six nights at the Los Angeles Universal Ampitheater. Six nights in the eyes of the stars. They all came out; David's show was *the* place to be and be seen. Our week was very bright and gay and wonderful, and David was showered with kudos, compliments, solicitations, and invitations.

One invitation he accepted with interest was to the Jackson family home. Like many British rockers, David had a firm grounding in the blues and the Stax/Volt soul school of black American music, but he didn't know his way around the Tamla-Motown neck of the woods from which the Jacksons had emerged; here, on a platter, was an opportunity to see into that world at close range.

He was also very flattered, I think. White British musicians have always believed that black American musicians far outrank them in soul, authenticity, and general worthiness, and David is no exception in that regard. So while many another summons to the soirées of Hollywood's finest competed for space in his trashcan, David accepted the invitation to the Jacksons' gratefully if somewhat nervously.

He needn't have worried. The senior Jacksons were warm and welcoming, very down-to-earth, and everybody treated him with great kindness and interest. Their house, rambling and modern, with a big yard and a pool, was somewhere up in the hills. It had great style – or rather, nonstyle. There was plenty of tufted carpeting throughout, and many gold records and such, but otherwise it was just your typical all-American mishmash; a house for a family to live in without thinking too much about it, as opposed to a European-style personal aesthetic statement or a show-biz-style declaration of financial success. It felt very natural to be bustling around, helping Mrs Jackson carry trays of snacks out to the menfolk.

I don't know what David learned or passed along during his visits (we were invited back, and we accepted) because I spent most of my time with Michael. He was fourteen or so then – or at least he *seemed* fourteen or so; he was probably older – and I related to him strongly as a mother. He was a charming, open boy, but not very happy with his lot, and that's what we talked about: how difficult it was for him to shop and date and have friends the way normal teenagers did. From what he said, I gathered that he saw the problem as a result of family policy rather than the forces inherent in his situation.

'Well, Michael,' I told him, 'it's a little like that for David too, you know. If he goes out in public, he gets gawked at all the time, and he could get mobbed and really hurt. It's probably the same for you, and your family is probably just trying to protect you. But you know, there are ways around those kind of problems. You shouldn't have to miss out on everything just because you're a star. I mean, this is Los Angeles. It's not as if you're the only kid in show business here. Maybe you could talk to your dad and come up with some creative ideas.'

That, when you consider what's been said about Joseph Jackson since those days, has to qualify as one of my more inappropriate suggestions. I should have perceived more than I did about the senior Jackson's parenting style from the depth of Michael's dismay and also, come to think of it, from the fact that at no time during our visits were any of the Jackson girls visible. I can't comment one way or the other on LaToya's stories of abuse by her father because all I know about them is the headlines they spurred, but I do find it odd that in that bustling household, when we were there the girls were invisible. At the time I didn't even know the Jacksons *had* daughters.

Another guest at the house during one of our visits was Diana Ross, who seemed quite friendly and unaffected, and whom Michael appeared to like a great deal. The boy really did cleave to older women.

I don't know about that lady. Her public persona is so outrageous – a compulsive self-promotional personality disorder bigger than all of them – but with Michael she seemed quite sweet. And she was wonderful with her own little girls.

But just imagine the warp in this boy brought up by Joseph Jackson, a star since he was a nipper, forbidden to date, who seeks teenage best-friendship with Diana Ross (and, a little later, Elizabeth Taylor). It really is a wonder, and a great achievement on his part, that Michael has grown into such a gentle soul. I think very fondly of him.

# $S$KIN $P$OUNDERS AND $H$EAD $B$ANGERS

$T$he current location of my story being Los Angeles, why don't I tarry there awhile and tell you some tales?

For a start, thinking about LA always gets me thinking about drummers – Mickey Finn of T. Rex, for a start, about whom I've already told you – and for me, thinking about drummers is a fascinating business.

There's just something about them. Well, actually, there are a couple of things. The first is how attractive I seem to find them. The second is how they seem to die rather frequently.

You can approach the latter subject on several levels, including the one chosen by the semi-retarded cosmic/metal rockers of Rob Reiner's brilliant *This Is Spinal Tap*: Drummers, they explain, just spontaneously combust more than most people (although most people spontaneously combust a lot more than we realize; there's a cover-up). But the question has forced itself into my life so personally that I have trouble addressing it in theory.

If forced, I'd have to guess that drummers die younger than singers or guitar players because they tend to live faster. Rock-and-roll drummers have a macho thing – they've chosen a very physical, driven form of self-expression – and perhaps they feel somehow *obliged* to drink, drug, and otherwise abuse themselves more spectacularly than their fellows. And of course, when you're in rock and roll, with its rather high median consumption levels for life-threatening substances, that's dangerous. Accidents happen. Down go the half-dozen 'ludes on top of the fifth of Jack Daniel's and the four or five speedballs; up comes the vomit, but not all the way; out the door on the gurney goes another dear departed skin pounder.

Gracious, what a tasteless subject. Let's raise the tone a touch, and lest we get carried away here, let's be sure to mention some rock-and-roll drummers who do not fit that profile: Phil Collins, for example, a person approximately as self-destructive as a (rather small) battle tank. And Charlie Watts, pottering about his garden and pruning his roses, grinning peacefully as some private little joke.

*My* drummers, though, the boys *I've* loved – well, a simple chronicle will suffice. There was Mickey Finn. Then, though, there was Billy Murcia, the drummer of the New York Dolls, a gorgeous guy with the cutest jet-black corkscrew curls – they looked almost like shiny plastic – who was my lover in New York for six weeks before he went on tour to London and died of an overdose. There was Robbie McIntosh, the drummer of the Average White Band, who was courting me in Los Angeles – we didn't sleep together, but I think we were going to – whom I left after three weeks to go back to New York for something or other; while I was gone, heroin killed him.

After Robbie died I felt a layer of discomfort over and above the basic sadness. The similarities between what happened with him and what happened with Billy got me feeling that maybe, besides the powerful mutual attraction between me and the boys behind the drum kits, there was something sinister going on, some weird kind of jinx or hoodoo or bad black magic. Maybe, in short, I was death to drummers.

The late John Bonham of Led Zeppelin was another man I loved and lost. He and I weren't physically intimate together, but in a way the bond between us was more valuable than what you can make with sex. He was a lovely, charming, strong, gentle, manly man, and I regretted his passing very much.

I really hated it when Keith Moon died too, but I didn't regret it so deeply. Moon was an incredible drummer and a divinely inspired clown – there never was nor will be a funnier man – but with him, you knew the score from the start. The only question was when the hands on the time bomb inside him were going to hit high noon.

Now that I've mentioned Keith Moon and Led Zeppelin, two of the most prolific progenitors of fast-lane legend and scurrilous anecdote in British rock history, I'd be seriously remiss if I didn't take the obvious cue. And I've got Moon and Zep stories that run together all in one day.

It's Hollywood, 1979, and I'm riding a limo down Sunset Strip in the company of Keith, heading for the Continental Riot (Hyatt) House. Naturally, the Moon is just as drunk and as stoned as it's possible for a human being to be. I'm assuming that he's been doing his usual combination of constant alcohol and periodic speedballs; he has that rational but totally, *totally* gone-from-the-here-and-now quality about him.

The limo pulls into the driveway, and the driver gets out and opens the door, and we proceed into the lounge; and Keith, figuring from the sequence of events so far that he's now at a gig, negotiates his way in wonderful weavings, boundings, and lurches to the stage.

It isn't his gig, though – there's a whole band already up there, with its own drummer and everything – but obviously this has happened before, and everyone knows what to do. The drummer simply vacates his position, getting up and going off to the bar without so much as a shrug, and Moon takes over. He plays, of course, fabulously; it's his usual astonishing exhibition of utter mania under unimaginable discipline.

I sit there and watch him, thinking, *Dear God, let me please remember this moment forever*. Keith, you see, is one of my great heroes, a man so brilliantly, wickedly funny that calling him the John Cleese of rock and roll seems inadequate, and so maniacally alcoholic that an hour with him can often feel like a week in an exploding Chinese fireworks factory. And now, all of a sudden he decides he's done enough drumming. He jumps up, leaves the stage, grabs me, runs me outside, whistles up the limo, and orders an immediate return to our hotel, the Beverly Hilton.

'No, no, Keith,' I demand. 'Wait a minute. We're supposed to go meet Richard Cole and Peter Grant and the Zep guys at the Rainbow, remember? That's where we should go.'

'Nah, nah! Don't wanna do that! C'mon! Let's go back to the Beverly Hilton and fuck!'

'No, Keith, really ... '

He's not listening. He starts into a long, passionate, disjointed ramble about how much he loves me from the depths of his soul, which is very funny, but I have to end it somewhere. This is as clear a case for my 'Never fuck 'em if they're too stoned to remember it' rule as any I can recall.

'You're being ridiculous, Keith. You don't even know me, for God's sake.'

'Yes I do,' he says. 'I've seen you around. I've seen you everywhere. I've seen you all over the world.'

This is true, of course, but irrelevant, as is the stuff he goes on saying until I simply take the necessary action and tell the driver, in no uncertain terms, to take us to the Rainbow, where the Zep are partying, as planned. Which he does.

Keith is still raving when we get there, so I tell the driver to keep him in the limo at all costs, and I slip away to get help. I've assumed my tour-manager role; I'm considering the greater good of everyone, and I'm thinking it wouldn't be too swell for Moon to come on the Zep's scene right at this moment. He's far too far gone to be fun, even for Jimmy Page and the boys (which is saying quite a lot).

Richard Cole is the man I need. He's been 'director of security' for the Zep for many moons (no pun intended) and now he's risen to the rank of tour manager, and he's a very helpful man. This is true in 1979, while he's still a rabid consumer of intoxicants, and it'll be just as true in 1992, when he'll be clean and sober out there on the road, helping recovering rockers such as dear old Ozzy Osbourne stay *away* from booze and drugs. I'm proud of him.

He looks a lot like Pete Townshend when he's wearing a beard, as he often is, but he's a fair bit more physically substantial than Pete; the figure he cuts, in fact, suggests a very intelligent Hell's Angel. I've always been a sucker for the biker type, and I find him just as attractive as have legions of Zep groupies over the years (When you're security director for a big British rock band, your sexual magnetism does get rather a lot of opportunities to establish its own status; your band's more serious young female fans do require screening, selection, and user testing before being passed along, if indeed you personally judge them worthy of such an honor, to the lads themselves.)

Richard appears before me after a brief search of the Rainbow, and I describe my dilemma. 'I don't know, Richard, I'm afraid

Moon's really far out, and he'll really misbehave if he comes in here.'

Richard gives me a look, then smiles. 'Angie, this is Keith Moon you're talking about. He's not David Bowie. He doesn't have to *behave!*'

I take umbrage at that – David doesn't behave at all, he's a raving paranoid coke freak! – but I see Richard's point, accepting that Moon is indeed in a class by himself and long ago earned a license for mayhem miles broader than anyone else's. So I calm down and decide to go with it: What will be will be. That which is destined to be broken will get broken, those who are fated to be puked on will get puked on.

Richard comes out to the limo with me, ready to embrace the hurricane, and the driver hops out and opens the door. Instead of a raging cyclone, however, we're greeted by the sight of the Moon at rest, passed out and gone, peaceful as a sunset on the ocean.

'Well,' says Richard, 'that worked, didn't it? Smooth move, Angie.'

'I guess so. Hmm. We'd better get him back to the Beverly Hilton now, hadn't we? Can you take him, Richard?'

He shakes his head regretfully but firmly. 'Sorry, luv. I can't do that, not under any circumstances. I've got hot babes going on in there, see.'

Oh, well. One tries one's best. Accepting the call of duty, I get in the limo, escort Moon back to the Beverly Hilton, negotiate him upstairs, and put him to bed.

And that, sorry to say, is the anticlimatic end of that. Rock-and-roll drunks can be a lot of fun, but sooner or later they fold up and pass out, even the semi-divine ones.

This is going to be the last time I see Keith, by the way. He'll die of too much of something a few months later, to nobody's great surprise. Certainly not mine. I always thought he was one of those characters never built for the long haul, and found it ironic that it was his band brother Roger Daltrey, a born survivor, who sang the line by which Moon lived: *I hope I die before I get old.*

Exit the Moon stage left; enter Led Zeppelin stage right, the scene the pool area at the Beverly Hilton a little later in the day, with the sun just beginning to lose its mid-afternoon power.

I'm relaxing with Richard Cole and our friend Biffo, of grievous-bodily-harm and three-pint-mugs-off-the-dick fame, who is working Richard's former job as security director in the Zep organization (a role for which he would seem to be supremely qualified), when Robert Plant, the singer I don't know very well but have always thought of, mistakenly, as the blond bimbo of the band, comes over and sits down with us.

Robert is the very model of charm and affability, as he chats away happily about this and that, and I find him quite engaging. Mostly we talk about what's going on back in London – whence I've just arrived; he's been on a US tour, which means weeks without cricket and Sundays without the *News of the World* – and all in all we pass the time very pleasantly indeed. The encounter has a flavor not uncommon between me and the boys in British bands; it's as if I'm their aunt or their sister, or maybe someone from their home office, with whom family language can be used and home turf trod for a while in comfort amid the strain of foreign strangeness. We talk about who just got a new song up to the top of the charts, who made a fool of himself at Tramp's last week, and so on.

After a little while Biffo goes off, then comes back and asks if Robert wants to talk to any of the girls who are trying to get at him. Robert declines: 'No, no, I don't think so, not right now. I'm talking to Angie.'

Quizzical looks pass between Biffo and Richard Cole, but they let it go. They can't however, ignore the uncharacteristic nature of Robert's next move.

'Well, come on, Richard,' Robert says. 'What are you doing just sitting there? Get the waitress, eh!'

Richard looks at him, stunned. 'Pardon? Did I hear you correctly? Am I to understand that you mean to actually *buy a drink*?'

Robert pretends he doesn't catch the drift – it's an article of faith in our circles that he, along with the Scottish Rod Stewart and my Yorkshire husband, is phenomenally tight with his money – and acting as if it's the most natural thing in the world, he forges ahead.

'Of *course* I'm going to buy drinks,' he says. '*Angie's* here. Get a waitress!'

This is done amid further protestations of astonishment from Richard and Biffo, and we all order tequila sunrises. One round leads to multiple others, as often happens with tequila drinks, and we begin to get pretty wrecked. Every so often Biffo or Richard launches a reprise of the Robert-as-tightwad theme – 'Do you realize how many times the man's put his hand in his pocket? I thought he kept the bloody thing sewn shut!' or 'Robert's poorly. He's not at all himself. We need a psychiatrist' – but Robert doesn't seem to mind. He appears to be having a wonderful time.

After a couple of hours Richard bestirs himself. 'Bloody 'ell, we're drunk,' he says. 'We'd better go upstairs and sober up a bit.'

An admirable idea, the rest of us agree, and off we go to Richard's suite, where our host pulls out his stash and chops up the lines. We take turns sobering up a little.

It strikes me at this point, with some force, that these guys are fun. They're so loose, so unlike David. If this were David and his little crew, nobody would be clowning around or sharing drugs: David would be off in the bathroom with his secret little vials while the others sat around waiting for orders, trying to figure out how to please the Great One. Fun would be the *last* thing on anyone's mind.

That's sad, I'm thinking, but I don't get the opportunity to dwell on it. My attention gets taken by another knock at the door.

Richard looks at me and starts laughing. 'What do you want to bet some bastard smelled some free charlie in here and came running?' he says. 'Which one d'you think it is?'

I go to the door, and Richard's right. It's Jimmy Page, guitar god, groupie magnet, and famous fan of the Antichrist, grinning from ear to cute little ear. I let him in.

Biffo takes one look and says, 'Oh, fuck me, Hoover Nose is here, hide the grams!' But before anything can get started, there's another knock at the door.

Interpreting this second knock as potential chaos, and sobered up to the point of pleasantly alert, not yet manic efficiency, I shift immediately into my crisis manager/tour director mode and begin handling things. I open the door just a crack and peer out, assuming the expression of slightly dangerous disinterest so familiar to anyone who has ever knocked on a rock star's door and had some bitch like me answer.

It's a girl, looking for Jimmy: the usual very young, very gorgeous stoned-out suburbanite, doubtless just as wanton and wet as can be this very minute.

I accept her inquiry, tell her to wait a minute, close the door òn her, and turn to Richard Cole. 'Richard! Lock this door. Take all the knocks at the other door, okay?'

Shifting into security mode himself, Richard comprehends immediately. We'll keep the door into the living room of the suite closed, cutting off any view of our action from outside, and use the door down the hallway of the suite, near the bathroom, as a blind checkpoint.

I tell the chick to go down to the other door, and Richard goes down there, talks to her a moment, and then lets her in. I watch as he ushers her into the bathroom and closes the door on her. I notice at this point that there's a pair of handcuffs hanging half out of the back pocket of his jeans.

He turns around and comes back into the living room. 'Jimmy, there's someone here to see you.'

Jimmy, who has his face down on the table, living up to Biffo's characterization of his suction power, is reluctant to be disturbed. 'What do you mean, "There's someone here to see you"? Who the fuck is here to see me?'

Richard is not to be deterred. 'C'mon,' he says, taking Jimmy by the arm and leading him down the hall to the bathroom. As they go I see him reach behind and whip out the handcuffs. Whatever this is going to be, I'm thinking, it looks like it won't be dull.

As soon as he gets Jimmy through the bathroom door he snaps one cuff around the guitar god's left wrist – a practiced gesture, deft and easy – and, before anyone has a chance to resist, whips the other cuff around the back of the toilet and snaps it onto the right wrist of the somewhat startled visitor. Jimmy and the girl are now manacled firmly together, and unless they somehow rip the toilet out of the wall, they're not going anywhere until Richard decides to let them. Which he's not about to do. He gives them a little wave, closes the bathroom door, and returns, whistling nonchalantly, to the vacuum party in the living room.

'Well now, that's good,' he says. 'We'll get some peace and quiet now that Hoover Nose is locked up for the afternoon. I tell you, you've got to be firm with these buggers. You've got to know how to *handle* them.'

Biffo is in stitches at this point, and I'm pretty amused myself – the good, clean, twisted balls-out fun these Zep boys are having is a very refreshing change from the paranoid, control-freak chill of David's road scene – and whatever happens next, it's obvious that peace and quiet aren't on the bill.

As if to emphasize that point, there comes yet another knock at the door, and off goes Richard to answer. It's Robert Plant, which reminds us that he hasn't been with us since we left the pool area, which in turn reminds us that we really are quite drunk.

'Where'd you all go?' Robert is saying in a breathless slur. 'Where's the girls? Where's Angie? I was right there at the pool and, like, you'd all just *gone*!'

'Sorry about that, Robert,' says Richard soothingly, thinking on his feet. 'We couldn't be sure you'd really pay for those drinks if we told you we were leaving, so we didn't. Come on, we're all in here.'

They both come into the living room, where Robert sees me and lights up. '*There* you are, Angie! I was looking for you all over!'

He moves to sit down with us, but Richard intercepts him. 'Robert, guess what's in the bathroom.'

'Wot?' says Robert confusedly, then comprehends the question. 'Well, what?'

'Come here,' says Richard, 'I'll show you.' And he takes him over to a large walk-in closet off the dining room and, despite poor Robert's continuing confusion – 'Wait a minute, this doesn't look like a bathroom' – ushers him gently inside and closes the door behind him. Then he comes and sits back down with us. 'Right. Now, where were we?'

'Oh, come on, Richard,' I say – I've begun to think this is all pretty silly – 'let Robert out of the closet, and go get Jimmy from the bathroom.'

Richard gives me an interesting look, but I never find out what it means, because here comes another knock on the door, and off he goes again.

Now it's Peter Grant, the Zep's manager, Richard's and Biffo's boss, another lovely man: a wonderful large-spirited lunatic, big, with receding hairline but hair long enough to be tied back into a ponytail; his pierced ears on this day feature a snake earring five or six inches long, studded with garnets and emeralds.

I have to tell you the Peter Grant story, just so you'll know why I love this man. There are a thousand stories, but this one gets to me the most. Some people say it never really happened, but Leee Black Childers, who told me the following version, swears it's true.

The boys in the band had been misbehaving a little in some deluxe hotel, and when Peter showed up at the front desk at checkout time to settle the bill, the reckoning really came. As well as the usual items on the bill, there was an additional $10,000 charge for renovation of one completely destroyed suite.

The clerk was very apologetic. 'Gee, Mr Grant, I'm sorry, but we really do have to add the damages to the bill.'

Peter didn't even bat an eye. 'That's all right, son, that's all right. Don't worry about it.' And he took a roll out of his briefcase and started peeling off hundred-dollar bills.

The clerk watched him, his eyes getting bigger and bigger. 'Thank you, Mr Grant,' he said. 'I'm glad you understand.... And really, Mr Grant, I have to tell you, it's been just wonderful, having you guys at the hotel. I'm the biggest Led Zeppelin fan. They're just incredible.'

He took the money, and Peter got ready to leave – and that would have been that if the kid hadn't added a final, wistful comment.

'It must be wonderful to be one of you guys, smashing up hotel rooms. Sometimes I get so mad and frustrated here, I want to go destroy one of these rooms myself.'

Peter looked at him. 'Really?' he said. Then he opened his briefcase back up, pulled his roll back out, peeled off another $10,000, and handed it to the kid. 'There,' he said. 'Go right ahead.'

Isn't that beautiful?

But back to the Beverly Hilton, where the lead singer of the world's first and greatest heavy metal band is still shut in the closet, the lead guitarist is still manacled to the toilet with his groupie, and Peter Grant has made himself comfortable.

'Have you seen Jimmy?' he asks. 'And where's Robert? We're supposed to go to dinner with Keith Moon, you know. He's gonna be here any minute. We've got to get it going here.'

Richard gives a little shrug, walks over to the closet, and lets Robert out. Robert's still a mite confused. 'I couldn't find the bathroom anywhere down that hallway,' he mumbles.

'That's all right, Robert,' I tell him. 'There's been a mistake, but it's okay now. Here, I've got something really funny to show you. You'll like this.'

I take him down the hallway to the real bathroom and open the door, and there's Jimmy sitting forlornly on one side of the toilet, the girl likewise on the other. 'I'm really over this, you know,' Jimmy's saying. 'I... Oh, hi, Robert. Hi, Peter. Richard, would you, er... ?'

Richard unlocks the cuffs once we've all had a chance to linger on the spectacle before us, and everybody saunters nonchalantly back into the living room.

Jimmy follows us quietly and calmly, as if he'd been washing his hands or taking a telephone call or doing something else entirely unremarkable. And I guess that is indeed the case. In the Led Zeppelin life-style, getting handcuffed for half an hour to a groupie in a toilet *is* pretty routine.

'Right, then,' he says. 'Where are we going to dinner?'


And speaking of dinner, I'm reminded of dear John 'Bonzo' Bonham, the Zep's great, unfortunately late, drummer. Bonzo, a gentle giant and gentleman lunatic, won my heart forever less than three years before he died his alcoholic death. He was killed by the reaction of Antabuse to large quantities of the alcohol it was supposed to prevent him from drinking – surely one of the most wretched possible ways to go.

I first met him during the 1977 Montreux Jazz Festival, when David and I were living in Switzerland (forgive me, for scrambling my chronology). The Bonzo story I'm about to tell took place almost two years after the point we've reached in the story of David and me, and two years before the high jinks at the Beverly Hilton.

I must confess that when Bonzo invited me to hang out with him at the recording studio where he was working in Montreux, I had my doubts. Like most people with more than a passing knowledge of rock and roll, I'd heard the mud-shark-meets-groupie, Jimmy-meets-Lucifer stories and therefore had an image of the Zep inclined quite sharply toward the distasteful and possibly even dangerous end of the spectrum: sexism, sadism, and satanism seemed the themes of the Led Zep life-style. Then too, David just *hated* them.

He had some semi-sensible reasons. Like more than a few rock critics and other cultural arbiters of the early seventies, he regarded the Zep as offensive throwbacks to pop's primitive past; his raised-in-the-sixties consciousness was much offended by their blues base and big, bad, balls-out bump-and-grind stage show. Like their other critics, though, he found them unusually fascinating in an awful way.

Another of his problems was a little closer to home. When Marc Bolan, his peer and rival, wanted to break out of the trippy-troubadour mold into that of the rock-and-sex god (which he managed to do with T. Rex and 'Bang a Gong' before David achieved a similar transformation via Ziggy Stardust), he went to none other than Jimmy Page for electric guitar instruction. David's ego bristled at that, and ever since he'd thought of Jimmy as a threat.

So much for the real world. Now for David's creative embellishments, which were sad but colorful. Basically, he thought Jimmy was in league with Lucifer, and was out to get him. When some nasty satanic business happened in Hollywood, for instance, about which more (much more) later, he was convinced that the human arch-agent behind it all was none other than Jimmy.

I don't think that was the case. I think that at the bottom David's real problem with Led Zeppelin was that the group always sold more records – millions and millions more – than he did. All his superheated Zepophobia was just the steam and smoke and shrapnel from a good old-fashioned battle of the bands.

Still, that was *some* pyrotechnic action, so I did wonder if there might not be some real fire behind it. And there was another intriguing angle to the question of whether or not to hang out with Bonzo. It was obviously something of which David would disapprove strongly, perhaps even find very threatening.

That's what settled it. I decided to accept the invitation.

Bonzo was a delight. He drank a lot and did a lot of drugs, but since he was working, absorbed in his music in the studio, he wasn't particularly far out on the chemical edge while I was with him. And as far as things satanic went, the Antichrist didn't even hint at putting in an appearance.

Bonzo was a funny man, sly and mischievous and quick-witted – like Keith Moon in that respect, although not nearly as manic (nobody on the *planet* was as manic as the Moon) – and I must say I really fancied him. I liked him more than I lusted for him, though, and I was having such fun being with him on a musical and professional level that I didn't want to muddy it up with sex. Besides, he was treating me like his favorite sister; moreover, he already had about four dozen other women hot on his trail – fans, groupies, debutantes, whoever. And anyway, I thought it wise to stop short, in my game of sexual one-upsmanship with David, of sleeping with a Zep. I didn't like to think about what David might do, or for that matter how he might feel, if I were to unite sexually with his own personal Lower Power.

So I hung out and listened to all that wonderful music and enjoyed dear Bonzo. It was one of those warm interludes in life, very precious, like an impromptu vacation in a place you love and will never see again.

To shift from the almost sublime to the not far short of ridiculous, though, I must add another element to this paean to dear dead Bonzo, namely, the Walls pork sausages. This is where we came in: dinner, or rather, breakfast.

It began when Gully, Bonzo's very Welsh and wonderful roadie, took me aside at the studio.

'Angie,' he said urgently, 'I've got this problem you might help me with.'

'What's that, Gully?'

'Well, we're staying at the Montreux Palace, and – well, you know, Bonzo's got to have his breakfast . . . '

It seemed to me, from the way he was looking at me, that some sort of penny should be dropping at this point. But it wasn't; I had no idea what he was talking about.

'What do you mean, Gully? This is Switzerland! They have the best food in the world here, you're staying at a five-star hotel, Bonzo can have whatever his heart desires.'

'No, no, no, dear, you don't understand. He likes his breakfast, see. He likes his *sausages*.'

Now the penny dropped. Gully was talking about English pork sausages – bangers – those gastronomic nuclear meltdowns, scorned and reviled by gourmands – and not just gourmands – the world over, without which the English national character would simply fall to pieces. A true banger, you see (and when you're talking purism in this league, you always end up at the classic English pork sausage of all time, the item produced – manufactured? assembled? – by the Walls food company), is what foreigners, especially Americans, always assume fish and chips or steak-and-kidney pie to be: the One True Food of the original English-Speaking Peoples. First fried up by King Arthur and Lancelot before they fell out over that woman, bangers caused the Norman invasion in 1066, fueled the Imperial exodus, precipitated both world wars, and are what gives the royal family their peculiarly depressive cast; being German originally, they refuse to eat the One True Food of their subjects and therefore exist in a state of chronic disharmony with their environment, suffering accordingly.

The Krauts, incidentally, mock English bangers with particular vehemence, perhaps because they invest such extraordinary energy in holding up their own obsessively varied range of intestine-entubed pig-offal products as the standard by which such things should forever be measured, everywhere – or else. This is interesting at the level of national character – the Germans bellowing their sausagely virtue from the mountaintops, the English keeping their banger love private and guarded – and makes me wonder whose sausages really *are* the best. It wasn't the lads in *Feldgrau* camped out in Trafalgar Square in 1945, barbecuing their bratwurst in empty ammo cans, now was it? It was the Tommies in the Unter den Linden, frying up their bangers!

Whoops. 'Scuse me. Sometimes my cultural-historical bias acts up a bit. The voice of my father, the World War II colonel, comes through, as does my own undying love for the British, despite their 'class system.' But you can see, can't you, how it was that Gully had a real problem on his hands? How just about the only food a person *couldn't* order in a five-star Swiss hotel would be a Walls pork sausage, browned and sizzling in its own awesomely plentiful emanations?

'I see what you mean, Gully,' I said. 'How can I help? I can cook Bonzo his breakfast at the house anytime, if you like. I'd be glad to, really. We could get the sausages flown in, I'm sure.'

'No, no, that's not the problem,' he replied. 'I've already got the sausages. I've got forty pounds of them in the hotel room cooler. Bonzo doesn't go anywhere without his sausages, see. And I'm okay cooking them myself, too. I've got a little barbecue set up on the balcony of the suite, and I do a fry-up there every morning.'

I let that image sink in for a delirious moment or two, dwelling on the wonder of a world in which a full-blown rock megastar could and would have sausages hauled around the world in bulk for him, and also marveling that some Montreux SWAT team hadn't responded in force to a gastronomic crime as outrageous as that featured each morning on Gully's balcony.... Then I returned, still somewhat perplexed, to the task at hand. 'So what *is* the problem, Gully?'

'Well, I'm frightened, Angie. The sausages won't keep in the cooler in the room, so I need to put them in a freezer. If I put them in the freezer at the hotel, though, some bastard is bound to try them and like them. Then they'll scarf them all up, and Bonzo won't have his bangers, and there'll be hell to pay. He'll go off like he does.'

It was a great privilege to help forestall such an evil. I granted Gully space for forty pounds of Walls pork sausages in my freezer, gave him spare keys, and told him he could come and go as he pleased.

Which he did. Bonzo got his bangers every morning, and didn't go off.

# 13

# THE DEVIL COMES TO HOLLYWOOD

*B*ack to the central, now sorry saga of David and me, and a very major development on that front: a new true love. Kyrk was his name – just Kyrk, no surname.

He was Todd Rundgren's hair and makeup artist, among other things, and that's how I met him; Todd's girlfriend, Bebe Buell, put us together at Max's Kansas City in the spring of 1974, just after David had established residence in New York.

It was Leee Black Childers who really introduced us, though. Drifting past as a companion and I laughed and parried, getting to know each other at the bar, Leee said, 'Before you get too excited about that girl, Angie, you'd better feel between her legs.'

I looked up, a little dazed from all the fun. '*What* did you say?'

By then Leee was already gone, so I looked inquiringly at the lovely young thing I'd been romancing. And she really *was* lovely: shoulder-length ash-blond hair, turquoise eyes under high arched brows, a fine nose, full lips, a sweetheart chin, perfect makeup, tight black Glitter-and-leather rock-and-roll clothes; in short, luscious.

She spoke. 'I think that, ah, what he was trying to tell you is that I'm a boy.'

I *almost* couldn't believe it, even after I'd slipped my hand down to his package and checked for myself. He was just so utterly lovely: the only man I'd ever met, in fact, who was as purely pretty as David. And like David, he was as strong and athletic as he was lovely; my initial impression of a slight, delicate physique was surprisingly far from the reality of his supple, well-muscled body. David's graceful strength came from dancing the boards of English stages; Kyrk's came from dancing the surf of his native Florida.

There, however, the similarity ended. When Kyrk fell in love with me, he looked on it as a commitment. He wanted to be monogamous, and to make me happy, and to support me in my career. He paid attention to me and took me seriously and let me have as much power and space in the relationship as he had. And he was a strong, subtle, powerful, sensitive, brilliant lover who really wanted me, in the best of ways.

Feeling his warmth turn toward me was like being carried out into the Mediterranean sun from a cold gray English sick room, and the chills and fevers of my love for David began to fade away beneath this new, sweeter, simpler spell. My feelings for David were still very strong, especially my loyalty to his art and my profound concern for his well-being, and from time to time he and I were even warm together, achieving brief moments of the kind of instinctive communication we once had every day, but more and more, the chill won out. David had become terribly hard to love.

I fell for Kyrk, then, and fell hard. Soon I realized that Kyrk was the big time; that this was real love.

He and I were together whenever our other commitments allowed, through 1974 and into 1975; that is, whenever he wasn't on the road with Todd or some other rocker in need of high-styling, and whenever I was in New York. Most of our time together was spent at the apartment I'd had Main Man rent for me on Twenty-first Street, near but far enough from David's house of chilly horrors on Seventeenth, and it was in that apartment that Kyrk's realistic support and counsel began to convince me that when the chips were really down concerning my career and indeed my life – my future – I might actually be better off without David and Main Man than with them.

'I mean, what are they really doing for you?' Kyrk asked. 'Is Tony helping you get work in the theater? Is David giving you the love and attention a man owes his wife? Does either of them really give a fuck about you, other than having you available when they need something done?'

The answers to those three questions, I had to admit, were no, no, and no. This was food for thought, and my thoughts were indeed nourished. The idea of bailing out from Starship Bowie – just walking away from the chill into warmth and freedom, and to hell with the so-called wealth and secondhand status of the pop star wife – became quite attractive, and I started to consider it seriously.

It was partly at Kyrk's prompting, and with his whole-hearted encouragement, that in the first months of 1975 I secured a booking on *The Mike Douglas Show*. This time I wasn't appearing just as a David Bowie shill or substitute (although I was doing that; his album *Young Americans* needed promoting) but, for the first time, as a performer in my own right. I was going to sing 'I've Got a Crush on You' to Mike, and use every ounce of craft I'd learned over the previous two years from my Hollywood voice coach, the wonderful Harriett Lee. Our sights had been set on the Broadway stage, so that song was perfect for my debut in a singing career before a national TV audience.

Kyrk came with me to Philadelphia for the taping, and of course he made me up and styled my hair exquisitely. He was proud of his work, and justifiably so, but on this occasion, in my opinion, his ego got a bit too involved. When the Douglas people wanted to add their own makeup work to balance me for the studio lighting, he objected huffily.

I saw their point and supported it, and he didn't like that, and I didn't like him not liking it, and soon we had ourselves a little tiff. I went ahead and sang my song (and did quite well, thank you), but that wasn't really the end of our fight. The whole silly subject came up again when we were back at our hotel. It was nothing, of course, but it created a tension between us, and the tension turned into something. And how.

The spark was a story in that day's *Philadelphia Enquirer*, a cute little paparazzo special that was to ruin the next few years of my life. Kyrk handed it to me in our room, and I felt my blood go from warm to boiling hot by the time I'd read the lead. My husband, it seemed, had been spotted on the Spanish Riviera in the company of our son, Zowie, and Mick Jagger's wife, Bianca.

I just exploded. 'That prick! That fucking slut! Mick writes "Angie" and tries to get in my pants, so Mr Fuck Anything That Moves If the Rash Isn't Acting Up Too Bad has to drag that sorry-faced, sulking little bore of a woman around in front of every bloodsucker with a Nikon in southern Europe, just so he can feel like a bigger fucking billy goat than Mr Lips! And my son has to *witness* this!'

I wanted to kill him – not just because he was fucking Bianca, but because he was doing it in front of Zowie. For all my exploits, I always tried to shield Zowie from the more decadent parts of our life. He was, after all, still a child.

Kyrk made a big mistake at this point. Or maybe he didn't; I was so angry that probably I'd have turned on him no matter how he'd acted. Whatever the case, he started in on a theme he'd aired before.

'You should leave him, Angie,' he said. 'This is just another example of why. He can't treat you like this. You deserve better. I...'

That's as far as he got.

'You *what*?' I shouted. 'How are *you* any different? All *you* care about is your fucking art and your fucking ego and your fucking self and...'

And so on. I was out of control, letting it rip, saying whatever I thought would do damage; just lashing out because I was hurt and angry, and he was there. I raved until I felt my grand exit coming on, and then I stormed out of the room, slammed the door, went down to the lobby, had the hotel call me a cab, and took it all the way out of Pennsylvania and back up the New Jersey Turnpike to Manhattan.

That was a grand exit indeed, and evidently it made quite an impression on Kyrk. He didn't call, write, send a telegram, or even have a dozen red roses delivered in the next few days. I didn't go out of my way to reach him either, and that's where things stood when my schedule called for me to go back to London.

That's where they still stood when I got a transatlantic phone call from Leee a week or so later. Kyrk was dead, he said. He'd been drinking with a couple of gay guys in their apartment, a fifth-floor walkup, and he'd fallen from the fire escape and been killed instantly.

Maybe he'd fallen, Leee said, maybe he'd been pushed. The word was that maybe those guys had wanted to fuck him and he wouldn't go along, and they'd gotten angry, and they were all drunk... or maybe it was just that they were all drunk... or maybe...

It didn't matter, did it? Either way, Kyrk was *dead, gone!* His beautiful head had been cracked and crushed – smashed open, all his warm, wonderful life exploded out of it – on the street of that wretched cesspool of a city.


I can't even begin to describe the black plague of despair, depression, and guilt that came into me.

I didn't recover; I denied. I drank my PMA-laced fruit juice in my lovely house with my lovely friends, and had a lovely time. And everything was just fine. My husband had seen my performance on *The Mike Douglas Show*, he told me, and had written a new song for me: 'Golden Years.' He sang it over the phone for me just the way, all those years before, he'd sung me 'The Prettiest Star.'

It had a similar effect. I bought it. Even if David was never actually there with me, I thought, we'd always be together, just as in the song. I had a very great need, you see, for things to feel all right.

I didn't take any action, then. I remained Mrs Bowie and stayed at my post.


Things were not just fine at all, though. They were, in fact, going to hell. Literally.

I found that out, once again, via a transatlantic telephone call. This time it was David on the other end, or at least the creature David had become, a friend-abusing, sense-mangling, money-bleeding, full-fledged Vampire of Velocity. Like coke addicts long before and after him, he'd learned to travel far and fast, to keep his mind spinning in tight circles even when standing perfectly still, to arrange an existence almost entirely devoid of daylight, to assume a worldview of utter paranoia (in his case, no great stretch), and to start slowly sucking the life out everybody close to him.

He was calling me from Los Angeles, only half a world away from Oakley Street, but from the way he sounded, he might just as well have been off in the emptiness of some awful cold black hole, out there in the timeless infinity far beyond the reach of warmth and earthly human feeling.

He said he was with the devil, or more specifically that he was *about* to be with the devil. He was in a house somewhere – he didn't know exactly where, except that it was in LA – and three people (a warlock and two witches) were holding him for some terrible Satan-related reason he kept trying, very incoherently, to explain. He wanted to get away, he said, but he didn't have any money, and he didn't know where he was, and anyway, the witches wouldn't *let* him leave. He was talking in slurred, hushed tones, and hardly making sense, and was crazed with fear; he sounded really spooky.

I'd heard David speaking from some pretty cold, strange places, both by telephone and in person, but this sounded different, worse than I'd heard before. I got scared, and insisted that he give me the number where he was, telling him he couldn't keep it a secret the way he liked to. It's a measure of how frightened he was that he gave it to me before he hung up the phone, or someone hung up for him.

Rattled, I called Los Angeles immediately, and much to my relief reached Michael Lippman, the new manager with whom David was rearranging his affairs.

I should relate to you the story of Michael's entrance on the scene and the sorry, sorry tale of David's ultimate disaffection with Tony Defries, but not in detail. It's entirely too tedious. Essentially, David tired of having no access to his money, particularly since he needed such large amounts of it so frequently, in cash, without a paper trail. For his part, Tony tired (or so I gather) of the way David resented him, refused his advice, and behaved in the standard out-of-control addict/alcoholic fashion, which is to say paranoid, compulsive, abusive, and irrational; Michael Lippman, who had finessed the Wonder Woman scam, saw an opportunity opening in David's career – yawning, actually, ready to accommodate an airship or ocean liner, at least – and took it. These simultaneous strands worked themselves gradually together until fully intertwined, at which point (sometime in January 1975) David sent a telegram from Los Angeles to Tony at the Main Man offices in New York, telling him his management services were no longer desired and instructing him to contact Michael for further details.

As I saw him, Michael was an intelligent, stable, decent, and ambitious fellow. He presided over an extraordinarily difficult period in David's career, to put it mildly, and he didn't last very long (with David that paranoid, who could have?), but I think he did well. He certainly treated *me* a lot better than Tony had – which isn't saying much, given that Tony the Nose handled me a little less graciously than Vlad the Impaler might have – and I'm sincere when I say I like him. He survived his experience with David, by the way, and these days he manages George Michael.

Tony did okay too, retaining the Main Man name and organization and, unlike David, experiencing no sign of anything remotely resembling insolvency or even financial inconvenience during the separation proceedings.

But back to Los Angeles, where we left David still detained by witches in an undisclosed location, and me on the phone with Michael Lippman, giving him the telephone number David had given me. Since Michael was both on good terms with David and in the same city, I told him, maybe he should call the number; maybe he could get a better fix on the situation than I could. He agreed, and I hung up and waited.

When he called me back, he too was worried. He hadn't liked the way David had sounded, he said, so he'd told him just to walk out into the street wherever he was, find a taxi, and go straight to the Lippmans' house in the Hollywood Hills. That way, Michael could pay the taxi off, and he and his wife could help chase the witches away if they followed. David had agreed to that.

Praying that David had taken Michael's advice, and determined to motivate him out the door if he hadn't, I called the witches' number. A woman answered, but I couldn't get any sense out of her – I couldn't even tell if she was speaking English, or any language I recognized – and I could hear people laughing crazily in the background. I listened to the gibberish coming at me across the Atlantic from that house in California, feeling a great sense of dread, and right then I decided to catch a plane. Duty, very plainly – unavoidably – had called.

I phoned the eminently sane Michael Lippman again, looking for a reality check. It wasn't good. He was disturbed. He thought I should get to California as quickly as I could.

I left that night. Looking down at the receding lights of Heathrow, I knew I was saying good-bye to civilization, or at least to a nice life in a sublimely special sector of a very sophisticated society, and heading into who knew what – hell on earth, or Hell on Earth? – in Hollywood.

It's not as if the Beast is any stranger in the Hollywood Hills. Wherever you have a concentration of exceptionally ambitious, utterly amoral egomaniacs locked in throat-slashingly ruthless competition with each other, which is as good a description of the Los Angeles movie 'community' as any I can think of, some genius is going to hit on the idea of a career boost from Satan. You want some mid-level toot-dipper at Paramount to read your script for *sure*? Call up the powerful patter of cloven hooves! You want your rival for that career-breaking new Disney feature out of the picture, into Betty Ford? Go for it – snuff a virgin!

Really. I'm not kidding. Hollywood is very likely the most active occult area on the planet, and it's been that way for decades. The black arts are established to the point of being ingrained, and in the mid-seventies they were thriving as never before or since. There were almost as many occult bookstores as health food joints.

I knew that, so it wasn't any great surprise when, transported intercontinentally to Michael and Nancy Lippman's house, I heard David's explanation of what went on between him and those witches (from whom he'd escaped just as Michael had advised, by walking out and hailing a cab).

Unlike David's usual stories of his adventures, this was not mild-mannered; this was heavy. The deal, he said, was that those people wanted his semen. They wanted to hold him and cast a spell over him – again, I'm not kidding – so that he could inseminate one of the witches in a ritual ceremony on All Saints' Eve, and thereby bring an offspring of Satan into the world.

Well, I thought. Fancy that. The things a few grams of cocaine can do to inspire people! David's tale had oodles of color, and even greater grandiosity, but like most coke fantasies it lacked any real spark, any true imagination; it was just puffed-up, superheated, secondhand bullshit. You watch *Rosemary's Baby*, then spend two days snorting three-inch lines every fifteen minutes in the company of some scumbag dealer and his coke whores, and – perhaps with encouragement from your company, though not necessarily – presto! now you're poor little protesting Mia Farrow and the big ol' power-procreatin' Beastman rolled into one, with all indicators pointing toward an exceptionally interesting outing for the Lance of Love. Even in his paranoid fantasies, David was leading with his dick.

I didn't know whether to laugh in his face or go cry in a corner. The idea that anyone would think of actually having to *force* David Bowie to exercise Lance was pretty funny under any circumstance, but on the other hand the spiritual degradation demonstrated by his story (true or false) was really sad. So I just straightened up and did my job. Angie would fix things, be the nurse and the cook and the voice of reason, make it all okay until next time. That was the way it went. Despite my unsuitability as a drugging companion, David found me very acceptable, even indispensable, when too much got to be too much and he started scaring himself.

My first task, I perceived, was to get some food into him, the idea being that food might slow him down enough to consider the even better idea of sleep. I had to buy and prepare the food myself, though, since, so David explained, Michael and Nancy would try to poison him if given the chance. Having communicated that essential item, he went off to the guest room to do some more toot. I went off to the supermarket.

When I came back, loaded with all his favorite delicacies, he was in a state of utter panic because I'd been gone so long. I calmed him down a little, then put a foot wrong.

'Babe, I think it might be a good idea if you stopped doing the cocaine for a little while. You know how it takes your appetite away, and you need to eat, so you might want to let up until you've eaten.'

Dumb mistake. 'Don't tell me what to do!' he yelled. '*Don't* you tell me what to *do*!' And he went into his room, slamming the door. Sniffing noises ensued.

As the afternoon wore on, he wouldn't come out of his room. Finally, after endless soothing talk from Michael and me, he opened the door. Very soon we wished he hadn't.

The problem was straight across the hallway, on the wall of a room Michael and Nancy were using as a home office: a photograph of David and me taken in Paris in happier times, with him in a white suit and me in a white dress.

David took one look at the photograph, and freaked right out. He stood there death-white, rigid and shaking, pointing at the picture with a look of total horror on his face. And it got worse; the shaking intensified very quickly, and I began to lose it. It occurred to me, in a wave of sudden fear, that David was plunging into a cocaine-induced epileptic seizure, which could kill him. People die in such states, literally shaking themselves to death, snapping their heads back and forth so hard that they break their necks.

It didn't get that far, though. With Michael, Nancy, and me in his face demanding to know what was going on, David was able to spit it out. In the photograph, he told us in his terror-stricken tremor, my arm circling his waist was *black*!

Well, so it was, or at least it was dark. And although that was no big deal to anyone else – it was a shadow, a quirk of exposure or printing, whatever, who cared? – to David it was the kiss of death. In *his* scheme of things, the fact that my arm around his waist was black meant that the witches were going to kill me as a way of getting to him. It signified, moreover, that their thrall had penetrated into his immediate environment. So back into his room he ran, and the door slammed shut again.

Creative solutions were called for now. If David couldn't save himself by making a transition to my rationale, then I had to adopt his. I had to jump into that nest of spooks and demons with him, and deal with them on his terms.

Fortunately I had the means of doing that. In my address book was the telephone number of Walli Elmlark, a very respectable white witch whom David and I had met in London while she was working with Robert Fripp on some weird ESP album project. Walli was great; she really knew her stuff, and she even looked the part – very pale and gothic, with good Gypsy-Slavic cheekbones – and to my great good fortune, she was home to answer my call. I explained the situation to her, and she gave me a prescription over the phone: the ritual scattering of household herbs, she said, together with certain readings from the Tibetan Book of the Dead (which David had kept handy since his Buddhist monk-wannabe days), should temporarily restore a relatively even keel.

The news that I had a plan from Walli was in itself comforting to David, and he began to calm down. He even agreed to eat – if, that is, I and only I touched his food. I went into the kitchen, prepared him a tray, and took it to his room.

I didn't notice it at first. David had to point it out to me. On a nice balmy Hollywood late afternoon, a storm was going on outside his window: rain, thunder, lightning, the works. Outside all the other windows in the house there was calm and sunshine.

I stood there looking at this thing, sort of numb, but then snapped out of it, resumed my Angie Fix-it role, and proposed reassuring points about the eccentric California climate and the deceptive topography of the Hollywood Hills.

I did a pretty good job, but all the same it took a long time to pacify David after this latest manifestation. He didn't get to sleep until quite late that evening. And before I myself went to sleep, I had to struggle for some time with the thought that my explanations weren't as convincing as I'd have liked them to be. That storm was weird. It cast a persistent, troubling shadow on the notion that cocaine paranoia was David's only enemy.

The next manifestation deepened my doubt. It suggested, in fact, that the Beast might really have come among us.


The household on Doheny Drive, where David, Zowie, his nanny Marion, and I settled, had a rhythm typical of its time. In the early seventies, when constant chemical mood alteration was the rule rather than the exception among the music business elite – virtually everyone was very stoned all the time, and at least half crazy half the time – there were rock-and-roll households around the world functioning very much like the courts of mad kings.

The arrangement was schizophrenic. The king (rock

star/breadwinner/drug addict) sat enthroned in his chambers, receiving vassals and emissaries and occasionally other royal personages (band members, roadie/groupie/drug dealers, other rock stars) and conducting the affairs of state (that is, scoring drugs and doing them). In other parts of the palace, meanwhile, beyond sight and sound of the Exalted One, the queen and her assistants concentrated on the little things: business, family, survival. That last was especially tricky, since the king was, after all, mad and often behaved irrationally, self-destructively, and dangerously. Therefore the queen and her people, including her children, learned that their best chance of survival lay in avoidance and evasion.

Thus you ended up with two separate households coexisting under one roof, and while that was usually very unpleasant emotionally, it wasn't impossible from a practical point of view. Often the king kept his court in an area the queen didn't need to enter in the regular course of her business; and it helped that while most drug addicts and the people who service them are nocturnal, most mothers, homemakers, and business people work by day.

Basically, that describes the rhythm of our household on Doheny Drive. David would rise sometime in the middle or late afternoon and spend the evening and night doing drugs. Occasionally he'd get involved in a little music or business, but his most compelling activity was receiving roadies of famous bands who would arrive with fat packages of best Peruvian flake in their hand-tooled leather shoulder bags and leave with fatter little rolls of his money, after which he'd chop and line and snort until dawn or later with his closest sycophants and whatever semi-famous show biz coke whores happened by. I instead would wake early in the morning, go about my own and David's business while His Highness was still passed out, and then try to stay out of his way as our timetables overlapped in the late afternoon and evening.

One rumor in particular about David's Doheny Drive life-style has circulated ever since those days, its most recent resuscitation in a profile/interview on David in a 1992 issue of the Hollywood monthly *Movieline*. The article poses the question: Did David *really* take to preserving his bodily fluids in jars in the refrigerator?

I guess this is the moment of truth, isn't it? Who would know better than I (apart from David, who isn't telling; who chose to toy with his interviewer on the issue)? Am I going to tell you?

Sure I am. As far as I know, David didn't preserve his bodily fluids, by which I assume urine is meant. There were only two refrigerators in the house on Doheny, and as you might imagine I visited both of them often, and I never saw any jugs, jars, vials, or other containers full of urine or anything resembling it.

And yet the notion does have a certain logic to it. David was definitely hip to the fear that one's cast-off bodily matter – hair, nail clippings, blood, and maybe urine and feces too – could be used by witches in spell-casting rituals. For one thing, my Polish mother had taught *me* always to burn the hair left behind in my hairbrush, and I know David was aware of that. Then too, he had lots of books on occult practices, some of which he might even have read, so I'm sure he was forming ideas about how to stay out of the clutches of the hellhounds on his trail. So I don't know. . . . Maybe he had a secret stash of his fluids somewhere (he *was* ingenious when it came to hiding things) . . . or maybe he used just one big jug to pee in, and scattered the urine in the garden in the dead of night (except that the garden did very well, which wouldn't have been the case if it had been dosed nightly with urine – or is piss harmless to plant life when it's as heavily cocaine-laced as David's must have been?).

There really are a lot of possibilities, aren't there, and I can't rule any of them out. So next time you see David, just ask him.

Back to the scene of the crime, now, the house itself. It was a rental property reasonably well suited to our purposes. I'd had to settle on it faster than I would have preferred, because I couldn't stand staying at the Lippmans' with David in such a ridiculous state. Michael and Nancy were very good to us, but you just can't abuse people's hospitality that way. David, however, had balked at the ideal home my best efforts had found for us. That was a beautiful Art Deco house on six acres, an exquisite property and a terrific value at just $300,000, but he took one look at a detail I hadn't noticed, a hexagram painted on the floor of a circular room by the previous owner, Gypsy Rose Lee, and got hysterical. Now *Angie* was in league with Satan. Why else would she try to lure him into such a trap?

A great deal of coddling and reassurance got us through that crisis, and I went and found the Doheny Drive house. Built in the late fifties or early sixties, it was a white cube surrounding an indoor swimming pool, with the pool accessible through sliding glass doors from most of the rooms. David liked the place, but I thought it was too small to meet our needs for very long, and I wasn't crazy about the pool. In my experience indoor pools are always a problem.

This one was no exception, albeit not in any of the usual ways. *Its* drawback was one I hadn't encountered before and haven't seen or heard of since: Satan lived in it. With his own eyes, David said, he'd seen Him rising up out of the water one night.

Back to Walli Elmlark I went, this time with a tall order. David wanted an exorcism.

A Greek Orthodox church in LA would have done it for us – there was a priest available for such a service, the people there had told me – but David wouldn't have it. No strangers allowed, he said. So there we stood, on that more than usually interesting night, with just Walli's instructions and a few hundred dollars' worth of books, talismans, and assorted other items from Hollywood's comprehensive selection of fine occult emporia.

I say 'we,' but to most intents and purposes I wasn't involved. My mission, going out into the world where David feared to tread and buying the paraphernalia, was over. Now I was just an observer. Whatever active assistance he needed would come from whatever coke whores and sycophants he had on hand that night.

There he was, then, primed and ready. The proper books and doodads were arranged on a big old-fashioned lectern, the necessary megalines of cocaine were laid out on the billiard table at his side: everything was prepared. I took a stab at suggesting that given the adversary he thought he was facing, he might be better advised to go at it on some night when he wasn't quite so stupendously stoned, but that didn't sit too well. If looks could kill, I'd have been dead meat right then and there.

The intonation began, and although I had no idea what was being said or what language it was being said in, and I questioned the effectiveness of a supposedly solemn ritual interrupted every few minutes by sudden lurches toward the billiard table followed by loud, vacuum cleaner-like noises, I couldn't stop a weird cold feeling rising up in me as David droned on and on.

There's no easy or elegant way to say this, so I'll just say it straight. At a certain point in the ritual, the pool began to bubble. It bubbled vigorously – perhaps 'thrashed' is a better term – in a manner inconsistent with any explanation involving air filters or the like.

As David watched this happening in absolute terror, I tried to be flippant – 'Well, dear, aren't you clever? It seems to be working. Something's making a move, don't you think?' – but I couldn't keep it up. It was very, very strange; even after my recent experiences I was having trouble accepting what my eyes were seeing.

I helped myself to a big rail of cocaine from the billiard table (a new policy of mine: Try to lighten up on disapproval of David by doing a little toot now and then), and that seemed to clear my mind from the miasma threatening to overtake me. I decided to take action.

I made a circuit of the house, peering at the pool from behind the sliding glass doors of each room, getting different angles on that crazy thing. But nothing changed it; the pool was definitely, absolutely, no doubt about it, bubbling with an energy for which there was no possible physical explanation.

After some fifteen minutes, by which time David had done about another gram of cocaine and made it to the end of his ritual intonations, the water began to calm. Soon it was back to normal, just another indoor pool in Hollywood.

I kept my eye on it for the next forty minutes or so, and nothing unusual happened, and so with my heart in my mouth I slid one of the glass doors open and, ignoring David's panicked screams, went out to the edge and looked in.

I saw what I saw. Nothing can change that. On the bottom of the pool was a large shadow, or stain, which had not been there before the ritual began. It was in the shape of a beast of the underworld; it reminded me of those twisted, tormented gargoyles screaming silently from the spires of medieval cathedrals. It was ugly, shocking, malevolent; it frightened me.

I backed away from it feeling very strange, went through the doorway, and told David what I'd seen, trying to be nonchalant but not doing very well. He turned so white I thought he might die on the spot, but he managed to stay with us and even revived enough to spend the rest of the night doing more coke. He wouldn't go near the pool, though.

I still don't know what to think about that night. It runs directly counter to my pragmatism and my everyday faith in the integrity of the 'normal' world, and it confuses me greatly. What troubles me most is that if you were to call that stain the mark of Satan, I don't see how I·could argue with you.

David, of course, insisted that we move from the house as quickly as possible, and we did that, but I've heard from reliable sources (Michael Lippman for one, that property's real estate agent for another) that subsequent tenants haven't been able to remove that shadow. Even though the pool has been painted over a number of times, the shadow has always come back.


All Saints' Eve passed without further incident, and David began to break free from his satanic obsessions. As I prospected for a new house, it seemed as if we were to be spared further problems with demons, warlocks, and witches.

That did nothing for my personal circumstances, however; in that area things simply got worse and worse. Only a week or two after the exorcism a new malevolence invaded our household: the film director Nicolas Roeg, arriving to work on *The Man Who Fell to Earth* with David and bringing along both his own dark, drunkenly twisted spirit and the wanton recklessness of Candy Clark, his starmistress of the moment. At the same time, a threat already in place began really asserting itself: the awful Corinne Schwab fired up her campaign for exclusive rights to David Bowie, body and soul.

My troubles with witches may have been over, but my troubles with bitches had only just begun.

# 14

# QUEEN BITCH AND THE
# MAN WHO FELL

Corinne Schwab. It was I who first marked her as a potential candidate for the job of David's personal assistant. I noticed how hard she worked when she first showed up as a temp at the London Main Man office – she had both devotion and determination, and would surely get done what you asked her to do – and so I befriended her and recommended her to David. It didn't hurt, I thought, that she seemed to get along quite well with Tony Defries; all kinds of static could be avoided if David had a go-between, loyal to him and also liked by Tony, in his dealings with Main Man.

And Corinne was indeed loyal to David. I figured she would be, right from the start, because she had that worshipful-doggie look in her eyes whenever the Great One came within her orbit. Hers wasn't any passing adulation either; she's still with him today, having stuck like glue through absolutely everything.

Of the many acolytes at the altar of the Church of David Bowie, then, Corinne turned out to be both the most enduring and the most privileged. Whether she's ever been admitted to the tabernacle and tasted the holy loins, however, I don't know.

Corinne was a person of medium height with curly brown hair and brown eyes. She had few distinguishing features other than a rather thin upper lip. All charm and sex appeal, in other words. She was an American, brought up in France by her photographer father and psychiatrist mother; among other things, this enabled her to say 'I need another Valium prescription' in fluent English and French and adequate German. Her habits seemed connected with her single-mindedness; control freaks often exhibit the kind of intense focus with which she concentrated on David, hearing his voice to the exclusion of all others. Or maybe not; maybe she was just obeying the dictates of her basic nature.

You get the idea, then. The woman was bad news: bad news for people wanting something from David, because they'd have to go through her to get to him, and extra bad news for me for that same reason. David used Corinne for everything – fetching his drinks, summoning his concubines, doing whatever needed doing – but most especially he used her to restrict access to himself. She became his gatekeeper, and as time went on and his heart hardened further toward me, I became number one on her list of people to be turned away. I hope for your sake that you can't grasp exactly how bad that felt.

Her control of the space around David grew quickly during our days on Doheny Drive, and strengthened even more after the Beast in the pool indicated that our welcome might have run out. It was she, not I, who found our next house, in Bel Air, and therefore it was she who determined what the space around *me* was going to be like. And it was awful: a dark, horrible house, differing in layout and construction from the West Seventeenth Street house in New York, which Corinne had also chosen, but almost identical in atmosphere. Devoid of light and grace and color, it was the perfect environment for a cave dweller such as poor David.

In the same category as Corinne, though hardly in the same league, was Candy Clark. Chosen by Nicolas Roeg to play the motel maid who became the reclusive alien's lover/protector in *The Man Who Fell to Earth*, she dropped into my life with all the grace of an incoming Scud. She was drunk when Nick brought her to the Doheny house for her first meeting with David (and so was Nick), and from the bottle of wine she had under each arm (as did Nick), it looked as if she would be getting drunker.

It was so tacky. Nick kept making sly remarks about what he and Candy had been doing at their hotel before they came over, and dropping obvious hints about what they might get up to now.

I was mortified. I've got nothing against group sex, but this was something else. This was Nick going for dominance over David by offering him his woman, establishing right up front who the Svengali was around there. It was Nick's method in those days, as was his encouragement of line-blurring between movie script and reality. If Candy's and David's characters were going to be fucking in the movie, then Candy and David should be fucking in reality.

I've got no time for that bullshit – it's not art, it's only perverted ego-gamesmanship – so I turned on my heel and left them to it. It's probable that Candy and David didn't get it together.

I didn't want to be around that scene, even though I was the one who had made the original connection for David; I'd taken his case to the agent Maggie Abbott, and she'd matched him with Nick Roeg's search for a suitable alien. By the time shooting began in New Mexico, we'd moved to that awful Bel Air house, David's compulsions had progressed so far that all he did was work and toot, and Corinne's reign over his surroundings had grown almost absolute. You can see why I much preferred to spend my time elsewhere.

I was summoned, though. David wasn't satisfied with the local caterers, Corinne told me when she called me in New York; he (and a few others) needed the far superior culinary services of yours truly. So off I went to Lake Fenton, New Mexico, to join David, Corinne, Nick, Candy, Zowie, Marion, and all the happy movie-makers.

It was too much. Corinne had found David yet another abysmal house, this one featuring an abandoned swimming pool and a long-established nest of rattlesnakes in the crawl space beneath the floorboards.

'What the hell did you pick *this* place for?' I demanded.

The gist of her reply was that David *liked* the rattlesnakes and the empty pool. They were romantic. They had the right resonance; they fit with his feelings of ambient apocalypse.

'Well of course,' I said. 'How silly of me. I should have known.'

I doubt whether the sarcasm registered on Corinne. She was so firmly oriented toward David that nobody – the director, the other stars, the child, the nanny, the wife – ever really got through to her.

I catered, then: planned the menus, bought the groceries, got up long before dawn every day, cooked until daylight, drove to Lake Fenton, and served meals all day in the Winnebagos parked around the location. It wasn't my idea of a good time, exactly, and it's likely I was already a little testy when one day I walked into the back bedroom of the ranch house, where Zowie slept, and saw a rattle-snake making itself at home.

Zowie wasn't there at the time (thank God!), but for me that was it. I stormed off and found David, and had to brush Corinne away when she tried to keep me from getting to him.

'David, this *has* to stop,' I told him angrily. 'If this person is acting on your orders, and this is how you want to lead your life, that's fine, but you have no right to let our son sleep in a house full of poisonous snakes, right next to a big hole he can fall into and smash his skull, just because *you* get off on reptiles and desolation. That's insane!'

It didn't seem to make much of an impression – he looked at me with those coke-filled eyes, sort of registered what I was saying, and didn't like what he heard. Fancy that. It was just Angie breaking up the buzz with reality again, I guess. So I gave up and split. I went back to the Albuquerque Hilton, where most of the cast and crew were staying and the production office had been set up.

I allowed myself some fun there, and some spite too. I ran into a gaggle of young Bowie fans who'd traveled across the country on the chance of meeting him, and proceeded to buy them and myself margaritas until we were all very drunk. Then I took a few of the girls off to my bedroom and made love with them; then, the next day, I made sure they got to meet David; and *then* I decided I'd had enough of *The Man Who Fell to Earth* and went back to New York. Screw 'em all, I thought. Let 'em eat burritos.

When I watch the movie today, I'm amazed by how well it came out – not so much by Nick Roeg's work, which has been wonderful right from the start, his egomania and alcohol abuse not-withstanding, but by David's. Knowing how much coke he was doing and what kind of state he was in, I almost can't believe his performance. There's a core of talent in that man which endured no matter how he abused himself.

Talent, though, can't hug you and love you and make it all better.

I jet-setted around my world in the months following the wrap-up of *The Man Who Fell to Earth*, London-New York-Los Angeles being the basic itinerary, and as before, LA was my least amusing location. The same gruesome themes dominated the Bel Air house: obsessive drugging and drudgery on David's part (he was trying to work on three albums at once, one of them his never-released *Man Who Fell* sound track), and determined guardianship by Corinne.

I learned how strong the tie between her and David had grown when one day I questioned Corinne rather sharply about the amount of baggage she'd assembled for a trip to Jamaica, where David was going to record. She snapped at me, so I snapped back at her – 'Don't you *dare* talk to me like that!' – and suddenly David hurtled across the room, grabbed my throat in both hands, and started to throttle me.

He was blindly angry, yelling at me as he tightened his grip, and I started panicking. It didn't feel as if he were going to stop . . .

Corinne pulled him off and saved me. So it's possible, irony of ironies, that I owe her my life.

I guess she was just doing her job, though. The Great One on trial for murder or manslaughter, or even tainted by some mysterious misfortune visited on his wife, would not have been cool. Too much hassle in a scenario like that, *far* too high a price. A better way could surely be found.

I don't mean to suggest that Corinne was the one who hatched the whole Switzerland scam. She didn't have the vision for something like that; she was born to follow direction, not give it.

It started, I think, with Stan Diamond, the lawyer brought into the picture by Michael Lippman as an outside opinion on the draft of a management contract between Michael and David. Stan came up with the idea of Swiss residency for David as a solution to a pressing tax problem. If David were to remain a resident of California, he would have to pay a hefty tax bill – $300,000 was the figure I was told – with money he didn't have. As I understood it, these were tax debts accumulated over the previous few years, during which time vast quantities of taxable cash he had generated had vanished into various murky areas, David's nasal cavities being only the most apparent. Now, as part of the legitimization of Bowie affairs under Michael Lippman's caring stewardship, the piper had to be paid. It was a big, bad problem.

I kept hearing about it in bits and pieces, as overheard remarks and passing references, until I got very tired of that. I invited Michael and Stan over to dinner and broached the subject head-on.

They were reluctant to tell me, but I pressed them and got at least the bottom line of the problem.

'Is the income tax situation in England so bad that there's no way of going back there?' I asked, knowing the answer already but hoping it wouldn't be so.

'Right,' replied Stan. 'England's out of the question.'

'Well, that leaves Ireland, Switzerland, or one of those places in the Caribbean, doesn't it?'

Stan made a face. 'We've tried Switzerland, which is by far the best option, but no go. We can't get residency there.'

That got my goat. I almost couldn't believe they could be so naive, or so shortsighted.

'Look at me,' I demanded. 'Do I look like some cute little decoration David has lying around the house? Who's gotten him out of every jam he's been in *so* far? Who went to *school* in Switzerland? Who knows just exactly how things get done there, and who you bribe to make them happen?'

They looked at me as if all this really *was* news to them, and I realized that things were worse than I thought. David and Corinne had been keeping me out of his affairs very well.

I was thinking about Switzerland, however, and seeing some positive possibilities. Demons and witches and roadies with bags full of cocaine were in short supply there, and the opposite was abundant: the Western world had been sending its sick, drunk, and addicted for treatment in Switzerland for a hundred years and more.

'Okay,' I said. 'This is going to cost some cash, but I guarantee you, if you want it, I'll get it done.'

Michael and Stan agreed, and so did David when he came back from the bathroom (he went to the bathroom a *lot*, and came out with his nose running).

So off to Switzerland I went, straight back to the obvious starting point, the bursar at my old school, St George's. She connected me to a lawyer specializing in residency situations, and he laid it all out for me. There was much to lay out, for the Swiss are incredibly particular about who gets in, and where and how they can live once they're there.

Now, the story of how it all worked, and what sharp turns and gentle curves were taken along the way, is a lot of fun if you like that kind of thing, but perhaps it's a touch too far from the mainstream of sex, drugs, and human drama for detailed treatment here. Suffice it to say that after much exquisite and very enjoyable negotiation, I got what we wanted, and better: legal residency in Blonay, a charming village above Lake Geneva, near Montreux in the French-speaking part of the country (*not* the German-flavored section), and an almost ludicrously low tax rate of about ten percent.

It was that low because I'd sold the Swiss a bill of goods they found attractive. They loved the prospect of big money flowing their way once David's income, currently low because of the ravages of his former management, was rehabilitated by a new recording deal. But of course, I pointed out, it would be very foolish of my husband to sign any such deal until he sheltered himself under the tax protection of Swiss residency, so for now... They understood the point immediately, having had long experience of potential cash cows in just such situations, and welcomed us aboard.

I wish *I* had understood the damned point. In addition to the tax benefit he could gain by delaying a new recording deal until he was a Swiss resident, David would also benefit from making another kind of move under Swiss law. In California at that time, divorce courts were recognizing the concept of communal property and beginning the bargaining at the fifty-fifty line. But in Switzerland the male still reigned supreme. If he played his cards right, any man could get rid of his wife for a song.

I didn't know that, but I'm certain everybody else at my little Bel Air dinner party did.

Not all those diners were still on board when the move to Blonay took place. Corinne the human limpet was still firmly attached, of course, and Stan Diamond too, but Michael Lippman had been shed.

The whole affair made me want to puke. Stan, to my great surprise, had advanced the opinion that Michael had behaved unethically, and David had decided that he wouldn't sign the management contract with which Michael had presented him. The 'unethical conduct' in question, though, centered on a short-term loan Michael had taken from the Bowie account for the down payment on a new house. It was all perfectly aboveboard, but David was so cocaine-paranoid (and manager-burned) that when très Stan Diamond brought the matter to his attention, he lost control. Now, he said, Michael was ripping him off, just like everyone else!

I think Michael was in fact his good ally. The real bone of contention between David's coke-clenched jaws was the sorry fate of his *Man Who Fell* soundtrack, which he blamed on Michael; and in his chaotic mental condition, with a paranoid resentment building, he'd either forgotten or conveniently ignored the fact that he gave Michael permission to borrow that money.

Corinne supported David's judgment, as usual, and so he fired Michael – who subsequently sued him and won, but no matter: Lippman was out and Diamond was in. Stan ascended to the manager's seat and Starship Bowie rattled on toward Lake Geneva.

And there, in contrast to acrid, acrimonious Los Angeles, the air was sweet, the scenery lovely, the society serene. The place I'd found us was a commodious cuckoo-clock of a house, *très* Swiss indeed, with seven or eight bathrooms, a caretaker's lodge, and a half-dozen acres of prime real estate above Blonay. It even had a name, Clos des Mésanges, and it was more than just suitable. I had our furnishings brought from Oakley Street, and Marion and Zowie moved in, and there we were: back in the high life again. *This* was no cocaine cavern.

That was its problem as far as David was concerned. When, eventually, he showed up with Corinne, after clinging for months to his precious coke connections in LA, he walked through that gorgeous house and couldn't stand it. He tried to pretend he liked it, but you could see the horror in his face. It wasn't his scene at all.

And that was his vibe while he lived at Clos des Mésanges: resentful, uncommunicative, inclined to be somewhere else entirely. He took the first chance he got to bug out of there, which happened to be a deposition on Michael Lippman's lawsuit against him. Dealing with that freaked him out, he said, so he had to be by himself. He ran off to some hotel, and told Corinne to tell *me* she didn't know where he was.

He came back, but at that point I couldn't handle his presence, so I took off for Morocco with Roy Martin. And after that, although David and I spent short periods in the same house sometimes, we really lived separate lives. Whenever I was at Clos des Mésanges, he wasn't, and vice versa.

That worked out fine in a coldhearted way, because even if my deepest emotions *were* rushing headlong into an abyss, at least David wasn't hanging around to put a damper on the hardcore fun I was using to get me through the night. I suspect that he knew about it, or perhaps just knew he *could* know. Roy, you see, wasn't just my lover. He was also David's friend. I don't know where his loyalty really lay. To himself, I suspect. I do know that David trusted him to watch over me, however, and when I think about an incident that was to prove significant to my fate a little further down the road, Roy's continuing loyalty to David seems more than mildly relevant.

The incident was par for the course, really, just some high-gear sex involving me, Roy, and D, a female heroin dealer, but this time Roy jumped up at a certain moment and said, 'Hold it, girls, hold it! You look so fucking good I've just got to get pictures!' I was so stoned I didn't even think twice about it, and cooperated as Roy went through a pack of Polaroid film. When it was all over and I sobered up, I got responsible. I couldn't leave those pictures around the house, I realized; Zowie might see them. So I put them in the house safe.

There they were, then, secure from little eyes, waiting for whenever they might prove interesting, entertaining, or stimulating.

In the months that followed, David gravitated toward Berlin while I headed for London. Neither of us *lived* in those places, of course, because the Swiss take their residency requirements seriously and demand that their resident foreigners spend significant amounts of time at 'home.' Therefore you 'stay' or 'work' or 'holiday' in your London flat, Berlin garret, or wherever, and return to Switzerland when you have to. It's like being on work release from a very nice, court-ordered health resort.

My scene, in London but also in New York and other places, wasn't the stuff of fond memory. I could see the writing on the wall for my marriage, so I was trying to establish a separate and independent life for myself – I got a little flat in London and I worked theatrically in *Krisis Kabaret* with Roy Martin and others – but deep down I didn't want to deal with what was happening in my life. I was angry, sad, and starting to get crazy, and so I turned to drugs. I began doing heroin, which I'd been sampling recreationally since I'd been introduced to it, on a habitual basis, and I found the perfect companion for that life-style: a New York musician then working as a sound man for the Heartbreakers, Johnny Thunder's out-of-control New York Dolls offshoot of seminal Glitter/ punk/junkie hard-rockers. He was experienced with heroin – he knew the life, he knew the ropes – and so it all worked out fine: there we were, the archetypically trendy mid-seventies match, just another couple of pale, desperate, black-leather music-biz junkies in . . . love?

David's scene was just as raunchy, but its themes were different. Berlin for him was the terminus of other obsessions of his: German Expressionist art, Nazism, and the mystical under-pinnings of Master Race culture. I first heard him talking about the whole dark underworld of Nazism with Lou Reed and Iggy Pop when they came to London; it seemed to have held his imagination, with growing power.

He wasn't, as the English tabloid press suggested, infatuated with the more simpleminded, racist aspects of Nazi ideology, and indeed he was furious when one London newspaper ran a photo of him apparently giving the stiff-armed fascist salute after arriving at Victoria Station from Berlin. The photographer had caught him in mid-gesture, he explained, and he disavowed any embrace of Nazism in general and one recently attributed declaration in particular. 'I believe Britain could benefit from a fascist leader,' he was reported to have said. 'After all, fascism is really nationalism.'

Whatever. I don't happen to think he ever really bought the geek-with-a-gas-chamber version of *Herrenvolk* philosophy. I think his real interest lay first in causing a stir and second, as he explained it, 'in mythology... about the Arthurian period, about the magical side of the whole Nazi campaign.' That sounds like the David I knew. And besides, as he later clarified, 'I was out of my mind totally, completely crazed.'

Berlin called to him in other ways. He was attracted to the ambience of 'a city cut off from its world, art and culture, dying with no hope of retribution' (this was of course before the wall came down and Berlin became once again the powerhouse of Europe), and he chose to live in a section of the city as bleak, anonymous, and culturally lost as possible: Schöneberg, populated largely by Turkish immigrants. He took an apartment above an auto parts store and ate at the local workingmen's café. Talk about alienation.

I couldn't even begin to relate to either his fascination with the magic behind the Holocaust or his affection for grim, gray places - and that's putting it very mildly indeed; I couldn't *stand* all that crap - but when he started talking about Romy Haag and her cabaret theater, I got interested. The fact that he was having an affair with Romy was neither here nor there. Sexually she was just one among many, since he also had his usual selection of black women and rent boys on tap (although since Romy was a woman impersonating a female impersonator, she *did* represent a rather intriguing new twist). But the fact of Romy's talent, as well as the fabulous theatrical action on the stage of her little club, was impressive. Walking into that place was like going back decades, to the Berlin of Christopher Isherwood, the glory days of avant cabaret before Adolf, the Soviets, and the Americans turned underground Berlin into little more than an anything-goes meat rack. Romy was *very* wild and *very* sophisticated.

Musically, David was in one of his regenerative periods, filling himself back up with something fresh after exhausting his previous obsession. This meant attaching himself to a new source of ideas and energy, in this case Brian Eno, whom he'd known since Roxy Music opened for Ziggy and the Spiders on the triumphal British tour of 1973. He and Eno created the appropriately titled *Low* in Berlin. And he was working a lot with Iggy, producing Iggy's *Lust for Life* album among other things.

Maybe he was reaching a turning point in Berlin, or at least groping for his bottom. Significantly, he didn't seem to be doing as much cocaine as before, if any; Corinne had found him a therapist in Switzerland, and that might have had something to do with it. But while this revealed a change in consciousness – *Gee, maybe this stuff is bad for me*! – it hardly mattered operationally. Virtually every time I saw him in Berlin he was drunk, or working on *getting* drunk, and his stress level seemed as high as in his gram-a-night days. On one of my visits he got so worked up he thought he was having a heart attack. I rushed him to the British military hospital, where the doctors checked him out and told him his heart was just fine, but maybe he should relax a little.

I didn't enjoy my visits. It was painful enough seeing David, but even worse seeing Zowie – enrolled, much against my wishes, at a British boarding school. Or rather, seeing Zowie was great; it was leaving him I couldn't stand. At those times I couldn't avoid being fully conscious of what, exactly, was going on: David was casting me off, and that meant he would be taking Zowie with him.

Zowie had always been my gift to David, you see. By bearing my fragile husband a child, I was giving him someone to live for. And now – especially now, in David's darkest hour of need – I wasn't going to back out on that commitment. I knew I wouldn't fight for Zowie's custody, and therefore I knew I was going to lose him. This was the worst thing possible for me. It felt like performing an amputation on myself.

My anger was very deep and very strong. It went inward and did its work there, poisoning me, but it also had to get out, and in that direction its proper target wasn't within range. David had only two possible responses to anger, as I'd learned from long and bitter experience, and neither did me any good at all: he would become neutral and distant, and begin planning your cancellation, or he would snap into violence. The latter had happened with me only once, but it had been enough.

Corinne, on the other hand . . . Corinne was his tool. She was the gatekeeper and the assassin; she did his dirty work for him and took all the consequences. With her by his side, he could behave however he wanted without accepting the responsibility for his actions. In politics and government they call that being insulated.

Corinne, then, became my focus. Recognizing that David and I couldn't deal with each other as long as he could insert her between us, I made my decision and took my stand. One night during dinner at one of the revolting, typically German organs-and-offal restaurants he enjoyed, I stepped out over the abyss.

'David,' I said. 'I need you to fire Corinne.'

Gravity worked. No angels came to save me. He refused.

We talked about divorce then. He asked me to divorce him, and I said no: The commitment I'd made at Plaistow Grove, and before the registrar of marriages, didn't include giving up and walking away. That left him only one course of action, and he took it. *He'd* divorce *me*, he said.

It was so strange. To have it all finally dealt with was liberating. It lightened the mood. My mind, I think, was doing a particularly efficient job of assimilating the new information, rationalizing it, and giving it just the right spin to keep my emotions from killing me . . . *Now that we're not married, it'll be different*, went the appealing little refrain. *We can be friends and partners again.*

I don't know why David was feeling lighter – it was probably simple relief at having finally spoken his mind – but he brightened considerably, and soon we were getting along better than we had in years. The offal on the plates before us even looked like food. It combined badly with the large volumes of alcohol he drank, however, and turned on him before the night was over. The wee hours found me holding David up on the street outside his apartment while he vomited all over his shoes.

It was one of those weirdly honest moments between people. Holding him, watching him, I suddenly knew how much I still loved this man, and at the same time I tapped into an amusing vein of irony. The vomit dribbling from David's lips to the Berlin pavement brought to mind those innumerable occasions over the years when the press, or even fans or musicians of lesser stature than he, had come before him, pens and microphones poised, to await his precious words.

I shook my head, laughing, and grimaced at him. 'Well, I don't know, babe,' I managed to say. 'I guess this just proves that not *everything* that comes out of your mouth is worth recording.'

He looked up at me, blankly at first, but then started giggling too.

At that moment we were truly together again. We went up to the apartment and made love for the first time in years.

It went on for three days, and those were good times. They had a strangely erotic quality, almost illicit, as if the decision to divorce had changed us from man and wife into brother and sister behaving very naughtily with each other. I started to think that maybe, as in the beginning, we were adventuring into something new, untried, exciting.

But that was a fantasy. The reality was Corinne. I'd had a confrontation with her about something or other, and it had ended with her fleeing the apartment (where she had her own room). That was fine as far as I was concerned – the less I saw of Corinne the better – but David was very upset. He turned his attention from me to the telephone, and while I listened, he called around Berlin looking for her – anxiously, with far more concern than he'd shown for *my* welfare since our Haddon Hall days. Finally he found her, and left the apartment to meet her.

I stood there letting it sink in. Then I went into Corinne's room, gathered up her clothes and some of the gifts I'd given her in better times, threw them out of the window into the street, and called a cab and caught a flight to London. And for David and me, that was the end.

# POSTSCRIPT

$D$avid divorced me under Swiss law, the decree becoming final in 1980. He granted me a settlement of $750,000 over ten years, and nothing else.

Because of the bias of Swiss law, the fact that I didn't claim custody of Zowie, and crucially, the Polaroids which Roy Martin supplied him with, David probably didn't even have to give me *that* much. He insisted on a gag clause stipulating that I could not discuss our marriage in the media for the term of the settlement, which has now expired.

David is alive and healthy. He is still living in Switzerland and still inventing fashionable versions of himself with which to keep us entertained.

Zowie stayed with his father, the court ordering that he be available to me twice a year. After living in Berlin he went to school in Lausanne, then attended Gordonstoun, the ultra-exclusive boarding school of the British elite in Scotland. Around that time he decided he would be called Joe (wouldn't you?), and a few years later decided he didn't want to see me or talk to me. Now twenty-one, he's a man I don't know.

After Berlin, I saw David one last time, in Lausanne, in a café midway between our respective lawyers' offices. He was open and even kindly with me, but in the end he was there to sign divorce papers.

I was low and sad and confused and stoned. At heart I felt like killing myself, but I knew I wouldn't. I'd already tried twice, once in Switzerland at Christmastime in 1977, when I arrived to find that Zowie, contrary to my expectations, was in Berlin with David, and once in New York three or four months later. The second time I almost made it. Only an unexpected visitor saved me; he called the paramedics when he found me in my bathtub, comatose from an overdose of Equanil. Then the paramedics unceremoniously dropped me down two flights of stairs on the way to the ambulance, breaking my nose. I wonder if they were trying to tell me something: *Suicide isn't pretty, babe. Either do it right or don't do it at all.*

I ran away from New York, the junkie life, and clinical depression after that, headed for California, good friends, and new beginnings. I quit trying to kill myself and found new adventures, lots of them, all over the world, with all sorts of wild and wonderful people. I lived through some simply terrible times (another failed marriage, for one) and I was given some great blessings (my daughter Stasha, above all), but that's another story. Suffice it to say that the years since I was with David have not been dull. And if I have anything to do with it, the future won't be either.

Looking back, I can see that my life with David was molded by forces beyond my control and even my understanding. I never realized how powerless I was against his secretiveness, his emotional frigidity, or his addictive nature. Now I know that there was nothing I could have done, and also that nothing I did do really mattered. He had a date with his own personal hell no matter what. *C'est la vie.*

I truly regret, though, that he never came out and told me what he wanted of me until it was far too late. I'll never really know whether I'd have been willing to play a traditional wife and mother's role in a conventional marriage with him, but I sure would like to have been offered that option. I *might* have taken it. As it was, I got neither real marriage nor real openness out of the open marriage I thought we had, and in the end I was shut out of everything.

Still, I don't regret trying. I still believe in the principles I brought to our relationship, and I still practice them. And I'm still proud of what I did to get those ideas heard. Regardless of his performance with me, David *did* do a wonderful job of broadcasting sexual freedom and personal liberation. He shone his light into a lot of dark places in people and helped them see themselves, and maybe love themselves, a little better.

And even though it hurt sometimes, I wouldn't have missed it for the world. It *was* one hell of a party.

# $D$ISCOGRAPHY, 1969–1978

All release dates are for British albums unless otherwise noted, and all songs are by David Bowie unless otherwise noted.

## DAVID BOWIE

November 1969 (released in the United States as *Man of Words, Man of Music*, 1970). Produced by Tony Visconti.

*Songs*: Space Oddity; Unwashed and Slightly Dazed; Letter to Hermione; Cygnet Committee; Janine; An Occasional Dream; The Wild Eyed Boy from Freecloud; God Knows I'm Good; Memory of a Free Festival

*Musicians*: David Bowie, Keith Christmas, Mick Wayne, Tim Renwick, Honk, Tony Visconti, Herbie Flowers, John Cambridge, Terry Cox, Rick Wakeman, Paul Buckmaster, Benny Marshall and friends.

## THE MAN WHO SOLD THE WORLD

April 1971. Produced by Tony Visconti.

*Songs*: The Width of a Circle; All the Madmen; Black Country Rock; After All; Running Gun Blues; Savior Machine; She Shook Me Cold; The Man Who Sold the World; The Superman

*Musicians*: David Bowie, Mick Ronson, Tony Visconti, Mick Woodmansey, Ralph Mace

HUNKY DORY

December 1971. Produced by Ken Scott (assisted by David Bowie).
*Songs*: Changes; Oh, You Pretty Things; Eight-Line Poem; Life on
Mars; Kooks; Quicksand; Fill Your Heart (Rose, Williams); Andy
Warhol; Song for Bob Dylan; Queen Bitch; The Bewlay Brothers
*Musicians*: David Bowie, Mick Ronson, Trevor Bolder, Rick
Wakeman, Mick Woodmansey

THE RISE AND FALL OF ZIGGY STARDUST AND THE SPIDERS
FRCM MARS

June 1972. Produced by David Bowie and Ken Scott.
*Songs*: Five Years; Soul Love; Moonage Daydream; Starman; It
Ain't Easy (Davies); Lady Stardust; Star; Hang onto Yourself;
Ziggy Stardust; Suffragette City; Rock 'n' Roll Suicide
*Musicians*: David Bowie, Mick Ronson, Trevor Bolder, Mick
Woodmansey

ALADDIN SANE

April 1973. Produced by David Bowie and Ken Scott.
*Songs*: Watch That Man; Aladdin Sane; Drive In Saturday; Panic
in Detroit; Cracked Actor; Time; The Prettiest Star; Let's Spend
the Night Together (Jagger, Richards); The Jean Genie; Lady
Grinning Soul
*Musicians*: David Bowie, Mick Ronson, Trevor Bolder, Mick Wood-
mansey, Mike Garson, Ken Fordham; (backup vocals) Juanita
Franklin, Linda Lewis, Jeffrey MacCormack

PIN-UPS

October 1973. Produced by Ken Scott and David Bowie.
*Songs*: Rosalyn (Duncan, Farley); Here Comes the Night (Berns);
I Wish You Would (Arnold); See Emily Play (Barrett); Every-
thing's Alright (Crouch, Konrad, Stavely, James, Karlsen); I Can't
Explain (Townshend); Friday on My Mind (Young, Vandam);

Sorrow (Feldman, Goldstein, Gottherer); Don't Bring Me Down (Dee); Shapes of Things (Samwell-Smith, McCarty); Anyway, Anyhow, Anywhere (Townshend, Daltrey); Where Have All the Good Times Gone (Davies)

*Musicians*: David Bowie, Mick Ronson, Trevor Bolder, Mike Garson, Aynsley Dunbar, Ken Fordham; (backup vocals) Jeffrey MacCormack

## DIAMOND DOGS

April 1974. Produced by David Bowie.

*Songs*: Future Legend; Bewitched, Bothered, and Bewildered (Rodgers); Diamond Dogs; Sweet Thing; Candidate; Sweet Thing (reprise); Rebel Rebel; Rock 'n' Roll with Me (Bowie, Peace); We Are the Dead; 1984; Big Brother; Chant of the Ever-Circling Skeletal Family

*Musicians*: David Bowie, Mike Garson, Tony Newman, Aynsley Dunbar, Alan Parker.

## DAVID LIVE

October 1974. Produced by Tony Visconti.

*Songs*: 1984; Rebel Rebel; Moonage Daydream; Sweet Thing; Changes; Suffragette City; Aladdin Sane; All the Young Dudes; Cracked Actor; When You Rock 'n' Roll with Me (Bowie, Peace); Watch That Man; Knock on Wood (Floyd, Cropper); Diamond Dogs; Big Brother; The Width of a Circle; The Jean Genie; Rock 'n' Roll Suicide

*Musicians*: David Bowie, Earl Slick, Michael Kamen, Mike Garson, David Sanborn, Richard Grando, Herbie Flowers, Tony Newman; (backup vocals) Pablo Rosario, Gui Andrisano, Warren Peace

## YOUNG AMERICANS

March 1975. Produced by Tony Visconti, David Bowie, and Harry Maslin.

*Songs*: Young Americans; Win; Fascination (Bowie, Vandross);
Right; Somebody Up There Likes Me; Across the Universe
(Lennon, McCartney); Can You Hear Me; Fame (Bowie,
Lennon, Alomar)

*Musicians*: David Bowie, Carlos Alomar, Mike Garson, David
Sanborn, Willie Weeks, Emir Ksasan, Andy Newmark, Dennis
Davis, Larry Washington, Pablo Rosario, Ralph McDonald;
(vocals, guitar) John Lennon; (backup vocals) Ava Cherry, Robin
Clark, Luther Vandross, Jean Fineberg, Jean Millington

## IMAGES

May 1975 (Deram); all material recorded before 1969. Produced
by Mike Vernon.

*Songs*: Rubber Band; Maids of Bond Street; Sell Me a Coat; Love
You till Tuesday; There Is a Happy Land; The Laughing Gnome;
The Gospel According to Tony Day; Did You Ever Have a
Dream; Uncle Arthur; We Are Hungry Men; When I Live My
Dream; Join the Gang; Little Bombardier; Come and Buy My
Toys; Silly Boy Blue; She's Got Medals; Please, Mr Gravedigger;
London Boys; Karma Man; Let Me Sleep Beside You; In the
Heat of the Morning

*Musicians*: David Bowie, Dek Fearnley, Derek Boyes, John Eager,
session musicians

## STATION TO STATION

January 1976. Produced by David Bowie and Harry Maslin.

*Songs*: Station to Station; Golden Years; Word on a Wing; TVC 15;
Stay; Wild Is the Wind (Tiomkin, Washington)

*Musicians*: David Bowie, Carlos Alomar, Earl Slick, Roy Bittan,
George Murray, Dennis Davis

## DAVID BOWIE SPECIAL

March 1976 (Japan only). Produced by David Bowie, Tony Visconti; Gus Dudgeon, and Ken Scott.

*Songs*: Starman; Moonage Daydream; Five Years; Hang on to Yourself; Suffragette City; Rock 'n' Roll Suicide; The Jean Genie; Time; Let's Spend the Night Together (Jagger, Richards); The Prettiest Star; Watch That Man; Aladdin Sane; Space Oddity; The Man Who Sold the World; The Wild-Eyed Boy from Freecloud; Cygnet Committee; Changes; Life on Mars?; Fill Your Heart (Rose, Williams); Andy Warhol; Black Country Rock; The Width of a Circle

### CHANGESONEBOWIE

May 1976. Produced by David Bowie, Ken Scott, Gus Dudgeon, Tony Visconti, and Harry Maslin.

*Songs*: Space Oddity; John, I'm Only Dancing; Changes; Ziggy Stardust; Suffragette City; The Jean Genie; Diamond Dogs; Rebel Rebel; Young Americans; Fame (Bowie, Lennon, Vandross); Golden Years

### LOW

January 1977. Produced by David Bowie and Tony Visconti.

*Songs*: Speed of Life; Breaking Glass (Bowie, Davis, Murray); What in the World; Sound and Vision; Always Crashing in the Same Car; Be My Wife; A New Career in a New Town; Warszawa (Bowie, Eno); Art Decade; Weeping Wall; Subterraneans

*Musicians*: David Bowie, Brian Eno, Carlos Alomar, Dennis Davis, Ricky Gardener, George Murray, Roy Young, Peter and Paul; (backup vocals) Mary Visconti, Iggy Pop

### 'HEROES'

October 1977. Produced by David Bowie and Tony Visconti.

*Songs*: Beauty and the Beast; Joe the Lion; Heroes (Bowie, Eno); Sons of the Silent Age; Blackout; V-2 Schneider; Sense of Doubt; Moss Garden (Bowie, Eno); Neuklon (Bowie, Eno); The Secret Life of Arabia (Bowie, Eno, Alomar)

*Musicians*: David Bowie, Carlos Alomar, Robert Fripp, Brian Eno, George Murray, Dennis Davis; (backup vocals) Tony Visconti, Antonia Maass

PETER AND THE WOLF

1978. Produced by Jay David Saks.

David narrates Sergei Prokofiev's *Peter and the Wolf* and Benjamin Britten's *Young Person's Guide to the Orchestra.*

*Musicians*: David Bowie with Eugene Ormandy and the Philadelphia Orchestra

STAGE

1978. Produced by David Bowie and Tony Visconti.

*Songs*: Hang onto Yourself; Ziggy Stardust; Five Years; Soul Love; Star; Station to Station; Fame; TVC 15; Warszawa (Bowie, Eno); Speed of Life; Art Decade; Sense of Doubt; Breaking Glass (Bowie, Davis, Murray); Heroes (Bowie, Eno); What in the World; Blackout; Beauty and the Beast

*Musicians*: David Bowie, Adrian Belew, Carlos Alomar, Simon House, Sean Mayes, Roger Powell, George Murray, Dennis Davis